Simple Mindedness

Simple Mindedness

In Defense of Naive Naturalism in the Philosophy of Mind

Jennifer Hornsby

HARVARD UNIVERSITY PRESS

Cambridge, Massachusetts
London, England
1997

Library of Congress Cataloging-in-Publication Data

Hornsby, Jennifer.
    Simple mindedness : in defense of naive naturalism in the
philosophy of mind / Jennifer Hornsby.
        p.   cm.
    Includes bibliographical references and index.
    ISBN 0–674–80818–5 (alk. paper)
    1. Philosophy of mind.   2. Naturalism.   I. Title.
BD418.3.H667   1997
128′.2—dc21   96–40847

Contents

Contents

Acknowledgments

I thank the editors and publishers who have kindly granted permission to reprint the following essays: 'Which Physical Events Are Mental Events?', *Proceedings of the Aristotelian Society*, 81, 1980–81, reprinted by courtesy of the editor of the Aristotelian Society, © 1981; 'Bodily Movements, Actions and Epistemology', *Midwest Studies in Philosophy*, vol. X (University of Minnesota Press, 1986); 'Physicalism, Events and Part-Whole Relations', in *Actions and Events*, ed. E. LePore and B. McLaughlin (Oxford: Blackwell, 1986); 'Physicalist Thinking and Conceptions of Behaviour', in *Subject, Thought and Context*, ed. P. Pettit and J. McDowell (Oxford: Oxford University Press, 1986); 'Semantic Innocence and Psychological Understanding', in *Philosophical Perspectives, 3, The Philosophy of Mind and Action Theory*, 1989, ed. James E. Tomberlin, reprinted by permission of Ridgeview Publishing Company; 'Descartes, Rorty and the Mind-Body Fiction', in *Reading Rorty*, ed. A. Malachowski (Oxford: Blackwell, 1990); 'Agency and Causal Explanation', in *Mental Causation*, ed. J. Heil and A. Mele (Oxford: Oxford University Press, 1993).

A version of Essay 10 was presented at a conference on naturalism and normativity at Scarborough College, University of Toronto, in April 1993. Sonia Sedivy deserves thanks for making that a good occasion. A version of Essay 11 was presented at a workshop of the Spatial Representation Group, King's College, University of Cambridge, held in September 1992. Bill Brewer deserves thanks for making that a good occasion.

I am grateful for financial support provided by the Andrew W. Mellon Foundation in conjunction with my fellowship at the Center for Advanced Studies in the Behavioral Sciences, Stanford, during which I wrote Essay 12.

Preface

When the essays in a collection span a number of years, the author sometimes starts by acknowledging their inconsistency—if also by regretting it: 'I wish I could stand by everything I say here'. Although most of the material in this book has been published previously, and some of it as much as fifteen years ago, I need not set out in this way. I have selected essays for inclusion on the basis of what I see as a common message: all of them attempt to discourage problematizing the mind in the manner that is most common in contemporary analytic philosophy. I don't claim any peculiar consistency: I have certainly not held a steady view about every philosophical thesis in the areas the material covers. But in retrospect I like to see such changes of mind as I have gone in for, not so much as the relinquishing of something I used to believe, but as the result of an increasing willingness to voice dissent.

Apart from one year spent at the Center for Advanced Studies in the Behavioral Sciences, in Stanford, California, I was at the University of Oxford, at Corpus Christi College, when I wrote the material here. I owe the College particular thanks for granting me leave of absence in my last term there (Fall 1994), during which I put the pieces together.

For comments on earlier versions of one or another essay, I am grateful to Bill Brewer, John Campbell, Bill Child, Donald Davidson, David Finkelstein, Lizzie Fricker, David Lewis, John McDowell, Nigel Shardlow, Christopher Peacocke, Philip Pettit, Sonia Sedivy, Paul Snowdon, Helen Steward, Michael Smith and David Wiggins.

Simple Mindedness

Introduction

1

The essays in this book are not set out in the order in which they were written, but are organized to address three questions, each of which presents some aspect of the philosophical question of 'the place of the mind in nature'. The first is a question in ontology. Among the things there are are things with the mental lives distinctive of ourselves, of people. How is our overall conception of *what there is* affected when we appreciate this? The second is about human agency. People have reason to intervene in, and they make a difference to, a world which operates according to natural law. How do their actions fit in there? The third question is about everyday psychological explanation. People understand each other on the assumption that we are all subjects of experience, with thoughts and wants and hopes and fears. What kind of explanation is then made use of?

These questions inform the essays that make up one or another of the book's three parts. Each part starts with an introduction of the material in it. I have added postscripts sometimes where the essays have been previously published and there are links to be traced now between their different arguments. I have done some cutting to simplify or to avoid repetition (and I have shifted some of the material—in both directions—between Essays 3 and 4). But in case there were anyone who would like to know that she could safely avoid any rereading, or anyone else who wanted to find a self-contained version of something, I have left the essays more or less intact, and relied on separate new material where I wanted to bring another argument in. (In order to preserve some sense of chronology of the recent work I comment on, I have used original publication dates for citations, even where the source for page references is a later, reprinted version.)

The purpose of this Introduction is to show how the parts cohere: I want to situate the view they all represent in relation to contemporary philosophy of mind.

2

By collecting these essays together, I hope to encourage a particular attitude to questions about 'the mind's place in nature', and to recommend a distinctive position in philosophy of mind. For the sake of contrasting it with others, I have given the position a name—*naive naturalism*.

The word 'naturalism' is appropriated: it is commonly used nowadays for the position that the mind's place is *in* nature, that conscious purposive subjects are simply elements of the natural world. The presumed alternative to naturalism in this sense, branded Cartesian Dualism, holds that minds are unnatural things—that conscious purposive subjects are not through and through a part of the natural world. My shared opposition to such an alternative view can be signalled by my use of 'naturalism'. But I have to qualify the 'natural' of 'naturalism' with 'naive', in order to indicate my opposition also to what is usually defended in the name of 'naturalism'.

Where naturalism and Cartesian Dualism are taken as opposites, it cannot be quite right to say that the two positions differ in whether or not they hold that minds are natural. For anyone who sets herself against Cartesian Dualism denies (in some sense) that there *are* minds. (There is a sense in which to say that there *are* minds is to aver the existence of one of the dualist's two sorts of thing.) This is why the formulation of naturalism above carried the gloss, with 'conscious purposive subjects' replacing 'minds'. But there is another way to avoid prejudicially dualist ontological assumptions in raising the general question of '"the mind's" place in nature'. Instead of taking this to be a question about entities of a particular kind, we can take it as a question about a particular kind of subject matter—suited for talking about, as one might say—minded beings. And indeed philosophy of mind's central metaphysical question, which used often to be put as the question of the 'relation of mind to body', is now often put as a question about the status of commonsense psychology, or of folk psychology.

There is a good question here. But it needs to be raised without prejudice in favour of what have come to be the standard answers. If the general question is to be put as one about commonsense psychology, then we should mean by 'commonsense psychology' the subject matter which people use in understanding one another, which we all use all the time, usually quite unreflectively. When its claims are made explicit, commonsense psychology employs terms like 'sees', 'thinks', 'wants', 'means', 'says', 'feels', 'depressed' and 'irascible' (or when marked out by philosophers, more likely, 'perceives', 'believes', 'desires', 'intends', 'asserts', 'emotions', 'moods' and 'traits'); these are terms for so-called intentional mental states, for sentient states, and for more or less enduring psychological characteristics of people. Using these terms, we regard ourselves and others as experiencing, rational beings, and we can give explanations at least of what is thought and said and done. Our explanations are not usually formulated: when we take people to see or feel or think or want things, for instance, we don't for the most part actually enunciate what they see or feel or think or want. Nevertheless, we rely on people as being perceiving subjects with thoughts and wants and feelings, who think things and do things for reasons. In communicating with others, for instance, we rely continually on their being such as to be interpreted as purporting to say how things are—on their being commonsense psychological subjects like us.

Some philosophers employ a different term, saying 'folk psychology'. But if 'folk psychology' is construed by analogy with 'folk physics' or 'folk linguistics', then it carries the implication that folk psychology is the perhaps defective version of a subject matter that others (physicists, linguisticians) study with more appropriate methods than the folk. The implication is to be shunned: we ought not to assume at the outset that the basis of our everyday understanding of one another is susceptible of correction and refinement by experts in some specialist field where empirical considerations of some non-commonsensical kind can be brought to bear. So I avoid 'folk'.

Commonsense psychology, on the present account of it, is a pervasive subject matter, more easily gestured towards than precisely delimited: in practice it cannot be separated off from all the other subject matters that people engage with in everyday life. In the use of many philosophers, though, 'commonsense psychology' is made to stand for something much more restricted than this. It may be made to stand for some set of generalizations which are supposed to underlie all the everyday commonsense psychological truths. Or again it may be made to stand specifically for the part of commonsense psychology which employs the so-called propositional attitude verbs (verbs like 'thinks' and 'hopes', which fit into the construction 'Person———that p'), or even for a part of this, for so-called belief-desire psychology.

When the first restriction is imposed, an assumption is made—that commonsense psychology is susceptible to a sort of summary, so that any everyday psychological truth about a person can be seen as an application of a generalization to a particular case. The difficulty of stating any general principles which are true, precise and interesting must count against this assumption.[1]

The second restriction makes it seem as if the propositional attitude states were the only mental states of commonsense, or, even less plausibly, that belief and desire were the only such states. Davidson spoke of holistic theory construction in respect of the attribution of propositional attitudes in 'Mental Events' (1970); and the 'holism of the mental' has been taken ever since to stand for a claim about the interdependencies between the propositional attitude states (or between some of them). The effect is that the true holism of the mental, constituted by interconnexions between the various propositional attitude states *and others*, is ignored. With this restriction in place, the question of commonsense psychology's status seems no longer to raise a version of a longstanding metaphysical problem. It is made to seem as if we had to decide on the merits of a certain mode of explanation, used when 'belief-desire psychology' is practised; and as if, having made a decision on this, we could then simply declare commonsense psychology O.K. or not O.K.

Usually when a question is asked about the 'status' of commonsense psychology, it is out of a desire to know how commonsense psychology matches up against some *other* subject matter. Usually the question is raised by those who are happy to suppose that commonsense psychology consists of some definite set of statable propositions, so that to ask it is to set one 'theory' against another. But we can talk about commonsense psychology without making that assumption, so that we do not have to confine ourselves to its putative summary. Nor need we confine ourselves to what is only a part of its subject matter. We can ask how one should think of the relation of the total subject matter, used in understanding people, to the subject matter of, say, the sciences.

3

It is rare these days to find the claim that the *laws* and *terms* of commonsense psychology reduce to the laws and terms of physics. But it is not at all rare to find the idea that commonsense psychological explanations ultimately can—or ought to—fall within the scope of natural scientific ones. The 'ought to' comes in here because of the belief on the part of some philosophers that any real phenomenon, however we may actually understand it, is intelligible from the 'objective, third-personal perspective' that natural scientists adopt. This belief may be thought to be essential to a naturalist world view. Commonsense psychological phenomena, then, from this view, 'ought to' be amenable to explanations of some kind that scientists give, because it would count against them—against their 'reality', or against naturalism—if they did not. Once this view is taken, there is the possibility that commonsense psychology fails to live up to a standard which the metaphysician sets. If so, commonsense psychology might be refuted.

There would be massive repercussions if someone could demonstrate that commonsense psychology both required vindication of a certain sort and lacked vindication of that sort. For if we could not take seriously the notions that we apply to one another in putting commonsense psychology to work, then we could not take ourselves seriously—as perceivers, as cognizers, and as agents (still less as social beings). Yet we have to take ourselves seriously to take, for instance, the projects of science seriously: it would be strange to allow that human beings have come to understand quite a bit about the world's workings if we also held that human beings have never been such as to perceive or understand anything (still less to communicate with one another). If commonsense psychology were false, then even if a world of objects did exist independent of us, that world would not be something of which we really had any conception of ourselves taking any view, nor something on which we could have a conception of ourselves as having any influence. We have to envisage a scepticism far more devastating than any with which we are familiar. In sceptical philosophy as we find it in recent history, psychological truths are taken as assured (even if they are truths about the mind of a solitary enquirer merely), and to entertain scepticism is to doubt the existence of further truths about the world (or about the existence of other minds within it). But a sceptical position based upon suspicion of the psychological, which overthrew commonsense psychology, would leave nothing assured; it would be a sort of nihilism.

Some philosophers are committed to this nihilism. There are eliminativists who tell us that commonsense psychology is straightforwardly false (e.g., P. M. Churchland, 1981).[2] But it is not only philosophers holding such devastating views who are implicated in a potential threat to commonsense psychology. Many think that commonsense psychological explanations work through their connexion with theories in physical science, without contemplating the possibility that the connexions do not exist. Functionalists may provide an example. Few actually speak of commonsense psychology as needing vindication; they take it for granted that there are projectible psychophysical correlations, and that through them (along with some specifically semantical correlations, perhaps) commonsense psychology is grounded in physical science. But presumably if there were no correlations of the sort that they themselves assume, our use of commonsense psychology would be, so far as they are concerned, merely 'fictionalizing and contrivance' (as Brian Loar, 1981, p. 15, put it).[3]

Some philosophers, though, are simply content to allow that our common faith in commonsense psychology is misplaced: they don't balk at the thought that we regularly fictionalize. Believing that commonsense psychology lacks the vindication that a realistic view of it would require, they make play with its seeming invulnerability. Quine (1960) held that we may continue to use 'the intentional idiom', because we cannot abandon it even on discovering it to be false. When we engage in science, he thought, we are on firm, true ground; but we must use a double standard to give credence also to what is said using the intentional idiom, and treat that as 'drama'.[4] Dennett too, more recently, suggested sometimes that attributions of states of mind to people must be viewed instrumentalistically rather than realistically; or that they need to be understood less than fully literally: where Quine spoke of drama, Dennett now speaks of 'fiction' (Dennett, 1987a).[5] But it is not easy to see how we could work to a lower standard in interpreting ourselves than in understanding anything else. If you have to engage in dramatic fiction in order to suppose that someone is telling you that *p* (as Quine says), then how do you extricate yourself from the drama so as to be in a position to feel assured that (really) *p?* If you cannot take it to be literally true that *x* thinks that *p* (as Dennett sometimes says), then how could it ever be that *p*—literally—is what you come to think when *x* (as it seems) tells you that *p?* The same point that led us to think that we should be taken to a sort of nihilism if we convicted commonsense psychology of falsehood must lead us now to wonder how it could possibly be accorded an inferior place in our world view.

Of course there is no danger of commonsense psychology's having an inferior place, still less of its being eliminated, until some standard invoked from outside it is set for it. The assumed standard when it is *naturalism* that is defended is got from an idea of *nature*. And a particular assumption about the world of nature appears to go along with the use of 'naturalism' that has grown up in recent philosophy of mind—the assumption that that world for its part is a world free of norms, a world such as scientists describe. A defense of naturalism is then thought to require the carrying out of a project of 'naturalizing' the subject matter of commonsense psychology—either of showing the fitness for scientific treatment of psychological attributions, or of showing some sort of link between everyday explanations using psychological vocabulary and explanations given from an 'objective third-personal' point of view. (A defense of naturalism turns into a defense of eliminativism when such projects seem doomed to fail.)

But the particular assumption about 'the world of nature' is not obligatory. And this is why there can be what I call *naive* naturalism, distinguishable from the more usually defended versions. When it is allowed that not everything in nature is visible from the perspective adopted by the naturalizer, we can see ourselves as inhabitants of a natural world without thinking that our talk about ourselves needs to be given special treatment to make this possible. Marx said, 'Man is not only a natural being, he is a human natural being' (Marx, at p. 169 in 1971).[6] There can be a conception of 'nature' to which humanity is not inimical. This, in my terms, is naive nature.[7]

If 'scientific naturalism' were made the name of the version of naturalism that is usually defended, then the contrast between the position I oppose and the one I embrace would correspond to a 'scientific'-'naive' distinction. But it might be tendentious to label my opponents' position 'scientific'. For although many of them may frequently remind us of science's triumphs, some of them may deny that any thoughts about scientific discovery impel them towards naturalism. True, the idea of science has loomed large in my characterization of what non-naive naturalists think; but it has entered only in order to make allusion to a kind of subject matter (nature, on one understanding of it) on which a certain perspective is taken, and for which certain styles of explanation (those which, actually, scientists use) are appropriate. What places commonsense psychology under threat is the thought that it might be impossible to take the relevant perspective on ourselves, and that the relevant sorts of explanation might not be forthcoming so far as the subjects of commonsense psychology are concerned.

The 'naive' of naive naturalism, then, is to be understood as qualifying 'nature' in the first instance: naturalism in philosophy of mind is tenable only if a conception of naive nature is introduced. But if the 'naive' of 'naive naturalism' resonates with its use in 'naive realism' as this is defended sometimes as an account of perception, then that need be no bad thing. For the naivety of naive realism consists in its claim to leave in good order what we ordinarily, innocently think; and so it is meant to be with naive naturalism. This version of naturalism avers something that someone without any philosophical agenda could without any second thoughts aver about herself and others. That is not to say that someone without any philosophical agenda would immediately accept naive naturalism: the doctrine is meant to bear on what philosophers take to be a problem. But it is to suggest that some sorts of philosophical sophistication make their own problems, bringing standards of theory, or assumptions from metaphysics, which are out of place. Commonsense psychology is to be deemed trustworthy, not because it leads to scientific theories or is founded in their truth, but because it stands with all of our beliefs about the natural world which fall without it.[8]

4

It is only relatively recently that *naturalism* has been the position presumed to be proof against the errors of Cartesian Dualism. In the 1960s and 1970s, one or another variety of *physicalism* or *materialism* was what a philosopher was supposed to make out her title to if she was not to be convicted of subscribing to any unnatural dualist tenets. At least I take there to be this continuity in the use of the different terms, because I think that a certain outlook encourages much of what has gone by the names of 'physicalism', 'materialism' *and* 'naturalism'.[9] Today, after the expansion of various engineering and computer sciences and of cognitive science, the words 'material' and 'physical' serve less well than perhaps they once did to convey a demand to accommodate everything from a perspective such as scientists adopt; and 'natural' comes better to do the work to which 'material' or 'physical' used to be put. (I allowed that it may be wrong to call the going naturalism *scientific*. But I suspect that, whether or not appeal is made to science, the actual progress of science combines with the prestige that it has in some quarters to make the outlook congenial to many philosophers.)

My need to distinguish *naive* naturalism corresponds, then, not just to my opposition to some ideas that have come into favour recently, but to the whole drift of the last thirty or forty years in philosophy of mind in the English-speaking world. It will be clearer why I say 'the whole drift' if I now connect up my reaction to reductionist thinking, which I have mainly had in mind above, with my reaction to the non-reductionist position of Donald Davidson, which is the position most often addressed explicitly in the essays that follow.

Davidson developed and defended his anomalous monism before 'naturalism' had its current use; and on the face of it, anomalous monism affords no threat whatever to anything in common sense. Davidson believes in the central importance of a normative conception of rationality in psychological understanding; and he believes that the understanding of rational beings is governed by its own principles, not by the laws of science. So far from trying to connect up common-sense psychology with some more scientific subject matter, Davidson uses the anomalousness of psychological truths, which is their failure to fit with accounts of the world as working according to natural law, as the ground of his physicalism.

The mental's irreducibility is then the key to Davidson's attitude to commonsense psychology. But his particular version of physicalism nevertheless rests on a metaphysical thesis—about causation. In Davidson's case it is not, as it is with many naturalists, that metaphysics reveals a standard to which commonsense psychology is supposed to conform. But still, the thesis about causation is introduced from outside of psychological understanding, as it were; and it gives us the sense of 'physical' by reference to which we are to understand Davidson's physicalist thesis, which says, about mental events, that they are (in this sense) physical. When I question this thesis in Davidson, I am resisting the idea that the events we recognize in taking a view of minded beings are available to a conception of how things are in nature independent of the minded beings there—of how things are, not naively, but according to, so to speak, objective metaphysics. (The thesis is the Nomological Character of Causality; the details are in Essays 3, 4 and 10; see also postscripts to Essay 2 and to Part I.)

Davidson's position has been subjected to a certain line of criticism in the last ten years or so. Critics have doubted whether his view of rational explanation can be combined with his view of causation; and many have said that his anomalous monism renders the mental causally powerless—that his position in truth is epiphenomenalist. Now the critics may be wrong; there may not be the instability in Davidson's position that they allege. (Again the details can wait; see Essay 8.) But the fact that there is such criticism helps to make it clear why I should see fit to assimilate Davidson's physicalism to the positions which I described as potentially endangering commonsense psychology. The criticisms show that our ordinary attitude to psychological explanation might be undermined by setting a general thesis about causality to work on an account of mental events. The premises Davidson uses to establish his monism, then, may, after all, pose a threat to common sense.

In the context of the present literature in philosophy of mind, Davidson's own claim about how things work causally can seem to introduce just one among a number of ideas of what is required of a causally efficacious item, all of which ideas have been thought to have epiphenomenalist tendencies—to cast doubt on the causal relevance of mental properties, that is. (For example, it is sometimes said that only the 'intrinsic' properties of something could determine its causal powers, and that the mental properties of people are not 'intrinsic' properties.) So the threat of epiphenomenalism, which is the position that the critics say Davidson's thinking leads to, is by no means an isolated threat in fact. And I think it is a symptom of prevailing attitudes not only how regularly the threat is presented, but also how lightly it is usually taken. Epiphenomenalism, like eliminativism, may be introduced as just one more in a catalogue of options in philosophy of mind, unattractive to be sure, but available to those whose arguments lead that way. Yet epiphenomenalism in truth is an incredible position, committed to the kind of nihilism that bothers eliminativists so little. For it holds that nothing that we think (for instance) makes any genuine difference to what we do or say. Once again, commonsense psychology is rendered worthless. It becomes impossible to see how we could have any view of *anything*. If, for instance, you seem to be told that p by x, you cannot suppose that x's own acceptance of p could account for what x says. Of course many of the critics pay little attention to the threat, because they deny the mental's anomalousness and think that nothing should prevent commonsense psychology from taking its place in the world objectively viewed. The fact that this is a fairly standard reaction only shows how strong and how ubiquitous the 'naturalizing' tendency has become.

The mental's irreducibility—which is the anomalousness, as opposed to the monism, of Davidson—is taken more or less for granted in the essays that follow. Although I often point to features of the mental as ensuring its irreducibility, I rely on Davidson's arguments rather than rehearse them. If one wants to see signs of the mental's irreducibility (as opposed to arguments), then one need only look to the work of those of eliminativist or instrumentalist persuasion (see §3 above). If these philosophers thought that reduction of the mental was a genuine possibility, then they would not call for its elimination or its treatment as fictional, or whatever. This will be true at least if the relation 'is reducible to' between two subjects is defined for the purpose (and vaguely enough), so that one subject is reducible to another if it so relates to that other that the other's metaphysical standing is conferred upon it. Davidson's belief in the anomalousness of commonsense psychology ensures that commonsense psychology is, in this extremely vague sense, irreducible to any subject matter suited to the formulation of natural laws. A comparable thesis of 'irreducibility', although it may not be explicitly embraced by them, is surely at work in the thinking of the fictionalizers and the eliminators—and of almost everyone.

5

Davidson himself is not the sort of 'naturalizer' I was concerned with in §3. But his theory can play a pivotal role in thinking about the various positions in philosophy of mind nowadays. This is because his is often supposed to be the weakest non-dualist theory there can be. If the critics of Davidson were right about an inherent instability in anomalous monism, then we could seem to have to choose between, on the one hand, a stronger position, having more metaphysical ambitions than Davidson's own and finding some sort of reducibility for the mental desirable, and, on the other hand, a position that gives up even on any ontological thesis about mental events and thus (supposedly) collapses into dualism. But these are not the only choices if naive naturalism is a possibility. For naive naturalism avoids dualism without advancing any of the claims of materialism or of physicalism or of naturalism as these have come to be known. The world in which mind is accommodated by the naive naturalist is naively natural: it contains the objects that we see and that we act on; no peculiarly scientific method is required to have knowledge of it.

Obviously everything here turns on what it takes to avoid dualism. Up to this point 'Cartesian Dualism' has been simply a name for what any naturalist rejects, something to be fended off. The negative and schematic characterization has been quite deliberate: in relation to the positions I have been discussing, the part assigned to Cartesian Dualism is the part simply of the enemy. But until we know what is so wrong with the dualism ascribed to Descartes, we cannot know what virtues accrue to a position through its avoiding Dualism. And until we have an idea of what it takes to avoid it, and can see that it is an erroneous position, the claim that naive naturalism partakes of any naturalistic virtues can only have the status of assertion. (Not that anything here has been argued for rather than asserted—I have only indicated where I want to stand.)

Evidently enough, I do not think that an ontological thesis like Davidson's, about mental events, is required to avoid a criticizably Cartesian position. In fact I think that Davidson's own ontological thesis can be a product of the 'naturalizing' tendency, and that many of those who call themselves materialists or physicalists or naturalists have not escaped from the features of Descartes's position which make it an untenable one. These are among the things that I hope are made out in the material that follows, and in whose light naive naturalism emerges as a positive position.

I

Ontological Questions

1

Introduction: Persons and Their States, and Events

1

Nowadays *consciousness* is sometimes presented as if it were a residual problem in philosophy of mind—as if we had reached a point at which a great range of difficulties has been taken care of, and a wide variety of mental states understood, yet at which consciousness still needs to be brought into the reckoning. I find this state of affairs at least as strange as I find consciousness mysterious. There surely is a problem about consciousness: there are no obvious answers to the question how conscious beings can have evolved. But is it right to suppose that we can have a good account of what are actually states of mind of conscious creatures—of people seeing things, or talking to one another—only the account needs supplementing because it omits the particular facts about their consciousness? How could filling out on an account of states and events ensure that the beings who possess the states and participate in the events are conscious beings? (I do not think it could; and "the problem of consciousness" is not addressed until Essay 10.)

The present sense of philosophical mystery surrounding consciousness is, I think, attributable partly to a line of thinking which allows questions about consciousness to arise detached from questions about the beings that are actually conscious. The line of thinking may be

17

promoted (for instance) when a philosopher seeks a treatment of intentional mental states. On the list of the intentional, she will almost certainly include 'believes that' and 'desires that', perhaps 'hopes that', and 'fears that', and possibly 'knows that' and 'is aware that'.[1] Her question then may be about how to characterize 'the causal role' of these states.

Following this line, we are encouraged to focus on certain items. We want to be sure that everything that inhabits the causal world is in good natural order. So we had better make sure of this not only in the case of the grossly visible items such as people, but also in the case of the states and events they are involved in. It may be *someone's thinking something* which explains what she did, and it may be *her deliberately doing something* which had such and such consequence. To be certain of the natural character of everything, then, we must attend to these things, it is supposed. We have to ask about such things as people's thinkings of particular thoughts, and their doings of particular things, 'Are these states and events physical?'. (Notice that when such things are called states, 'state' has a different use from that of the philosophy that sought 'a treatment of intentional mental states': see further below.)

Undoubtedly, one pressure that there is to raise such questions is a desire to avoid dualism, which holds, as Descartes did, that two quite different sorts of thing occupy the spatiotemporal world—things of the mental sort and things of the physical sort. Non-theistically minded people mainly find such dualism rebarbative today. And in order not to take Descartes's side, it can seem that we must assure ourselves that *someone's thinking something* (which is mental) is actually of some same sort as, say, a door bell's ringing (which is physical).

But Descartes's own principal claim, which makes him a dualist, was the claim that there are spiritual *substances:* in Descartes the ghostly things were souls or minds, not entities in the category of state or event. It is true presumably that Descartes would have judged that there are states and events which are spiritual and non-physical, particular ones of these obtaining or occurring when people think thoughts and do things. But it is not as if Descartes first identified these problematic states and events and then deemed them spiritual. So there is the possibility that we may avoid Descartes's dualism without having anything very distinctive to say about the general nature of the states and events that people participate in. The material in this first part of the book tries to make this possibility good.

Philosophers who share my view that there is no need for any thesis of physicalism such as is usually supposed to be required to counter Descartes's dualism are Tim Crane and Hugh Mellor (1990). They consider physicalism to be 'a wrong answer to an essentially trivial question' (p. 206). If that were precisely right, then the present part of this book would be needless. I doubt that it can be precisely right, however, because I have found that it takes actual argument to refute the physicalist thesis in dispute in the next three essays. What *ought* to be needless is the line of thinking that I try to characterize here (and also the assumption to which I am opposed in Part II; see Essay 5). If it came to seem that those who go in for the line of thinking (and those who use the assumption) engaged in an 'essentially trivial', or anyway an idle, exercise, that would be fine.[2]

Most of the material in Part I speaks most directly to things in the category of events rather than states. When philosophers have raised general questions about identities for events *and states*, they have often assumed that things of both sorts are in the category of particulars— that both events and states belong in a domain of non-abstract objects which can be picked out now in this way, now in that. It actually seems much less clear that there are states which are particulars than that there are events which are. Of course there *are* mental states. But for someone to be in some mental state in the ordinary sense is simply for her to have some mental property. (Belief, say, is a mental state: people have the property of believing things.) In this ordinary sense, then, mental states are not particulars. Philosophers who notice that their purposes aren't served by the ordinary sense of 'mental state' may assure us that 'token' states are what they mean in identity theses: whereas belief that *p* is a type of state, *her* belief that *p* is a token, they say, and it is the token that we have to relate to some particular thing in the neurophysiological realm. We may have become inured to the putative tokens by habitual references to, for example, 'beliefs and desires as causes of actions'. But of course just writing 'token' in front of a phrase standing for a mental state (in the ordinary sense), or adding a possessive 'her' or 'his' to such a phrase, cannot bring an item of the kind in question into existence.

It is possible to be suspicious of the whole idea of token states.[3] My own suspicions will not come to the surface until Essay 8, and need not be voiced in Part I. In this part, I am often concerned only with events, although sometimes I find fault with identity claims made about items within a putative category of events *and* states. If the truth were that no items in that category are properly called states, then, in respect of those putative items, it would be overdetermined that the identity claims I object to are objectionable.

2

I call states and events *micro* things in Essay 2, thinking that they are thought of as, so to speak, much smaller than persons, who occupy the *macro*physical world. The essay was prepared for a volume on Richard Rorty's *Philosophy and the Mirror of Nature*, and it contains some more about Descartes; it attempts to bring out the extent to which his dualism was not an answer to a question about the micro things. I had been struck by the fact that, as Rorty says, it is pretty easy for a philosopher to avoid the dualism of Descartes. Yet Rorty also thinks that philosophy of mind has survived only because it is carried on in the Cartesian vein. There must in that case be more to the Cartesian legacy than the easily avoided dualist thesis. Well, one thing common to Descartes and some contemporary writers (I suggest) is a thesis of the mental's irreducibility. But Rorty for his part accepts this irreducibility thesis, so that this cannot be what he blames for the errors, or the needlessness, of post-1950 philosophy of mind. To understand what has been inherited from Descartes, I think we have to notice a way of thinking metaphysically which served in Descartes as part of the reason for his dualism; it is a way of thinking which actually gains ground in the late twentieth century, but which is used now as the route to various materialist theses (including, I maintain, Rorty's own).

Essay 3 shows that one need not side with Descartes to take exception to claims that are made about the physical nature of events. It suggests that an unduly monolithic conception of what there is is often at work when micro items are considered—or that, if the conception is not actually at work, then it would need to be called on in order to make out the usual physicalist claims about mental events. The conception is a mereological one, which (to put it roughly) takes the existence of larger things, occupying more room in the spatiotemporal world, to depend on the existence of the smaller things making them up. If we abandon it, then we may think of dependencies running the other way, so that, for instance, the presence in the world of the things that philosophers take to be candidates for 'micro'-identification depend upon the existence of people, and are not to be pondered about aside from thinking about what persons themselves are like.

Essay 4 was written at a time when it seemed to me a better project than it now does to conduct enquiries into the nature of the micro items that have come to concern philosophers of mind. Surely such items are contained in the physical world, I thought. But it struck me that the sense of 'physical' in which that can seem so obviously true might not be the sense that philosophers had brought to bear in making out their various physicalist identity theses. I wanted then to confront those physicalist theses, having fixed the sense of 'physical'—but to confront their consequences for particular cases rather than any of the sweeping arguments for them. I came to think that the usual physicalist theses must be rested more in philosophers' prejudice than in anything obvious. And I later tried to expose the philosophers' prejudicial outlook (in Essays 2 and 3). I hope that I can benefit now from time's passage, if not from hindsight, and that the argument of Essay 4 may be more persuasive, if less indispensable, in its new setting. At any rate I have placed the oldest essay last in Part I. The argument it gives is for the negative ontological conclusion which the essays here are meant collectively to support. That conclusion is that mental events cannot be regarded as physical according to any at all exacting conception.

3

If the arguments of these essays were ever worth rehearsing, then they still are. For the claim that they took issue with—that all the mental states and events are (in a certain sense) physical—is usually taken quite for granted these days. The claim has not been lent any actual support in the philosophical literature in the last ten years or so; but this is not because it has fallen from philosophers' favour, but because progress in neuroscience is supposed to have made it credible, so that it is no longer in any need of specifically philosophical defense. It has come to be assumed that people's dealings in a causal world, when they are not overt, are just the causal connexions between neural states and events inside them. Naturalism (which in the Introduction I characterized sufficiently imprecisely to bring in all its various proponents) is sometimes actually said to *be* the view that 'the mind-brain relation is a natural one. Mental processes just are brain processes'. Neuroscience has 'shown that the brain possesses both the complexity and the power to do the information processing that human minds in fact do' (Flanagan, 1992, p. xi).

Formulations like this give rise to the 'residual' problem about consciousness from which I began. If a question is raised now about the consciousness of something, we must think of it as having all of those sophisticated information-processing properties that brains have, and then wonder how it could also have the distinctive properties of a conscious being. This indeed is how the problem is often put: 'we do not understand how the brain could be conscious', it is said (Akins, 1993, p. 125, e.g.).

But should anyone be trying to show how *brain* consciousness is possible? *Of course* one won't see any signs of consciousness when one looks at (and tries to listen to?) a portion of gray matter. No wonder there is puzzlement. But *this* puzzlement may go away when it is realized that *if* an isolated brain could be conscious—which is not the least obvious—then that would only be because it was, or had been, or at the very least was such as to be, inside a conscious being. The things whose consciousness in the first instance we should seek to treat are surely those things encounters with whom we take to be encounters with conscious beings. And these, the actual, extant, visible, audible, beings who are subjects of experience, are not brains.

We come full circle at the point at which philosophers identify brains with minds. The micro items supposedly involved in a person's being the minded being she is have all come to be associated with a persisting entity on the macro scale. (True, we don't *see* brains in the ordinary course of things; but they aren't microscopic.) This is why I said that late twentieth-century speculation about the micro items seems to have helped a Cartesian way of thinking to gain ground. Descartes himself found no problem about our being conscious creatures, because his conception of a conscious creature just is a conception of a certain kind of thinking one *(a res cogitans)*. Having introduced souls, Descartes had something onto which sensations could be latched—where, for him, sensations are things like colours and odours and flavours, which, as he put it, 'exist in my thought'. But there was a cost in associating consciousness with thought in this way—in supposing that being a subject of experience can be accommodated simply as an aspect of a *res cogitans*. Descartes was committed to the view that non-human animals are automata: animals (except for people) are like fountains and clocks, complicated enough in their workings, but, because non-rational, wholly machine-like, insentient. Consciousness of the human sort cannot be seen as a development of animal nature when it is associated with a something which interacts causally with a body.

Of course Descartes's own thesis that minds are not natural things has been abandoned today. But even today the ontological claim presupposed in that thesis—that there *are* minds—seems to be endorsed in a sense which Descartes would have approved. It is endorsed when we are supposed to believe in things (brains, now) an account of which is the whole account of 'the mental side' of persons—set apart from what we might have taken pretheoretically to be 'their physical sides'. With the identification of minds with brains, a person's leading of a mental life comes to be treated as a separable side of her biography, conducted inside her.[4]

If Descartes was mistaken in making room for such a treatment, then his immaterialism is only one of the aspects of his position that we have to reject. We must also reject his idea of mental autonomy, which makes it possible to suppose that an account of mental phenomena can be an account of a certain sort of substance—immaterial substance in Descartes's own case. My attack on the idea of a realm of micro items identifiable with things in the neuroscientists' province is thus meant as an attack on a part of Cartesianism.

2

Descartes, Rorty and the
Mind-Body Fiction

Philosophers, having invented the mind, discovered some mind-body problems; then, relatively recently, they created the philosophy of mind. If we could gain the proper perspective of historical contingency on the mind's invention, then we should no longer feel that we needed solutions to mind-body problems. We should settle for materialism, but not the sort of philosophical materialism that has been fashioned in opposition to Cartesian Dualism.

This is the message I read in the first two chapters of Richard Rorty's *Philosophy and the Mirror of Nature* (1979).[1] As I have expressed it, in broadest outline, I find it congenial: I agree with Rorty that many of those who have fought against Cartesian Dualism have failed to realize that the battles have always taken place on territory of the enemies' making. But I believe that something different from what Rorty insists on will be involved in liberating ourselves from the oppressive forces of traditional conceptions of mind. In this essay I shall try to bring out the manner in which the historical picture in part I of Rorty's book seems to me to be partial. Lacking Rorty's command of the history, I cannot even try to present a complete picture myself. But I shall say some things about Descartes in order to make a suggestion about what I think is kept hidden by Rorty.

1

Rorty thinks that issues about materialism versus dualism would take care of themselves if only we could free ourselves from habitual ways of viewing the putative problems of the philosophy of mind. But he endorses a version of materialism himself—materialism without identities, as he calls it. It is supported partly by way of a thought-experiment about the Antipodeans, a race of creatures, very much like us, discovered on a distant planet in the twenty-first century, who got on quite as well as us, but who were fortunate enough never to have invented the mind, or to have participated in the '"idea" idea'. Thanks to technological progress, they could label their neurological states. And they found themselves indifferent to whether they reported (for instance), 'It appears to be red and rectangular', or 'It makes neuronic bundle G-14 quiver'. The Antipodeans are meant to show us (Terrans) that we should be *materialists*, because the mental can be renounced without loss; and that we should be materialists *without identities*, because, the mental having been thus renounced, we see that there should never have been any need to assert that mental things are identical with physical things.

Some people have suspected that Rorty is not quite the wholesale revolutionary that he presents himself as being. Suspicions arise from two quarters. First, Rorty's new doctrine seems uncomfortably close to his own earlier one, which it was natural to classify as eliminative materialism; and eliminative materialism was put together as a solution to the very problem that Rorty wants to show us we do not have to solve. So it can seem that Rorty's position is insufficiently radical for his own purposes. Second, Rorty's new version of materialism seems sometimes to be addressed only to such putatively problematic items as sensations, and to say nothing on what philosophers of mind would subsume under intentionality. So it can seem that Rorty's position is unduly narrow for his own purposes. I think that the first of these suspicions, on probing, will seem to be the reverse of the truth, but that the second, in the end, is much harder to remove.

To allay the first suspicion quickly for the time being, it may be enough to point out that eliminative materialism was always a revolutionary position (even if it has sometimes seemed like just one more in a catalogue of anti-dualist positions). We should not forget that eliminativists were always ready and willing to abolish the mind. (I shall return to this.)

The other suspicion was that Rorty's own position as arrived at in part I of the *Mirror of Nature* covers too little of what we have come to think of as mind. The suspicion is created in the first instance by Rorty's emphasis on *raw feels*. When he comes to say anything positive in the place of what is said by philosophers of mind, his only actual example of a putative mental attribute is 'having a sensation of *pain*'. And when he imagines his readers worrying about his Antipodeans (about whether they really have everything that we've got), their worries extend only to the existence or otherwise of *phenomenal* items in the Antipodean case. At first blush it may seem entirely appropriate that Rorty should put the emphasis where he does. After all, he believes that philosophers who have worried about mind-body problems have suffered both from the tendency to think of the intentional in a phenomenal way, and from regarding indubitability (which may strike us as more characteristic of the phenomenal than of the intentional) as *the* characteristic of mentality quite generally. So it isn't surprising that Rorty should think that mind-body problems are laid to rest when the phenomenal has been disposed of. If Rorty's own version of materialism does not seem to be addressed to intentionality, and to limit its scope to the more sensational items, this may only be because it is Rorty's view that the whole of our misconception of mind can be located in the phenomenal realm.

This can all be said. But it may still leave us wondering about the intentional. If we are concerned about whether the Antipodeans can be assimilated to us, should all of our questions really revolve around how things might feel for them—rather than around what things are like for them (in a sense much broader than how they feel)? The last decade of Anglo-American philosophy has seen an enormous amount of work devoted to the propositional attitude states and to representation. Rorty will tell us that historical accidents determine philosophical agenda from time to time, so that there isn't much to be made of the fact that philosophers in the 1980s have been obsessed with 'content' whereas philosophers of the previous two decades had been obsessed with 'raw feels'. Nevertheless, the recent work on intentionality has certainly developed inside the very subject—philosophy of mind—which Rorty is concerned to undermine. And Rorty must acknowledge that if the mind is a fiction, then, for better or worse, its authors and perpetrators have decided what features in it.

So what of the fiction's perpetrators? Rorty thinks that the myths of dualist thinking have survived for three centuries, and still pervade philosophy. According to him, even contemporary *materialists* show themselves as guilty of being under the myth's influence—in their wish to assert identities. But if we want to see manifestations of the distinctive ways of thinking owed to the invention of the mind, then the kind of philosopher we should look to is the *neo-dualist* of Rorty's book. The neo-dualists presumably (given their name) are those in whom the invented mind is at its most recognizable.

Yet when we look to Rorty's summing up of neo-dualism, it seems to be a doctrine with a fragile basis on which nothing much is built: 'contemporary philosophers, having updated Descartes, can be dualists without their dualism making the slightest difference to any human interest or concern, without interfering with science or lending any support to religion' (p. 68). Of course Rorty's thinking that dualism can very easily be dispensed with is all of a piece with his view that the mind might never have been invented. But it is mysterious why philosophers should cling so tenaciously to their invention if dualist thinking can be abandoned with so little loss. Can there really be so little to the Cartesian legacy?

At two points Rorty is more explicit about what neo-dualists actually believe.

1. According to Rorty, neo-dualists endorse a conceptual dualism along the same lines as that which is required by Descartes's substantial division of mind from body (p. 17; see also p. 65). In this variety of neo-dualism, ontological significance is accorded to a certain *conceptual* division.
2. A little later, neo-dualists are characterized as placing weight on two ways in which phenomena may be known about or understood (pp. 28–29). Their variety of neo-dualism accords ontological significance to a certain *epistemic* distinction.

In the following section, I shall discuss Descartes's views with these two varieties of neo-dualism in mind—conceptual and epistemic neo-dualism, as I shall call them. I shall suggest that it is not very likely that Rorty's conceptual neo-dualism is something that Descartes has left us with. Epistemic neo-dualism, though, which Rorty dismisses very rapidly, and which he does not connect with Descartes's thought, can be related to a Cartesian way of thinking. I believe that if we can see the relative unimportance dialectically of Descartes's dualism of substance as such, and the relative importance dialectically of views held by Descartes about how the world must be understood, then we may begin to understand better some of the feelings about Rorty's position that I have expressed. In particular, we may appreciate the true nature of its radicalism; we may see why intentionality is not quite as incidental to mind as (I have maintained) it appeared to be in part I of the *Mirror of Nature;* and we may understand how it can seem that in Rorty's view the mind is both very hard and very easy to be rid of. In the final section, I shall try to make some of this out.

2

One reason Descartes merits the title of dualist is that if he had been asked, 'How many sorts of substance are there in the natural world?', he would have answered, 'Two'. He thought that there are minds, whose essential nature is cogitative, and that there are bodies, whose essential nature is to be extended (or to occupy space in the world). One contradicts Descartes, and is a monist and not a dualist, then, if one says that there is only one sort of substance in the natural world. So in order to be a materialist, in one sense of that term at least, it is enough to deny that there are mental substances distinct from material substances—to deny that there are souls (or spirits or minds).

But Rorty's conceptual neo-dualists rely not on a distinction between soul and body, but on a distinction between mental and physical *properties* of people. How are the two sorts of dualism related? Are the mental properties simply the properties that substance dualists thought of as properties of minds and the physical properties those of bodies?

In fact it is hard to know what should be included in a representative list of mental properties. But suppose that our aim is to capture out intuitions about this (and Rorty admits we have such intuitions, wherever they have come from), but that we do not aim for anything distinctively Cartesian about our list (though Rorty thinks our intuitions lead us *willy-nilly* to draw lines in a roughly Cartesian way). Then we should presumably want to include among the mental properties at least those properties expressed by most of the following predicates:

is trying to hit the target
is intentionally annoying Mary
is aware of the blackboard
has a headache
knows that grass is green
believes that whales eat people
is cheerful today
is arrogant

It seems evident that all such properties are properties of people, who are things that have height and weight and move around in space, and thus are equally bearers of physical properties. And in the case of at least some of these mental properties, we can form no conception of what it would be to ascribe them to things of any other sort: we have no idea of what it would be for, say, 'is cheerful today' to apply except to something readily visible as it were. If the idea of possession of a mental life was meant to lead to the postulation of a substance leading that life, then the idea of possession of a mental life could not plausibly be equated with possession of properties that we feel inclined to put on a list of mental properties. The answer to our question, then, seems to be *No:* the neo-dualists' conceptual distinction does not connect straightforwardly with Descartes's distinction of substances.

In fact, and not surprisingly, Descartes would not have wanted to say that a person's possessing the properties in our list was a matter simply of a soul's having certain attributes. A Cartesian soul is a *res cogitans*, and, even though 'cogitare' has to be interpreted more broadly than 'think', not every property which is intuitively a mental one is a *cogitative* one in a sense that Descartes would have intended. Much of what we regard as mental is not to be accounted for in the Cartesian scheme simply by saying how things are with a soul. Descartes recognized a class of sensational properties, for instance, 'which arise from the union and, as it were, are an intermixture of mind and body'.[2] Sensations include pain, hunger and thirst, and sense perception. A person's seeing something is a composite fact, made up from a figure's being printed on her senses, from an image of the fig-ure's being imprinted on her pineal gland, and from the mind's attending to what is imprinted on the gland. Again a person's doing something intentionally is a matter both of there being a volition (which is a species of cogitation) and of there being some bodily movement. Presumably Descartes needs to be able to tell some such story about any property that we regard as intuitively mental—a story about how a person's possessing that property can consist in the possession of attributes by each of his two sorts of substance taken separately. In *The Passions of the Soul*, Descartes had much to say of a detailed sort under this head. But in spite of his furnishing detail, Descartes resorted to evasively vague suggestions in painting the general picture of how minds and bodies conspire to produce people with properties such as those in our list: he often alludes to the 'apparent intermingling of the mind with the body'.

There are then too many properties which we naturally conceive as mental but which on Descartes's own admission cannot be assigned either to a *res cogitans* or to a *res extensa* for it to be plausible that Cartesian Dualism is the substantial counterpart of a distinction we may now naturally make between mental and non-mental attributes of people. And of course we know in any case that Descartes himself wasn't led to introduce his soul in the *Meditations* because of some difference in two sorts of properties that he possessed. When he announced, 'Sum res cogitans', he was not at a stage in his project where he was entitled to believe in the existence of things having physical properties. He tells us that he had considered, before engaging in his doubt, that he was nourished, that he walked, and so on; but when he looked upon his own nature, these attributes were not in the picture. 'It is very certain that the knowledge of my existence taken in its precise significance does not depend on things whose existence is not yet known to me.'[3] The soul of the *Meditations* is not arrived at by way of thoughts about mental-physical difference as such.

Evidently Descartes ought eventually to make up his mind about how things turn out when physical things are acknowledged: he ought to be able to say whether he is his soul or whether he is the union of his soul and his body. In fact he settles for speaking sometimes of 'myself inasmuch as I am only a thinking thing' and sometimes of 'myself in my entirety inasmuch as I am formed of body and soul'.[4] It is as if we have to believe that Descartes is one thing inasmuch as he engages in the project of doubt, and a complex of two things inasmuch as he sits in his study while he does so. A soul conceived in the Cartesian way, then, so far from lining up with Rorty's neo-dualists' dualism between the mental and the non-mental properties (by providing a bearer for the mental ones), actually gives rise to a problem about 'mind' and 'body'—a problem about what persons are, about what in the world bears what sorts of properties.

This is itself a Cartesian problem, of course. My point has been that we do not automatically involve ourselves in it by making a distinction between mental and physical properties. In fact this problem is not much discussed nowadays. *Substance* dualism would seem to be thought to have been left behind. Nowadays questions about mental and physical things usually concern not substances (people, souls, people's bodies), but the states and events in which people participate. The identity theories that Rorty dismisses as superfluous make such claims as that every mental event or state is the same as some physical event or state. If we want to see connexions between these materialists and Cartesian ways of thinking, then we need now to appreciate that there was another route leading Descartes to his dualism—other than that which he followed in the *Meditations*.

We might begin here with a distinction between two sorts of ontological question: macro-questions (about people) and micro-questions (about events and states).[5] Present-day concerns, which lead to identity theories, are, it seems, concerns with micro-questions. And Descartes, whose views engender various macro-questions, did not even introduce the 'micro-entities'. Even so, there may be a point in using a micro-macro distinction in thinking about Descartes. For Descartes did concern himself with questions at the micro level, if not the explicitly ontological micro-questions of today's identity theorists; he thought that interaction between mind and body had to be dealt with from the perspective of someone looking at the inside of a human being close up. Present-day materialists speak of mental states and events in the brain: Descartes describes the soul's interaction with the body physiologically. He uses the same sorts of terms in treating of the mechanisms of blood circulation and digestion as he uses in describing, for instance, voluntary agency, where the soul determines 'the subtle fluid styled the animal spirits, that passes from the heart through the brain towards the muscles . . . to perform definite motions'.[6]

In order to see micro-questions as provoked by a problem of mind and body, we have to recognize a different sort of perplexity from that which led Descartes to say, 'Sum res cogitans'. Non-mental properties of people, which are properties also of things that do not have mental lives, may be regarded as properties that characterize a world of nature that can be conceived independent of the fact of its containing things with mental lives. They are Physical properties. (The 'P' of 'Physical' is sometimes capitalized in editions of Descartes, and I shall follow this.[7]) The question then may be how the mental facts fit into a Physical world. Can mental facts be viewed as constituting the same natural realm as is characterized by those who study the Physical world and generalize about its workings? Descartes's answer was 'No'. He was sure that mental phenomena were not any part of what it is the scientist's task to study, because scientists are concerned with an extended substance which has its own essence precluding the features of thinking beings.

Margaret Wilson has argued that 'a *reason* for his dualism may be found in Descartes' commitment to mechanistic explanation in physics, together with the perfectly creditable belief that human intelligence could never be accounted for on the available mechanistic models'.[8] Descartes claimed that no mere machine could use language. And he thought that our aptitude to respond rationally in very various circumstances also could not be accounted for mechanistically: 'it is morally impossible that there should be sufficient diversity in any machine to allow it to act in all the events of life in the same way as our reason causes us to act'. He concludes, 'The rational soul . . . could not be in any way derived from the power of matter.'[9]

At one point Descartes even explains his dualism as the upshot of a correct understanding of the Physical world. In the *Replies*, he writes that he has to confess that, despite the fact that his arguments for the real distinction of soul and body in the *Meditations* fully conform to his own most exacting standards, nonetheless he found himself 'not wholly persuaded'. But when he 'proceeded farther', and 'paused in the consideration of Physical things', he observed that:

> nothing at all belongs to the nature of essence of body, except that it is a thing with length, breadth and depth, admitting of various shapes and various motions. Its shapes and motions are only modes, which

no power could make to exist apart from it; and on the other hand
. . . colours, odours, savours and the rest of such things, are merely
sensations existing in my thought, and differing no less from bodies
than pain differs from the shape and motion of the instrument which
inflicts it.

Thus a demanding conception of the Physical leads Descartes to refer
to minds 'rather than to bodies' aspects of things which, before reflection on the essence of body, he says he had supposed to be corporeal.[10]

The particular treatment of the secondary qualities—of 'colours,
odours, savours and the rest of such things'—makes the line of
thought here more explicit. The scholastics, whose view of the secondary qualities prevailed at the time that Descartes wrote, held that
when someone perceived, say, a yellow book, there was something in
her mind resembling the yellowness of the book. Descartes not only
rejected the resemblance doctrine, but also gave a particular account
of what it is about the book which makes for its being yellow. The
book's yellowness is to be identified with a specific power to set the
nerves in motion in certain ways;[11] the phenomenal quality yellowness
is located in the mind's reading of what is delivered by the nerves from
the organs to the gland. Here it can appear that Descartes was under
pressure to think of what is external to the subject of experience in
terms that apply whether or not there are any minds: we can say what
yellowness is (insofar as it is a property of external objects) by allusion
to the nervous system, but without any allusion to experience itself. It
is as if everything that has to be said about anything that is yellow
must be said without assuming the existence of anything except Physical bodies. There being no place in the world of matter for the book's
appearing yellow, Descartes can then accommodate it only in something whose existence is independent of the existence of matter—the
soul, which 'does not perceive excepting in as far as it is in the brain'.
The only things in Physical reality that the mind is directly in touch
with are the mechanical perturbations of the pineal gland.

It seems then that a thesis about the self-standing character of the
Physical world as a subject of study serves for Descartes, just like the
Meditations' thesis about the self-standing character of the mind, as a
way of arriving at a view of the mental and Physical as autonomous
realms. As Descartes said (speaking now of human bodies, rather than
of bodies in the external world at large), 'Considering the body in it-

self, we perceive nothing in it demanding union with the soul, and nothing in the soul obliging it to be united to the body.'[12] What has become clear is the extent to which the two doctrines—about the body and the soul—though reciprocal, are independently supported in Descartes. Each can equally be seen as underlying his idea that all mental-physical transactions are located at a place where mind and matter meet.

3

If the quick categorization at the start of the previous section does everything necessary to say what constitutes the properly *dualist* element in Descartes's philosophy, then it helps to show how very little it might take to make some materialist position attractive. There is something right about Rorty's thought that once the seventeenth-century notion of substance is abandoned, dualism ought to seem easy to dismiss. The philosophers of today who call themselves materialists have indeed dismissed it. Why in that case should Cartesianism about the mind seem to Rorty to be so persistent?

No immediate answer to this question is given by considering the conceptual neo-dualism of Rorty's opponents. For we saw that a distinction between what are and what aren't mental properties can be dissociated from any specifically Cartesian conception of the attributes of a *res cogitans*. Until more is said about a dualism of concepts—so long as it remains the intuitive one we looked at—there is nothing to place it in a tradition in which Descartes is a central figure.

Nor does the egocentric pathway of the *Meditations* appear to have much of a following in contemporary discussions of materialism versus dualism. The egocentrically arrived at conception of a soul is a conception of a subject of thought, where a thought is an object of introspective awareness or 'internal cognition'. It is the putative self that in modern writings features under such descriptions as 'ultimate private objects apparently lacking logical connections to anything else'.[13] Each person is meant to have a grasp of what her self is through reflection on what she can mean by 'I', just as Descartes is meant to discover his essential nature while making no assumptions except for those that pure introspection reveals as indubitable. Of course the *Meditations'* conception of a soul or self has recurred often enough in the philosophy of the last three centuries that it is not to be dismissed out of hand. But it seems right nevertheless to dismiss the suggestion that it is Rorty's target when he speaks of neo-dualism. If present-day opponents of materialism persist in Descartes's errors, their fault is not to rehearse the arguments of the *Meditations*.

Selves arguably do recur in contemporary discussions—in discussions of personal identity. And it is curious, I think, the extent to which the literature on personal identity and the nature of persons and the literature on the mind-body question and materialism have come to be separated in our tradition. The separation is roughly that (spoken of earlier) between macro- and micro-questions. Recognizing the separation, and having seen an apparent overlap of Descartes's concerns with the concerns of those who address micro-questions, we should look for a different connexion between Descartes and the neo-dualists of Rorty's book.

This is where Rorty's *epistemic* neo-dualists seem relevant. Their distinction between mental and physical is not introduced by way of intuitions about what constitutes mental vocabulary nor by way of what characterizes the soul. Rorty does not elaborate on their position; but from his gestures towards it, we can extract for them a recognizable and distinctive conception of the mental as a putatively problematic category: it is a conception of the features of a subject of experience that she is recognized as having when she is made sense of as a subject of experience. These features, the neo-dualists may suggest, could not be perceptible from the perspective of a student of matter, because they are recognizable only from a particular point of view.[14] And here epistemic neo-dualists seem to be at one with Descartes in his thesis of the impossibility of accommodating the rational soul in a world of mechanistically explicable things.

Two obvious differences between Descartes and those whom Rorty calls neo-dualists should be acknowledged. First, Descartes's views about the essence of the Physical as mind-excluding are not based straightforwardly in any obviously *epistemic* distinction.[15] Second, Descartes relied for those views on a specifically mechanistic idea of the Physical world, and on his (historically inevitable) ignorance of what machines are capable of. But there need be no very exact parallels between Descartes and the epistemic neo-dualists for us to see that no Cartesian ontological doctrine needs to be grounded in their initially epistemic distinction. For if we take Descartes at his word when he says that he had found reasons for his dualism 'in the consideration of Physical things', then we may accept that there is a thesis which is a candidate for neo-dualist assent and which is extricable from substantial dualism proper. What the neo-dualists' reflections on two modes of understanding leads them to can be summed up, suggestively enough and without specifically epistemological or ontological overtones, as the irreducibility of the mental. Might not an irreducibility thesis be what Descartes expressed in saying that 'the rational soul . . . could not be in any way derived from the power of matter'? (The reference to the rational soul seems eliminable: Descartes's thought at this point might be captured if one replaced 'the rational soul' with 'features of people, who are rational beings'.)

Here Descartes was denying that a material thing could have the character of a rational one (as opposed to his more familiar denial that a *res cogitans* could have a material character). If epistemic neo-dualists find problems in modern materialism parallel to those which at this stage Descartes would have thought to threaten any alternative to his dualism, then features of rational beings have to be seen now as problematic *relative* to what they are putatively irreducible to. A problem arises (neo-dualists may say) when it is supposed that concepts used for understanding the Physical world are apt for understanding the subjects of experience as such. Perhaps Rorty's difficulties about characterizing the mental, about finding any coherent target for his remarks, derive from his thinking that he has to find a category of things which are problematic in their own right as it were, rather than a category of things which it is problematic to accommodate with other things—with items studied by science, or with bare extended and mechanical things, or with Physical things (depending on what exactly the mental is said to be irreducible to). Perhaps also we may be able to give a more revealing answer than Rorty's own to his question 'Why do we tend to lump the intentional and the phenomenal together as the mental?': they will be brought together by a good characterization of the mental as irreducible.

If Descartes bequeathed us a problem, then it seems possible now that we should want to fault him for his conception of the world in which minds had to operate as much as for his conception of mind. When this possibility is realized, the affinities of Descartes with modern materialists come to the fore. Modern materialists, like Descartes, work with an assumption about the natural world within, or on, which the mind operates. For Descartes, there are two autonomous realms; some of the items from each are 'made to be united' to one another, and they interact at points where mind and matter meet. For the modern materialists, there are the things whose identity with physical things needs asserting, and there are the unproblematically physical, external things; and the two meet up at the place where the central nervous system joins the visible body. For both Descartes and the materialists, location of mental phenomena is then achieved by slotting the mind in (as it were), and in such a way that its interactions with the Physical are intelligible in the terms in which the Physical was understood before the slotting-in. What is special about Descartes's position is that the very nature of what is slotted in is different from that of what it is slotted in to.[16] But it is not only what is special to Descartes about which the neo-dualist complains. In either case, a neo-dualist will question the suggested accommodation of the mind: the modern materialist purports to have done what the irreducibility thesis showed to be impossible; Descartes has recognized the impossibility, but drawn the wrong conclusion and ensured that the mind itself is not any part of the natural world.[17] In both cases, we may think, something that the neo-dualist objects to is the equation of the natural world with a Physical world.

If this were right, then the radical character of Rorty's own position would not need to be thought to result from his having freed himself from all Cartesian ways of thinking. It may result from his sharing with Descartes and the materialists the assumption to which the neo-dualist now seems to object. For Rorty, the metaphor of *slotting-in* is evidently inappropriate. But we might think of Rorty's refusal to endorse an identity theory as his own way of retaining the picture which in the presence of the assumption that mental phenomena were problematic led to the claim that they were simply to be slotted in among Physical phenomena: for Rorty, though, mental phenomena have been precluded from the picture before a question about their location can arise.

This diagnosis of Rorty's view might seem to fit ill with his claims that his version of materialism need make no appeal to the powers of science. But my idea is that there is no need for such an appeal on Rorty's part because the powers of science have been *presupposed.*

In order to see how and where 'the powers of science' enter the debate, it will be useful now to distinguish between two kinds of eliminative materialism; they might be called the vanishing kind and the banishing kind. According to the first, science is to be put to work to uncover materialist truths. Once the powers of science have been put to practical effect, and mental-physical identities established, we shall find that the mental was dispensable: it vanishes from the scene—or anyway it could vanish once the scientists have done their work. The powers of science come into the second sort of eliminative materialism not only in their practical, truth-uncovering capacity, but also at a higher-order level, to show us what sort of thing *can* be true. Proponents acknowledge that the mental-physical identities that their metaphysics seem to demand might not be forthcoming, and their reaction is to say so much the worse for the mental: if its concepts are not such as to provide the sort of understanding that science provides, then the mental must be banished from serious enquiry. These eliminative materialists suppose that a great deal of what we think about one another, which we express in everyday mental concepts, will, when not vindicated by science, be shown to be false.[18]

Rorty may now be seen as combining the optimism of the materialists who think that the mental can be made to vanish with the ruthlessness of the materialists who think that the mental ought to be banished. Rorty assumes that a certain style of investigation, such as his Antipodean neurophysiologists are supposed to have undertaken, is always suitable for gaining understanding. In assuming this, he sides with the banishers. But unlike the banishers (and perhaps because, unlike them, he does not make his assumption explicit), Rorty does not consider the possibility that confining investigation to the scientific mode could result in the rebuttal of any common wisdom. In not envisaging his assumption as possibly threatening, Rorty is like the vanishers, who simply place their faith in scientific investigation, as destined to free us from needing to use our common mental concepts.

Rorty's own claims that he does not need to appeal to science's powers are supported by such remarks as this: 'Science's failure to figure out how the brain works will cause no [real] danger to science's "unity."' 'Even if neurons turn out to "swerve"—to be buffeted by forces as yet unknown to science—Descartes would not be vindicated' (p. 124). Rorty speaks here as if his opponent had already conceded that the mind would have to be slotted in (i.e., to where the brain is); the opponent then is worried that Rorty himself has put unwarranted trust in present science. But the danger that an opponent may see is different. It is not that Rorty has taken science to be the best bet (as the vanishers indeed do); rather, in taking it for granted that the Antipodeans' mode of understanding once applied to the brain is adequate to the whole of human understanding, Rorty has rendered unthinkable the possibility of any other mode.

The state of present science is not to the point in any case. Even materialists who would wish to make explicit appeal to science's powers will allow that science might show us that the world (or the neurons therein) works in ways that we have not yet imagined. And although it may be natural to think of Rorty's presupposition in terms specifically of science, this is not necessary. The 'powers of science' can allude to a kind of finding which scientists make. It is a kind of finding which the neo-dualists might insist on contrasting with our finding one another intelligible as fellow subjects of experience. But one does not need actually to believe in the neo-dualists' irreducibility thesis in order to appreciate some contrast between Physical explanations of Physical things (not necessarily physicists' explanations[19]) and rational explanations of people's experiences, states and doings. Conceptions of the Physical vary no doubt: Descartes's was more mechanistic than anyone's is today; Rorty's is more pluralist than most; and Rorty is less willing than Descartes was to judge what an accurate conception might be. But Descartes and Rorty evidently believe in a Physical realm which might be characterized by thinking of scientists as, *de facto*, the specialists in it—a realm on which a certain perspective is appropriate.

The vanishing kind of eliminative materialist would have us believe that from our usual perspective, the mental need not come into view. (This is what science was to demonstrate.) The banishing kind of eliminative materialist would have us believe that we are in error if we take a perspective from which the mental does come into view. (This is what metaphysical reflection is supposed to persuade us of.) Rorty's radicalism consists in his belief that we were always in error if we had supposed the mental had come into view.

The reluctance of almost everyone to be as radical as Rorty may register in our thoughts about his Antipodeans. Rorty assures us that 'no predictive or explanatory or descriptive power would be lost if we had spoken Antipodean all our lives'. Of course this seems right when we are also assured about how much of what we do the Antipodeans also do. And if our doubts about the Antipodeans had extended only to what we think of as phenomenal features, then the assurances about the Antipodeans' likeness to us might have made the doubts seem out of place. (There is always the view that we should never have expected any explanation of the phenomenal.) But if we had wanted to be sure that the Antipodeans make sense of one another as subjects of experience, then in order to be convinced of what Rorty says about the explanatory power of Antipodean, we should need to be told how their ways of attributing beliefs to one another (as we should put it) are connected with their modes of describing the world that they experience and have beliefs about. The Antipodeans can use 'F-11' to report their being struck by the thought that elephants don't occur on this continent. It is hard then to see why they should not also use the vocabulary of 'Fs' and '11s' from the neurological language when they want to *state* something about elephants. If even the semantic properties of their states of mind are neurophysiologically formulable, why should they not restrict themselves entirely to a neurophysiological vocabulary? But the idea that everything is sayable in terms of how things are in our heads seems preposterous: it appears to preclude us from thinking that the external world is something on which we have a point of view.

Ensuring that the world is something we can have a point of view on is part of the problematic of Cartesian epistemology. The apparent affinity here, between Descartes and Rorty, results from what I have been suggesting is a shared assumption of the two philosophers—that if we are to find a place for mind, it has to be a place for mind in the world conceived independent of mind. The consequence both for Descartes and for Rorty, though they would put the emphasis very differently, is that there is no place for mind in the natural world.

Where does this leave neo-dualists?

Well, they cannot now be seen as holding a monopoly on the Cartesian legacy in philosophy of mind. And if they 'lump together the intentional and the phenomenal', this need not be because 'Descartes used the notion of the "incorrigibly known" to bridge the gap between them' (Rorty, p. 68). The neo-dualists in fact share with Descartes one, but only one, of the premisses (the irreducibility thesis), in one, but only one, of his arguments for his dualism (the argument from the Physical). And the premiss which they deny (which equates the natural and the Physical) is affirmed not only by Descartes but by Rorty. No doubt Rorty will continue to think that neo-dualism is pernicious; but perhaps he need no longer think of it as an inheritance of substantial dualism, nor as simultaneously pernicious and quite without consequence.

In Rorty's book the neo-dualist is an embarrassed figure—wanting to accept what Strawson and Wittgenstein have said about persons but to resist modern materialism.[20] But there need be no embarrassment about this if one allows oneself to reject the assumption that I have suggested is at work in Descartes and (behind the scenes) in Rorty. Resistance to a Cartesian view of mind need not be resistance to the whole idea of the phenomenon of mind, but only to a conception of the mental informed by a particular view of what the natural world can contain.

Postscript: Rorty on anomalous monism

This essay takes no account of what Rorty has written in philosophy of mind since the 1979 publication of *Philosophy and the Mirror of Nature*. A comment on his more recent views is in order here. What Rorty has come to support (1987) is the non-reductive physicalism of Donald Davidson, which is put in question in much of what follows (see Introduction, §§4 and 5 on Davidson's anomalous monism).

Rorty thinks that Davidson's position helps us to preserve a naturalistic perspective on human beings while getting past Enlightenment scientism.[21] 'Contemporary American philosophers such as Putnam and Davidson represent a strain of philosophical thought which makes philosophy no more the ally of science than of any other area of culture', he says. He explicates this: 'Davidsonian philosophy of mind enables us to treat both physics and poetry evenhandedly' (1987, at p. 113 in 1991).

When commonsense psychology is held to be reducible, some branch of science is what it is held to be reducible to, of course. Rorty is surely right then that anti-reductionism about the mind may be anti-scientistic. But his explication can seem to spoil the point. Why should one have to be *enabled* to treat different subjects evenhandedly if scientism has been left behind? Presumably the scientistically minded think that physics and poetry receive different treatments, and that poetry loses out; but when science is regarded as just one cultural endeavour among others, it is not clear that a philosopher needs to do anything to give (say) poetry the benefit of equal treatment. And, in any case, is evenhanded treatment what Davidson actually gives us? Davidson thinks that explanation in physics is of a different kind from explanation in commonsense psychology (which, for the purposes of this argument, we may take poetry to fall within). Surely that makes some difference to our treatments of the two areas.

Well, when Rorty speaks of Davidson's 'enabling evenhanded treatment' he could mean only that a proponent of Davidson's position is well-placed to avoid according a second-class status to a subject such as commonsense psychology: she can avoid any of the various species of eliminativism and irrealism and instrumentalism favoured by so many philosophers (see Introduction, §3). If we understand Rorty like this, then there is no incompatibility between the categorially distinct sorts of explanation which Davidson believes in and evenhanded treatment. For in this case Rorty is really telling us only that Davidson's non-reductive physicalism permits an account of the mental which is realist, in the simple sense of allowing that one can often get right what someone thinks or feels or intentionally does.

Such a simple-minded realism is welcome both to Rorty and to me. But if Davidson's views encourage it, then that is because, as Rorty explains, Davidson has helped us be rid of a certain metaphysical picture of what it takes to get something right, of what it is for something someone thinks to be true. The metaphysical picture, which calls truth 'correspondence with reality', and which sets facts apart from human thinking and places them in 'the uninterpreted world', has led to the idea that science sets the standard of truth. To those in the grip of the picture, science seems uniquely equipped to determine the facts. But once the picture is abandoned, science has no special status in telling us what are matters of fact. Without the picture, then, we are under no pressure to suppose that commonsense psychological phenomena 'ought' to be amenable to explanations of some kind that scientists give (see again Introduction, §3).

When we explain Rorty's attraction to Davidson's position in this way—in terms of the assault on 'correspondence with reality'—we make good sense of his remark about 'evenhanded treatment'. Given that 'correspondence with reality' was only an illusion, natural science is done no damage when it is held not to measure up to correspondence truth. It is no more to science's detriment, then, that subject matters irreducible to it are not demoted than it was ever to the detriment of those subject matters that they are not reducible to science.

But now, by Rorty's lights, what recommends 'Davidsonian philosophy of mind' is actually a metaphysical outlook. What enables Davidson to capture the high ground now is not the version of monism that he espouses—the doctrine which Davidson calls anomalous monism and which Rorty calls non-reductive physicalism. (The outlook is secured by abandoning the 'dualism of scheme and content'. For more on this, see Rorty, 1987, in 1991, and Davidson, 1974.)

Of course Davidson's non-reductionism continues to be very much to the point, because his metaphysical outlook makes such non-reductionism tenable. But this non-reductionism consists in holding (a) a thesis of the mental's irreducibility, and (b) an attitude towards an irreducible subject matter which ensures that it is in no way deprecated by being revealed to be irreducible. (I remarked in the Introduction that an 'irreducibility' thesis is accepted by eliminativists and instrumentalists. The reason we do not think of them as non-reductionists is that their scientism prevents them from simply endorsing an irreducible subject matter: they hold (a) but not (b).)

What Rorty takes over from Davidson, however, is not just (a) and (b), but also his particular version of monism. Indeed, Rorty seems to think that this version is part of the package: he writes of the 'ontological neutrality *characteristic* of a non-reductionist view' (p. 121, my italics). So Rorty accepts the claim that mental events are physical when read in Davidson's way, with 'physical' events in the domain to which the laws of nature speak. It seems that the 'evenhandedness of treatment' that he favoured amounts to more than holding simple-mindedly realistic attitudes to both science and commonsense: Rorty thinks, as Davidson does, that at the micro-level science and commonsense must share an ontology.

Rorty not only endorses a Davidsonian version of monism; he derives from it his own account of human beings. He writes: 'There is no harm in continuing to speak of a distinct entity called "the self" which consists of the mental states of the human being: her beliefs, desires, moods, etc. The important thing is to think of the collection of those things as *being* the self rather than as something which the self has' (p. 122). Rorty, then, in company with those who identify the mind with the brain, descends to a micro-level to locate mentality. We find once again what I have suggested (in the essay above, and in Essay 1) is a Cartesian idea: a person's leading of a mental life is treated as if it were a separable side of her biography.

There are differences, it is true, between Rorty's account and that of those who identify minds with brains. But the two most salient differences do not make Rorty's own account obviously more satisfactory. One of these differences is that Rorty drops the notion of "consciousness" (his sneer quotes, p. 121). But we may wonder whether Rorty does full justice to the facts of our being conscious when he tells us that 'ability to report is not a matter of "presence to consciousness" but simply of teaching the use of words' (p. 121). The other difference lies in the manner of forging a link between the micro-items and something on the macro-level. In both Rorty's and the mind-brain identity theorist's accounts, the goings on which make up a person's mental life are to be seen as activities of her brain; in Rorty's account, though, a bearer of mental properties is identified with a collection of some of these, rather than with the thing of which they are the activities. But it is really not plausible that a person, or "her self", is literally made up out of the thinkings and feelings and doings that we might think of as comprising her mental life—no more than it is plausible that (say) a football is literally made up of the events of its being kicked and thrown and caught that are parts of its history in games. (Rorty admits that his picture is 'hard to reconcile with common speech'; at p. 123 he counsels us 'to think with the learned'.)

The essay claimed that Rorty's materialism is more Cartesian than Rorty allows. These remarks may help to show why I do not want to retract that claim in the light of the development of Rorty's position, taking off from Davidson.

I hope that they can serve another purpose, too. I have suggested that Davidson's ontological claim that mental events are (in a certain sense) physical has nothing to do with the aspect of his philosophy in which Rorty rightly finds real merit. Davidson shows us how to 'eschew the impulse that leads to reductionism' (as Rorty puts it, p. 116). And, *pace* Rorty, eschewing the impulse does not take one in the direction of 'ontological neutrality'. Indeed, it is possible to think that the opposite is true: I suspect that the same pressures that lead to reductionism can work also to sustain a monolithic attitude to what there is. However that may be, it is good to have dissociated the ontological claim from other Davidsonian ones. The claim is in dispute in the next two essays. I am glad to be in a position to argue against it without disturbing any of the rest of Davidson's contribution.

3

Physicalism, Events
and Part-Whole Relations

1. Physicalism

At a certain high level of abstraction, we may think of the physical world as a world of space and time occupied by particular things, among them persisting things (such as a table or a carrot or a person) and events (such as the wind's once blowing, or a wedding, or someone somewhere's contemplating murder). At the same level of abstraction, we may think that singling out particular things is simply a matter of delimiting the regions of space and time that they occupy—of drawing spatiotemporal lines around them, as it were. In order to identify a particular table at a time, for instance, we might suppose that we had only to specify it as the occupier of some determinate region of space at some moment of time. Philosophers have challenged this conception of the identities of particular persisting things (or, as I shall say, continuants). In this essay I shall suggest that some proponents of physicalism employ a similar conception of the identities of *events*, and that this is wide open to a somewhat similar challenge.

According to the position I shall call *physicalism*, we are entitled to take a certain view of the relations between the entities spoken of by the different sciences and by common sense. Scientists speak about

46

events (among other things). What distinguishes the various sciences from one another is their employment of different vocabularies; they provide different ways of classifying events. Each science introduces some taxonomy of the events in its universe of discourse; the various taxonomies may not overlap or fit together at all neatly; but ultimately there is one common fund of events spoken of in fundamental science; and common sense, though not a science, imposes one more classification on the same set of things scientists describe in their different terms. Thus physics describes the same events as chemistry, chemistry describes events which include those of neurophysiology, and, more generally, the sciences redescribe the same events we all describe in the course of day-to-day life.[1]

According to this position, then, there need be no more events in the world than a physicist can descry within it. The doctrine is conceived of here as concerned specifically with what *events* there are, because it is commonly supposed that the laws of science speak of events. Given that supposition (which might be modified to embrace states, processes or whatever), physicalism, which is an ontological doctrine about the world's contents, leads naturally to a more substantial metaphysical doctrine about the world's workings, that 'under their physical descriptions, all events are susceptible of total explanations, of the kind paradigmatically afforded by physics in terms of physical laws and other physically described events.'[2]

An interesting special case of physicalism so understood is Donald Davidson's anomalous monism.[3] The events of which commonsense psychology speaks (mental events) are the very same events as those of which law-seeking scientists speak (physical events). It is held that it does not count against this at all that the taxonomies of commonsense psychology and of the sciences are out of harmony. Indeed, Davidson argues from the absence of close relations between scientific and commonsense languages to his thesis of identities between the items that are described in the two languages.

Many philosophers do not give any arguments for physicalism, but take some such position for granted in all their reasonings. My arguments here are meant to expose and criticize an assumption I believe they make. I shall not return until §7 to the argument that Davidson has offered for the position.

2. Physicalism, part-whole relations
and mereological conceptions

A first reaction to the physicalism just expounded might be this: 'Scientists look at things through microscopes, and we do not. The things they talk about are then much smaller than the things we talk about, and they cannot be the very same things.' This is certainly a naive reaction (we know that the microscopic is not the sole concern of fundamental physics). But there may yet be something right in the reservation that prompts it.

It would be natural to counter the naive reaction by saying: 'Even if the submicroscopic events of the physicists cannot *be* macroscopic events, still they can be *parts* of them. Allow the relation "is a part of" into the scientist's language, and then he will have all the resources needed to build up descriptions of everyday events.' More generally, it will be said that wherever the events isolated by two different subject matters are associated with different expanses of space and time, we can assert identities between *fusions* of the events isolated by one subject matter (i.e., events composed from the relevant microphysical parts) and the individual events isolated by the other.[4]

This response will be congenial to proponents of the conception of the physical world that was sketched at the outset. It is in fact found in the literature on physicalism.[5] And the same idea that underlies such a response is implicit in the doctrine that tells us that every entity is a (spatiotemporal) part of that whole which comprises (as their 'fusion') all basic physical entities. This sort of physicalism carries with it the idea that part-whole relations obtain between events not only in the cases where we naturally think of events as comprised from other events, and not only in the cases where there are special reasons for seeing events as comprised from other events, but much more generally.

This is the idea that I want to cast in doubt. So I shall begin by describing and criticizing what I call *mereological conceptions*. I shall take it to be definitive of the decision to adopt a mereological conception of things of some kind that one's theory of things of that kind should commit one to the following principle, and that one be committed to allowing it to play some significant role in determining the identities of those things:

(A) $(x)(y)\ (\exists!z)(z$ is a fusion of x and y).

Taken by itself, (A) could hardly constitute a complete theory of things of any sort.[6] But in practice there is no immediate need to speculate what other axioms might be present in a theory containing (A). For my aim is not to establish the falsity of any particular mereological theory, but to demonstrate and trace to their source the problems that (A) will bring to theories in which it is given a substantial role. In this way I hope to establish that there are problems with mereological conceptions (§§3 and 4) which rebound on the defense of physicalism (§§5 and 6).

3. Mereological conceptions of continuants

If commitment to (A) is diagnostic of the mereological conception, then we may enquire first what role if any it will play in a good account of continuants.

If one assumes the existence of the continuants that we ordinarily talk about, then (A) brings existential commitments far beyond any we ordinarily recognize. For instance, it guarantees that there is something composed from the Bodleian Library and some carrot, and something made up from my copy of *The Structure of Appearance*, Goodman's left arm and your right leg. Such examples, which can of course be multiplied indefinitely, suggest that (A) is simply false of continuants. But some people think that we should not concern ourselves about these weird things; they think that we can treat them as "don't care" cases and need not worry if our theories admit them. Goodman said, 'The supposition that bizarre instances demonstrate that two individuals can fail to have a [fusion] betrays a misunderstanding of the range of our variables'.[7]

Anyone who responds in this way to an attack on (A) must then be someone who understands (A)'s variables to range over a domain which includes more than continuants. And it seems he must allow that not everything in the ontology that can be constructed from everyday continuants is itself a continuant. For not every construct from everyday continuants is such that a principled account could be given of what it is for such a thing to persist: no autonomous principle of individuation through time can be specified for objects that are the

fusions of some library plus some carrot.[8] But of course (A)'s proponent will now introduce a new term for the items of his ontology—
'material thing', say. And then his claim will be that we are committed
to the existence of material things, and that in the presence of axioms
asserting the existence of (say) atoms, (A) simply defines the class of
material things. He will then say that our ordinary continuant things
are to be found *among* the material things, and that all he does in introducing (A) is to effect a certain generalization.[9]

In order to see what is wrong with such a proposal, it is helpful to
distinguish the two components of (A), namely, (E), which asserts the
existence of fusions, and (U), which asserts their uniqueness.

> (E) $(x)(y)$ $(\exists z)(z$ is a fusion of x and $y)$
> (U) $(x)(y)(z)(w)$ $[(z$ is a fusion of x and $y)$ & w is a fusion of x and y
> $\rightarrow (w = z)]$

What the introduction of material things is supposed to help us to see
is how (E) can be true. If I can show that (U) fails for material things,
however, then this will have the effect of showing that (A) is not true
where the domain is material things.

Counterexamples to (U) may be found wherever two distinct material things exist in the same place at the same time. The notion of 'part'
for material objects is a spatial notion to the extent that, if two enmat-
tered objects are in exactly the same place at one time, then at some
level of articulation of their parts, they must have exactly the same
parts at that time. Thus any case in which there are two objects in a
place at one time will be a case where (U) must rule that there could
be only one material thing. (At this point, one has to make some assumption about what will be combined with (A) in a theory. If (say)
chemical atoms are taken as the basic individuals, and everything can
be seen as some fusion of atoms, then if x and y occupy the same place,
they will have as parts exactly the same atoms, and will be identical.
[The mereologist may resist such an assumption: see below on temporal parts.])

The idea that two things can be in the same place at one time
should be a familiar one.[10] The contention is that we have to distinguish, for example, between a gold ring and the quantity of gold from

which it is made, because the quantity of gold is something that may exist before the ring does and may go on existing after the ring is destroyed. A similar point can be made about almost any continuant and the fusion of the molecules composing it at any particular time. Biological organisms, which survive through complete replacement of their matter, provide particularly vivid examples. And what leads one to distinguish two objects in cases like these is only an application of Leibniz's Law: x exists at t, y does not exist at t; so x is not the same as y.

Of course an advocate of the mereological conception is likely to claim that we misdescribe these cases when we say that we have two things in the same place at the same time. 'We shall see that in fact there are no counterexamples to (U) here,' he will say, 'if we realize that in deciding what parts an object has at any time, it is not enough to decide what its spatial parts are at that time. A violation of (U) would require the coincidence of the whole of something with the whole of something else; and in these examples we learn only that a part of a ring coincides with a part of something else. (U) does not commit one to identifying a fusion that exists after t with a ring which ceases to exist at t, because the imagined fusion in fact has *parts* that the ring lacks—namely, temporal parts.'

We are told now that what we naturally regard as an encounter with the ring at a time when we pick it out is really an encounter with a temporal part of the ring. So next the mereologist must show us how we can regard 'the ring at t' as referring to a temporal stage of something. And he must answer the formidable objections to the whole idea of continuants as things with temporal parts.[11] But even if a mereologist thinks that he can answer such objections, he will still have to say how he hits on the particular fusion which he wants to equate the ring with. What I cannot understand is how he proposes to dispense here with all considerations that concern the temporal dimensions of the *ring*. Surely he must avail himself of a prior account of the ring's identity and persistence conditions—something supplied from elsewhere, from our ordinary conception of what a ring is—to determine which things are parts of rings. So it seems that even if he persuaded us that we should 'admit as an object the material content of any portion of space-time' (as Quine puts it), he can scarcely claim that the conceptual resources of our ordinary vocabulary for continuants are simply dispensable. But how then can he allow (A) to play a constitutive role in the account of the identities of the continuant things about which we talk?[12]

No doubt the mereologist will want to present objections of his own to the very idea that there could be counterexamples to (U). He may say that he cannot understand how there could be two distinct (non-identical) things, the ring and the fusion, which are so very like each other whenever both exist. But it seems that it is in fact very easy to explain what he professes to find unintelligible. Many of the properties of a thing derive from the disposition of the matter that occupies the space that it occupies; thus things which are spatial co-occupants cannot help being alike in respect of numerous features that do so derive.

Of course if absolutely all of the properties of any object derived from such features as molecular arrangement at a moment, then there could not be cases of spatial co-occupancy. So it may be that the mereologist will want to redefine the notion of a property of a material thing so that properties depend entirely upon how the matter occupying the space that the thing occupies is disposed at any time. But in fact this notion of property is not the notion of a property that we apply to continuants. Simply examining a portion of matter at a single time cannot tell us everything about what a continuant's properties are. It is in the nature of continuants to persist. The whole continuant *can* be picked out at one time, and what is then picked out is the very thing that endures. We cannot then say that what it is for some continuant thing we have picked out to endure is something quite irrelevant to what it is, and to its identity.[13]

This shows that (U) fails for a domain that purports to contain continuants among mereologically conceived things. But (E) failed for a domain that purports to contain only continuants. The conclusion we reach is that (A) cannot hold true for any domain that includes continuants in it at all.

4. Mereological conceptions of events

The arguments of the preceding section were intended to serve as a reminder of what seems to be essentially at fault in the mereological approach. We aren't able to describe the world except in the terms *(inter alia)* of the continuant things that we find there; and we cannot replace continuants with mereologically conceived material objects, because we cannot understand continuants having the properties they do except by making reference to continuants themselves. The predicates that the champion of a mereological conception must take to suffice in determining things' identities do not in fact suffice for the singling out of continuants. Using Quine's distinction between ontologies (stocks of items) and ideologies (ways of characterizing items), we might put the point by saying that a barely spatiotemporal ideology is inadequate to the singling out of the ordinary items in our ontology; continuants can only be identified in the context of a richer ideology suited to them. Once the idea of bare singling out is discredited, we find that the question whether one and the same thing is singled out in this and that distinct ideologies has to be a substantial question.

How much of this has application to events? The physicalism we have begun from acknowledges the possibility of a certain incommensurability between different event ideologies, but it is not led by this into any consequential doubt about whether the very same entities are isolated within different ideologies. This question is sometimes not treated as the substantial one that the continuant case suggests it is.

Consider (A) with its variables taken to range over events. If one assumes the existence of the events we ordinarily talk about, then (A) now guarantees that there is an event of my reading in the library today fused with your writing a letter yesterday, and an event composed from the death of Julius Caesar, the Battle of Hastings and a recent speech by Edward Heath. Examples can be multiplied indefinitely. And again it seems we ought not to be too easily persuaded of the existence of these things.

The mereological conception of continuants was undermined by the thought that it is in the nature of continuants to persist: fusions of things with coherent, intelligible persistence conditions need not themselves have coherent, intelligible persistence conditions. A corresponding thought for the case of events might be that it is in their nature to cause and to be caused. And then the corresponding problem for a mereological conception would be that fusions of things which cause and are caused need not themselves be things which cause and are caused. This surely is a real problem. What on earth can we find to say about the causes and effects of a fusion of events whose parts occurred in 44 B.C., in 1066 and in 1984?

Well, those who think that the more bizarre things whose existence (A) guarantees are no great embarrassment will presumably say that we can perfectly well see the theoretical, constructed fusions as playing some role in the causal order; and perhaps they will propose some principle which has the effect that fusions inherit some of the causal properties of their parts, for example, something like this:

> (C) IF {event c causes event e AND $f = c + d$ AND [NEITHER d occurs later than e NOR d and e have common parts NOR part of e causes part of d]},
>
> THEN f causes e.

(C) would be meant to introduce enough in the way of causal relations between the entities that (A) imports to credit those things with a causal status of their own.[14] But (C) seems absurd. And certainly adherents of a typical counterfactual account of causation and of a typical regularity account of causation must reject it.

The simple thought behind counterfactual accounts is that if c caused e, then c made a difference to whether e occurred. Can one say then that f—the fusion of c and some arbitrary event d—made a difference to whether e occurred? Well, perhaps this seems innocuous enough. In typical cases, there will be a difference that c makes such that we can know that e would not have occurred unless c had. But if '$-C \square \rightarrow -E$' is true, then, provided that D is independent of E, we shall also have '$-(C \ \& \ D) \square \rightarrow -E$'; and this latter counterfactual is exactly what we shall expect to hold, assuming that the parts would not have occurred if the fusion hadn't. (I employ David Lewis's terminology here: '$\square \rightarrow$' is the counterfactual conditional; 'C' (or 'E') says that the event c (or e) occurred.) However, such a defense of (C) from a counterfactual theorist would ignore the fact that, in any particular case of c's causing e, it cannot be settled by sole reference to whether c actually caused e exactly which counterfactuals obtain. (It depends, for instance, on whether there was a fail-safe mechanism ensuring the production of e in the absence of c.) The difference which c as cause makes to e's occurrence is a quite specific difference.

Why should we think that, for any d, the difference made by $(c + d)$ to e's occurrence is such a specific difference that we can take the relation between $(c + d)$ and e also to be causal? Where c caused e, the occurrence of e must have actually depended crucially upon the occurrence of c, and although this may ensure some dependence of the occurrence of e on the occurrence of $(c + d)$, it cannot ensure that there is the same actual crucial dependence as in a real case of causation.[15]

Again, there are difficulties for someone who tries to combine (C) with a typical regularity theory of causation. Such a theorist takes the presence of an underlying regularity to be a hallmark of cases of causation: he thinks that what distinguishes between a case where e causes f and a case where f follows on e temporally but not causally is that in the first case, but not the second, there is some significant (lawlike or lawful) generalization that subsumes e and f.[16] The problem about (C) for such a theorist is that it requires him to accept generalizations of an *ad hoc* and apparently trivial kind as playing a role which he has to insist only significant regularities can really play. Try to imagine some regularity that subsumes, on the one hand, the fusion of Caesar's death and my striking the match, and, on the other hand, the match's lighting. Here you may assume that there is some significant regularity which deals with the particular striking/lighting sequence, and that there are significant regularities which deal with sequences that include Caesar's death and what we normally consider to have been its effects. On that basis, you must imagine an as interesting as possible (death + striking)/lighting regularity. But it is plain that *that* need not be lawlike.

These arguments against (C) suggest that within the domain of events (A) is incompatible with any plausible account of the causal relation: the difficulty with (A) now is that it introduces fusions which, having no place in the causal nexus, lack any title to be identified with events. And notice that it is not merely the more bizarre among putative event fusions—those which are strikingly irregular by virtue of their discontinuity, say—which are cast into doubt: even fusions composed from events that are closely related spatiotemporally are undermined. For surely bare spatiotemporal contiguity of the parts of some fusion cannot be what is needed to endow that item with a causal status.

5. Mereological conceptions of events and physicalism

Of course events do sometimes stand to one another in part-whole relations. And often there are arguments for seeing events as parts of others, or as fusions of others. These claims are not at issue. But if physicalism is allowed to be at issue, then we should not start with a presumption that exactly those event fusions exist which are required to make physicalism hold true. The physicalist of §2 said that if one imported the relation 'is a part of' into a scientist's language, he would then have all the resources he needed to build up descriptions of everyday events (mental events, say). And what the arguments against (A) suggest is that there isn't any reason to think that (putative) fusions constructed from events using the relation of parthood need themselves be genuine events.

To be clear how the argument against (A) rebounds on this physicalist's assumption, it is helpful to consider a particular case where the relation of *parthood* might be put to work in defending the claim that the same event makes its appearance in different ideologies. Consider then some arbitrary macro-event *e*. It could be an event of interest to economists—say, the Public Sector Borrowing Requirement's dropping by six billion pounds in a certain period. Consider also the (putative) fusion composed from those microphysical events which will be said to 'occupy the very spatiotemporal region that *e* occupies'.[17] Is there any reason to suppose that this fusion has any special claim to the status of event? Is it not on a par with some of the extraordinary putative items that (A) imports, which, in the light of the arguments against (C), we are confident are *not* events? But if the fusion is not an event, it cannot be the same as *e*.

We have no doubt that *e* itself in this example is a genuine event, because *e* is the sort of thing we might be able to learn the cause of: an economist might be able to cite features of *e* which bring it in the scope of intelligible, more or less projectible generalizations. And it need not be in doubt that the microphysical events whose putative fusion is coincident with *e* are also, severally, susceptible of causally interesting descriptions such as figure in counterfactual sustaining generalizations. But we know that in order to discover generalizations in economics, there is no need to investigate the physics of the regions that economic events occupy; and this suggests that it cannot be relevant to economic generalizations which sorts of microphysical events occur in the spatiotemporal regions in which we find events satisfying predicates from economic generalizations.[18] Thus the fact that *e* has an interesting description, in virtue of which we can appreciate its causal status, cannot in itself help to secure any description of the putative fusion (a description using microphysical vocabulary plus the word 'part') which would figure in some counterfactual sustaining generalization. It is surely because the fusion lacks all such descriptions that we feel it lacks any claim to the title of event.

More generally, I should suggest that the reason we do not tolerate the extraordinary events which (A) would commit us to, and that the physicalism of §1 apparently requires, is that these putative events lack any conceivable value to us in giving explanations. This provides a further point of parallel between continuants and events: inasmuch as it is in the nature of continuants to persist, we expect individual continuants to be members of kinds whose instances have intelligible, individuation-sustaining persistence conditions; inasmuch as it is in the nature of events to cause and be caused, we expect individual events to be members of kinds that pull their weight in illuminating accounts of why one thing followed on another. The items which are events, like the items which are continuants, need to be singled out not merely as occupiers of space and time, but by reference to a suitable ideology; and the suitable ideology for events is conditioned by the need to construct an explanatory causal nexus. If we take ourselves to recognize events in nature only as we come to understand their occurrences by finding ourselves in a position to supply explanations, then knowing that our everyday low-grade explanations and our use of concepts in exercising our ability to discern everyday events require only rough and ready generalizations and nothing like the laws of scientists, we shall be suspicious of any crudely realist theory neutral ontology such as (A)'s advocate purports to describe. If events *e* and *f* are such as to need to be singled out by different ideologies, it will take an impressive argument to show that *e* is nonetheless the same as *f*. Of course, if some reductive thesis connects the two ideologies, then that thesis may provide the premiss of the needed argument. But no actual argument is given when the word 'part' is introduced into the vocabulary of physics.

6. Physicalism and mereological conceptions reviewed

Someone who was sympathetic to the views about continuants outlined here, and who accepted the parallels between continuants and
events (such as they are), might think that to the extent to which this
conclusion is anti-physicalist it could not be correct. For he might
react by saying that the claims about continuants made in §3 do nothing to impugn the spirit of physicalism: why, then, should the claims
about events in §§4 and 5 be thought to present any sort of challenge
to any sort of physicalism about them?

Well, if he wishes to defend a doctrine about continuants exactly
parallel to the physicalism about events of §1, then he is simply wrong
if he thinks that the arguments against mereological conceptions do
not affect him.[19] The physicalism of §1 used a distinctive conception
of the *physical*, as that which a physical scientist is concerned with; and
it made claims of *identity*. If one uses such a conception, and one
makes such claims, then as a physicalist about continuants one will say,
for instance, that any gold ring is identical with some fusion of gold
atoms. But this is just the sort of claim disputed in §3.

If one is clear about this, but still feels that physicalism about continuants survives the arguments against mereological conceptions,
then one must have some different version of physicalism in mind—
perhaps a doctrine that employs a different conception of the physical,
or perhaps a doctrine that gives no special place to identity claims.

It may be that we do use some more relaxed conception of the physical than the physics-based one in assessing physicalism about continuants. Conceiving continuants as macrophysical things, we do not take
the fact that they are not the same as fusions of microphysical things
to cast any doubt on their status as physical in some sense. Of course
when it comes to events also, we might make use of a relaxed conception of what it is to be physical; and then there will surely be some an-
odyne physicalist position about events for us to turn to. What I have
been concerned with, though (in §§1, 2, 4 and 5), is physicalism as we
have it in the literature.

But some people will think that even if we take the exacting
(physics-based) conception of the physical, and even if we accept that
continuants are not the same as anything that is according to that conception physical, still physicalism about continuants holds true. What

these people want to say is 'Even if the ring is not the same as any fusion of gold atoms, still it is nothing over and above that fusion'. Now presumably what this means is that the ring and the fusion of gold atoms have the same parts: there may be rings *and* fusions of gold atoms, but there are not ring-atoms and gold-atoms besides. It seems, then, that where continuants are concerned, it is thought to suffice, in order to establish physicalism, to demonstrate that all continuants are related exhaustively by *parthood* to things in the scientist's world.

This is where the case of events is very different. The claim about *parthood* for continuants is available because, for continuants, it is arguably a sufficient condition of x's being a part of y (at some time) that x occupy some part of the volume of space that y occupies (at that time). The notion of part that is pressed into service, we might say, relies only on the spatial ideology, yet it seems to have enough substance to give content to something properly physicalist. In the case of events, however, the occurrence of one event within the spatiotemporal region in which some other event occurs does not by itself ensure that the one event is a part of the other. In the ordinary way, we see events as parts of others where that enables us better to explain things; support for particular claims about parthood is given by facts internal to some event ideology, and never by purely spatiotemporal facts. Think, for instance, of the kind of thing that would be brought to bear in deciding whether certain events were correctly regarded as parts of the event that caused economic event e. Of course someone might posit a spatiotemporal notion of parthood, saying that *any* event occurring within the spatiotemporal volume in which an event occurs is a part of that event. But if this stipulation exhausts the content of *parthood*, it is no longer clear that introducing parthood into physicalist theses gives them any distinctively physicalistic content. Perhaps physicists' events occupy the whole of space and time, and perhaps all mental or economic events are spatiotemporal particulars. Is that a doctrine worthy of the name of physicalism?

This difference between continuants and events, in the contribution that *parthood* can make to physicalist doctrines, is reflected in a difference in our attitudes towards the constructed items that (A) would introduce. Where a fusion is made up of microphysical events, we are not prepared (without further argument) to recognize it as any sort of thing. By contrast, where a fusion is made up of (say) gold atoms, the mere assertion of the fusion's existence seems less problematic: we know that the fusion is a portion of matter at least, and we may call it a 'material thing' (cp. §3). It is surely our conception of matter, as space-occupying stuff that is more or less indefinitely divisible, which gives us the idea of items made from matter as competing with one another for room in the spatial world, and makes such material things as intelligible to us as they are. If matter so conceived is something that concerns a scientist, and if matter is what all continuants are composed from, then that explains why the notion of *parthood* has a role to play in stating a physicalism of sorts about continuants.

But the absence in the event case of any analogue of the notion of matter (the fact, we might say, that there is no event stuff out of which occurrences are constructed) prevents the physicalist about events from resorting to any doctrine merely about *parthood* to register his convictions.[20] Such a physicalist seems bound to defend *identity* claims. In that case, he must either introduce a conception of the physical different from that of the physicalism of §1, or else he must find some actual argument for identities that does not simply assume a mereological conception.[21]

7. Anomalous monism

Davidson does not envisage extending a physical vocabulary with 'part'. And (in 1970) he does give a positive argument for his doctrine.[22]

Davidson employed three premisses: (i) there are psychophysical causal interactions; (ii) there are no psychophysical laws; (iii) wherever events are causally related, some law covers those events. He argued that if some mental event causes some physical event (by (i)), then there is no psychophysical law that covers that case of causal connexion (by (ii)). But some law must cover that case (by (iii)), and it must be a physical law, ensuring that the mental event is subsumed by a physical law, and is itself physical.

Notice that premiss (ii), which denies psychophysical laws, introduces the idea of a certain sort of incommensurability between different event ideologies, and that it was incommensurability of this sort that gave the lie to the mereological conception (in §5). Given that premiss (ii) (as Davidson acknowledges) already seems to cast doubt on the identity of mental and physical events, the real work in David-son's argument must be done by premiss (iii), which Davidson called the Principle of the Nomological Character of Causality. If David-son's argument for physicalism can stand, then, it seems that the Prin-ciple of the Nomological Character of Causality can do what others have relied on some mereological principle to do.

The notion of a law used in the Nomological Principle is not merely the notion of some counterfactual-sustaining generalization that we can use in explanation: if it were, psychophysical laws could be admitted. Rather, since the conclusion of the argument is to be that mental events are physical, and since this has to be established by showing that mental events can be described using the vocabularies in which laws are stated, a law must at least be this: a generalization stated in such vocabulary that what is described in that vocabulary is obviously physical in some sense of physical in which it could not be obvious before the argument was given that mental events are physi-cal. It seems, then, that we have to envisage laws as concerned pre-cisely with events that scientists describe.

But now we might wonder whether we can use again a version of the naive point that set all these considerations in motion in order to dispute Davidson's crucial premiss. If we take a view of events in the brain as related to one another by strict physical laws, then we shall probably be inclined to think of these as microscopic events, de-tectable only with a neurophysiologist's fine-tuned apparatus. Are these the things that we talk about as a result of our grosser observa-tions of people's impact on the world as they move about it? It will be said that if the brain scientists make more discriminations than we do, then that need only show that we may sometimes have to introduce the relation of *parthood* to ensure that mental events are among the things subsumed by laws. It seems, then, that someone who thinks that all causally related events can be subsumed by laws formulated by sci-entists will sometimes claim that events we recognize are in fact fu-sions of the events described in laws. Now I have heard it said, in re-sponse to the suggestion that this claim may be problematic, that it can easily be defended because we can always construct the necessary fusions from the events of science. But to say this is to suppose that Davidson's argument forces on us the mereological conception of events.[23]

No doubt the Nomological Character of Causality is meant to be an independently grounded principle in Davidson, a principle which in its turn could ground a belief that (say) a fusion of physicist's events is the same as some mental event. If the principle were defensible in its own right, then we could dispense with anything like (A) in arguing for identities. But if the principle were defensible in its own right, then we should have a perhaps unexpected disanalogy between continuants and events. We have a disanalogy, because we know that, using the exacting standard of the physical, there is nothing that can make us think that continuants are the same as fusions of microphysical things—nothing, that is, except an illicit importation of the mereological conception. This disanalogy may be unexpected, because we take it that there are relations of dependency between continuants and events. There are asymmetrical dependencies between the two categories of thing in respect of members' occupancy of space and time. And there are ontological dependencies between things in the two categories. We take it that many events can be seen as changes precisely of continuants: mental events, for instance, are changes to persons. It would be surprising if mental events could be accommodated to the mereological outlook whereas persons could not.

4

Which Physical Events
Are Mental Events?

1

Someone who believes in identities between mental and physical events taken as particulars obviously accepts a weaker form of physicalism than someone who also believes in identities between mental properties of events and physical properties, or between mental and physical states taken as universals. The latter, stronger physicalism, against which much argument has been directed,[1] has usually been based upon a view of everyday psychology as reducible to some branch of science. But many who uphold only the weaker version take over the conceptions of *mental* and *physical* implicit in the stronger; they take a *physical* predicate to be a predicate of physical science (or else they leave it crucially unclear what they mean by 'physical'). Then, identities between particulars being thought of as the minimum required for proper physicalism, a point is reached where adherents even of weak physicalism have no option but to assert that each mental event can be uniquely identified by a phrase making exclusive and essential use of predicates of some scientific theory (expressions that are proprietary to neurophysiology, or biochemistry, say). Here I shall deny that every mental event need be physical in this sense.

One way for us to discover whether there is any good reason to believe the commonly accepted mental-physical identities is to take as an example some particular mental event, imagine ourselves knowing all that we could about that event, and ask what grounds we should then have to assert such an identity. That at least is how my own argument will proceed (§3), relying at first upon the particular account I should give of the particular kind (viz. action) that the chosen event exemplifies (§2). I shall suggest that a putative identity claim would be groundless, and is not to be rescued (§4). If physicalism survives, it is not physicalism of the sort that most philosophers who call themselves physicalists ascribe to themselves. I end by considering what other sort there might be (§5).

2.1

There is a host of distinctively mental events that physicalists I am opposing in this essay are committed to conceiving of as identifiable by scientific descriptions supplanting common vocabulary. Among these are actions. The claim that actions are particulars that can be variously picked out is founded in the idea that when someone does something intentionally there is an event of his doing it, and that a person's doing of one thing can be the same as his doing of some other, different thing. However controversial this idea has sometimes been found to be, it seems to force itself upon us as soon as we try to be explicit about what we say when we say what people do.

Start with the thought that there are many things that people do—run to catch buses, move their arms, break glasses, open their mouths, contract their biceps, say that there are events, and so on. Then notice that sometimes, on occasion, there is some sort of connexion between these things: a person does one thing *by* doing another. For instance, he may break a glass by knocking over a jug, and do that by moving his arm. Now clearly this does not show that a certain relation holds once and for all between these three things that people do—between break a glass, knock over a jug and move an arm. For people can break glasses without knocking over jugs, and they can knock over jugs without moving their arms; it is only on certain occasions of people's doing things that there are connexions between the things that are done. But we get this across if we talk about the actions that occur on occasion (particulars), and avoid confusing those with the things that are done (universals). If we acknowledge that the agent's moving of his arm at a certain time, his knocking over of a jug, and so on are dated events, then we can ask once and for all about the relations between such events, of moving an arm, of knocking over a jug. Powerful arguments have been given that these particulars are related by identity where they are what occurred when someone knocked over a jug by moving his arm: his doing the one thing was the same as his doing the other.

How might "scientific" terms enter into the account of an action? Well, in the list of things done, we saw one thing people do that shows some actions to be describable at least in crude physiological terms— contract their biceps. And indeed contracting muscles of one sort or another is something that is done whenever a (so-called physical) action occurs: as physiologists tell us, it is impossible to move one's body without contracting muscles. All of us can move our bodies, and can get to do other things when we come to know how we need to move our bodies to do them; physiologists know in addition something about how the body is moved; one of the things that they know is that we move our bodies by contracting our muscles. If so, then contract the muscles is something else that someone does when he knocks over a jug by moving his arm; this is something by doing which he moves his arm. (Of course in the ordinary way we don't contract our muscles *intentionally*; nor, for that reason, do we *say* that we contract our muscles. But often there are things we don't intentionally do, and don't say we do, although our doing of them is our doing of something else that we intentionally do, and do say that we do.)

In order to show how an action is both a person's knocking over of a jug and his breaking of a glass, one need only point out that a single event may have more than one effect: it may cause a jug to topple, and if it does, and if it is an action, then it is someone's knocking over the jug; it may also cause a glass to break, and in that case, it is also his breaking of a glass. The same point explains how an action can be both someone's contracting of certain muscles and his moving of his arm: the action results in both a contraction of muscles and a movement of an arm. Because the contracting of the muscles *causes* the movement of the arm, the agent whose action it is can be said to move his arm *by* contracting those muscles. Compare: because the jug's toppling over caused the glass to break, he broke the glass by knocking over the jug.

The conclusion must be that an action—an event of someone's doing this thing, and that thing and that other thing, where he intentionally does at least one of these things—is an event that causes contractions of muscles, movements of bodies, and so on. But if actions are events that cause *(inter alia)* contractions of muscles, then one kind of physicalist will be bound to identify them with neurophysiological events.

2.2

It might be asked why anyone concerned about the status of *mental* items should worry about actions. 'Is it not agreed that actions of the kinds in question—people's movings of their bodies—are physical things?' Well certainly actions can be specified in (intuitively) physical ways. But equally we can employ psychological vocabulary in talking about actions—as when we say what someone *intentionally* did; and actions can be subsumed under concepts at least as obviously mentalistic, if, for example, they can ever be seen as events of people *trying* to do things.

Perhaps such considerations serve only to make you think that it ought to be a matter of indifference whether actions are regarded as mental or as physical things. If so, then for actions you may believe in physicalism of a kind I accept in spite of my opposition to one identity theory (see §5). But supposing that you persist in thinking that there are no interesting questions about the truth of physicalism of any other kind in relation to actions, I note now that any view taken about the relations between neural events and actions can be taken also about the relations between neural events and any of those other things—pains, perceptions, say—whose occurrence you may for some reason prefer to take as distinctive of the presence of mind (cp. §3.3).[2]

3.1

Pretend that a person could be wired up to apparatus that recorded the firings of his neurons (in the relevant bit of the cortex) and displayed a record of brain events on a screen. We can then imagine ourselves having sight of a chain of causally related events culminating in a bodily movement that occurred because the subject intentionally did something. The neurophysiologist may give a detailed story of events in the chain. But what we shall say about many of them is simply that they are events that the subject brought about. His bringing them about is his causing his body to move, his moving of his body, his action of doing something intentionally.

A question about scientific descriptions of actions can now be made rather precise. We can ask at what stage in the neural chain we find the man's action. Where is the action itself, as distinct from its effects, as distinct from the events that the agent brought about? To be in a position to answer such a question, or to say how to set about answering it, would be to know, or to know how to look for, some actual identities between events of someone's intentionally doing something and events that the neurophysiologist studies. But even as this question about identities becomes precise, we discover that our concepts of action may not contain the precision needed to determine an answer for it.

One may feel some pressure to say of each one of the events leading to the movement of his body that the agent brought it about, so that however far back one goes in tracing causes of his body's movement, one finds something to say about his action seen as the cause of events encountered there. The pressure operates, I think, because we are so used to employing the language of people's causing things when describing their actions that we tend to think that we can proceed to employ it indefinitely. But obviously we cannot: there was an action, which caused what the agent brought about in acting; in that case, there must be some point at which the action occurred, at which there occurred the cause of whatever had the effects (the muscles' contracting, and so on) by means of which we can recognize the action as the agent's bringing about of those things. So we know that we cannot say of *all* the neural events we observe that they are effects, or things the agent brought about.

But then there is a problem for the physicalist who supposes that we must be able to identify the action with some specifiable neural event or with some determinate collection of neural events. He assumes that we can distinguish sharply between those events which compose any action and those which result from the action. And the problem is that it comes to seem quite an arbitrary matter where we draw the line between the action and its effects. 'Is this a part of his action?', we can ask of an event that we see on the screen, 'or is it rather something that the action caused?'. We run out of answers and of places to look for answers when, having changed the focus, we examine events at a degree of resolution that we never need to achieve in order to make sense of one another.

3.2

If scientists of the brain develop their classification of events independent of our interests in recounting people's actions, then why should we presume that what they single out is the same as what we single out when we speak of actions? The point of the example is to arouse our suspicions of that presumption. But to establish that it is false, the case must be developed further. For someone may object that something so far left out of account could assist in locating the action among the neurophysiologically identified events. He claims that we need a full account of what is characteristic of actions; the account should say how actions, by virtue of being actions, are connected with events and states of other kinds; when complete, it will then record in schematic fashion all of the properties of actions that flow *a priori* from the fact that they are actions, so that, as applied to a particular case with suitable instances filled in for the properties, it will enable us to reduce to a minimum any indeterminacy that attaches to questions about how actions are matched with neural events. I shall try now to supply such an account. But I claim that it will not enable us to reduce that indeterminacy to nil.

An action *a* is an event of a person's doing something, where

   (i) *a* has various effects of a kind which qualify *a* as the person's doing this or that or the other thing;
   (ii) for at least one thing that the person does, *a* gives rise to a non-inferential belief that he has done it;
   (iii) at least one thing is done intentionally, and (appropriate) beliefs and desires of the person causally explain his doing it.[3]

Condition (i) merely captures the idea that actions are spoken of in terms of effects; and we have already seen that this feature of actions alone does not lead to neural identities. Condition (ii) relates to the agent's awareness of his action, and assumes that there is some direct route from an action to his belief that he has done something. (A direct route in the sense of one that is causally independent of the agent's perception, including proprioception, of those effects of his action to which condition (i) already alludes.) This means that, in addition to those events that lead away from any action via the muscles to the body's moving and further effects, there must be events leading away from the action which account for the agent's special awareness. And so it may be thought that, although it appeared indeterminate precisely which events were actions when we were confined to the language of bringing things about and found it undecidable exactly which neural events could be said to have been brought about, we now have a new sort of grasp upon the distinction between actions and their effects.

But here I would ask how knowledge that another chain leads from the action is supposed to enable us to say of specific events whether they compose actions or not. In applying condition (i), we knew of certain events that they caused things that were definitely effects of actions, but could not tell whether they were themselves parts of the action or events that mediated causally between some part of the action and other events that were its effects. Matters are not improved by our finding more events that partake of the same indeterminate status. To be justified in thinking that some event was an action, we should need a reason for thinking that everything that happened beyond it not only caused what that action caused but also was caused by the action. Yet whether we consider events belonging to chains that lead to movements of the body (to which condition (i) directs us), or whether we consider chains that lead to bits of the brain (to which condition (ii) directs us), we still lack any method for determining whether events are correctly reckoned parts of actions.

Conditions (i) and (ii) might have helped us say where an action finished, as it were. Condition (iii), by contrast, points us to causes of actions, and would help, if it helped at all, to say where the action started. On occasion it may tell us of a vast number of different states from which an action sprang. But, speaking as it does of mental *states*, however much it reveals about the agent it is of little avail in making the neurophysiological location of his actions definite. Even granting some strong physicalistic assumptions, according to which the mental states of an agent are realized by easily specified neural properties of his brain, there is still a problem of finding systematic and traceable connexions between the agent's possession of such states and the spatiotemporal particulars whose identities are the present concern. It may be held that wherever a state is said to cause an event e (as a belief may be said to cause an action), some event in which the state can be said to participate is a cause of e. But if we are hoping to latch onto actions by way of causes, then what we need is specific information about particular causes expressed in the same sorts of terms as those in which we hope to frame identities; and this tenet about state-event causation so far tells us no more than that an action, being caused by various states, is caused by some event or other.

Nothing we can squeeze out of condition (iii) in a particular case enables us to mark out the first point of the action; and nothing we can squeeze out of conditions (i) and (ii) jointly enables us to mark out the final point. This means that if we construct fusions of neural events, in the general neural region where the action might have been supposed to be, we shall have a number of events, each composed from neural events, but none a stronger candidate than any other to be the action.

3.3

Some writers about action have spoken of 'the initiating event in a neural sequence leading to the movement of the body', and have taken it that a unique denotation for such expressions is automatically guaranteed. Their assumption about such phrases is easily made in a variety of cases. Consider 'the event that was caused by the pricking of the skin with a pin and that caused the withdrawal of the hand', or 'the event that led to the belief that p and was caused by its being the case that p'. Those who use these expressions take them to designate neurophysiological events, and argue to neural-mental identities between things picked out in this fashion (by way of causal relata) and events of feeling pain or of perceiving objects.[4] But if a neurophysiologist can distinguish between many events that are causally intermediate between what happened at the surface of the skin when a pin pricked it and a motion there a little later, or between an object's being present and a person's first coming to think that it is, then there are too many possible denotata for such expressions, and the easy assumption is false.

Of course events may be introduced by way of their causal relata even when we are not doing philosophy of mind. Phrases on the pattern 'the cause of ———' do not occur only in descriptions constructed for the sake of arguments (such as 'the cause of the withdrawal of her hand'). So some account is needed of how we secure the determinacy of reference that we do when we speak of events via causes and effects. I should suggest that phrases like 'the cause of [the fire]' are understood to name that event causally closest to [the fire] which can be described so as to give an explanation of why [the fire] occurred. On this account, such phrases may refer quite determinately on particular occasions of use by speakers with particular explanatory concerns. But that does not ensure that, for example, 'the cause of the bodily movement' determinately refers *both* to something in the extension of an action predicate *and* to something in the extension of a neurophysiological predicate. For if the explanatory concern were a specialist scientific one, there would be no reason to suppose that the phrase picks out an action; and if the explanatory concern were a commonsense psychological one, then (I have argued) we should be at a loss to find one neural event a better candidate than any other for the reference of the phrase.

In the case of action, it may be especially clear that we cannot secure a determinate reference for a piece of commonsense psychological vocabulary when confronted by neural events. If this does seem especially clear, then that may be because it is especially clear-cut how a detailed causal account of *action* should go. Action concepts equip us to describe what impact the agent had on the world, but they do not provide us with anything exact to say in the language of neurophysiology. We should reflect more generally upon the point of our psychological concepts. Perhaps we shall see, more generally, that they need not have provided us with any need to say anything exact outside of common sense.

4.1

If nothing establishes that some one claim of identity between an action (or a pain, or a perception) recommends itself more than all the others, then we should do better not to assert any claim of identity. Benacerraf reached such a conclusion in respect of numbers and sets.[5] But other reactions to the indeterminacy may be thought appropriate where mental events are in question; and I now attempt to rule these out.

The considerations of §3 might be thought to show that action descriptions fail to refer (as Benacerraf's arguments seem sometimes to be taken to show that numerals lack reference). This extreme view of the matter may appeal to someone who starts with the prejudice that mental events simply have to be neurophysiological events, and then comes to be persuaded that there are no neurophysiological events that mental events have to be. Yet it is surely only under the sway of a prior conviction that identities must be discoverable that one would be moved from thinking that there are no identities to thinking that there are after all no actions or events of perceiving things or of feeling pain.

According to a second reaction, mental events are things of such a sort that identity relations do hold between them and neurophysiological events, but they hold indeterminately. Concerning some action a, for example, it is indeterminate whether it is b. But this isn't something we say about a thing of any sort. For a is determinately the same as a, and thus has a property that b hasn't; b isn't, though a is, determinately the same as a; and, by the non-discernibility of identicals, we may conclude that a is not b. Truth-preserving steps take us from the indeterminacy of the identity statement to its falsehood, and we cannot rest with the claim that identities themselves are vague.[6]

The last reaction of someone who wishes to persist with identities will be to have the indeterminacy which characterizes the case reside in the part-whole or 'composes' relation that is taken to obtain between mental and physical things. Then he can agree that actions are not the same as determinately constructed fusions, but maintain that they are the same as indeterminately constructed fusions, without allowing that it is ever indeterminate whether they are the same as fusions of any sort. By identifying actions (and so on) with fusions built up using a vague relation, he avoids denying the existence of mental events, and avoids the consequences of having indeterminacy attach to identity itself. But what this physicalist cannot avoid is a mereological conception of events. For on the account he gives, the domain of events marked out by neurophysiology and the domain of events marked out by commonsense psychology have members in common only so long as identity may be seen as a limiting case of the relation of composition: any fusion constructed from neural events as parts must itself be an event and the very same event as any, however articulated, that has those same parts. Such constructionalism was refuted in the last essay.

4.2

The vain reactions that we have just encountered are reactions to the problem of making out a mental-physical identity in a particular case. But those who accept the identities are likely to rely on general arguments, rather than to treat particular cases—arguments such as that of Davidson, which rely on the Nomological Character of Causality (Essay 3, §7). One of the things counting against a mereological conception of events was the difficulty of reconciling it with any plausible account of causation (Essay 3, §4). It is worth turning now to Davidson's own account of causation, which is a species of the regularity theory whose compatibility with mereological conceptions of events was cast in doubt. We need to look at a particular difficulty that it faces, a difficulty which is at its most acute when mereological conceptions are not taken for granted.

Davidson's principle of the Nomological Character of Causality holds that a law subsumes any two events between which a causal relation obtains. ('L subsumes a and b' is shorthand for 'There are descriptions of a and b that instantiate L.') The initial difficulty I find with that emerges from asking how we are meant to accommodate certain cases where a causes b and b causes c, and where, in virtue of that, it is also true that a causes c. If we think that a law subsumes a and b, and that a law subsumes b and c, we have no reason yet to assume that some law subsumes a and c. We have no reason even if we accept that, if a bi-conditional relating F-events and G-events is lawlike, and a bi-conditional relating G-events and H-events is lawlike, then a bi-conditional relating F-events and H-events is lawlike. This point does not meet the difficulty, because three causally related events a, b and c need not be connected by any pair of bi-conditionals which both show b as effect of a and show b as cause of c; the feature of b which we need to discern in order to link it by law to a may be different from that which we need to discern to link it by law to c. And if no property G of b ensures its lawful connexion both with a and with c, then a and c are not subsumable under one law. (One may not be persuaded of this if one thinks only of "short" causal chains, and thinks of them in abstraction. One needs to consider ordinary examples, and to remember that many causal chains have many links, and that every chain is part of a network and not insulated from every event that isn't a link in that chain.) We might call this the problem of transitivity. More strictly it should be called a problem of non-intransitivity, because it will afflict Davidson's account so long as the causal relation is not *in*transitive, and it is allowed that *a* might cause *c* "via" its causing *b*.

The view that *causation* is intransitive is not without adherents. But it is not a view one can take if one accepts Davidson's claims about causation. There are events (such as avalanches) which are causally related to other events, but which are, as it were, too big and too rough-hewn to be picked out simply in the vocabulary in which laws are stated. In order for such events to be brought into contact with laws, presumably they need to be seen as composed of parts that can be brought under laws. But if the parts whose descriptions are found in laws are to do their job, then it has to be seen how they in turn are causally connected. Granted transitivity (and granted some mereological principles), it would be easy to say how causal connexions in the small make for causal connexions in the large; but in the presence of intransitivity, there seems to be no way in which one might seek to show how the causation of rough-hewn everyday events was grounded in connexions between their law-governed components. Then Davidson's view is not only faced with the transitivity problem, but also gives rise to it.

It now appears that someone who defends the identities in question here, and who uses the Nomological Character of Causality, requires a mereological conception of events not only to support identities where we have (intuitively) smaller and larger things, but also to make good his account of causation itself. The problem now is not just with the mereological conception, nor just with Nomologicality. Each of these appears to be required by, but incompatible with, the other.

5.1

I can imagine someone saying that to deny the identities that I have argued we have to deny is to make only a very weak claim. Why should we say that mental events are not physical events because we see that they are not the same as the neurophysiological events which exhaust them?

If this is to point out that no concession to traditional dualism is made by me here, then it is true. But if it is meant to suggest that a denial of identities is not damaging to what physicalists have believed about mental events, then it is not true.[7] For philosophers have found mental objects problematic enough to give rise to a need for *arguments* to their physical character. Pains and perceptions, it is thought, are not obviously physical—or at least they are not obviously physical until it has been demonstrated that there are obviously physical predicates that apply to them. I claim that it may be that no obviously physical predicates apply to them; and if that is not to accept dualism, then it must be to say at least that the brand of monism which is called physicalism has been misconceived.

5.2

Everything here has concerned a thesis in ontology. But it is widely accepted that any doctrine capable of capturing what the physicalist characteristically believes must also include a thesis about the relations of the concepts that mental and physical predicates stand for. Davidson's argument for his ontological thesis about mental particulars relied upon a rejection of nomic ties between mental and physical concepts; but a different conceptual thesis, of supervenience, figures in his version of physicalism. Quine has held that a purely ontological thesis establishes so very little that 'ontology is not what mainly matters': almost everything turns on a physicalist's further claims. And Hellman and Thompson hold something very similar: 'An ontological component is necessary for physicalism', they say, 'but it is insufficient'.[8] Now all of these writers believe the ontological thesis that I have denied. They believe that mental events are physical, in a sense of 'physical' fixed by science. Moreover, they all formulate the extra, not purely ontological, component of physicalism so as to ground it in that ontological thesis; the extra is always stated as some claim about relations between mental and physical (scientific) classifications of a domain containing things picked out by predicates of both sorts. But if all these formulations are set in this way against the background ontology

I reject, then it may seem that I have renounced the whole of physicalism, at least as that has come to be understood.

In fact, someone who denies the identities I deny can make distinctively physicalist claims outside ontology, if not of the currently orthodox kind. Statues are different from their matter, but features of statues depend upon features of the matter that composes them (and not conversely). So it might be, much more generally, that there is some exigent notion of the physical according to which the way anything is in any mental respect depends upon the way things physically are, without there being a single domain all the members of which can be isolated by predicates counted as physical by the exigent standard. Of course if this claim is to characterize physicalism, then it is important to say more exactly what might be meant by uses of 'depend' such as these. But there is a difficulty for everyone in stating in what sense the physical fixes the mental, or the mental depends upon the physical.[9] And certainly no contribution is made (the task is only made to seem as if it were more smooth or simple than it actually is) by presupposing that a common ontology has to underlie dependencies between the two realms.

This cannot be the end of the matter, though. A monist of any sort surely does take an asymmetrical attitude not only with respect to what determines what, but also to ontology. And if a doctrine of monism is to deserve the title of physicalism, it must find in some claim to the effect that all mental events are physical some merit which it fails to find in any claim that all physical events are mental. I have blocked one kind of strategy that might be used to establish such an asymmetry. Here one starts with a class of obviously physical predicates, and then works hard to show, what wasn't obvious, that there are identities between each of the mental things and some item picked out by those obviously physical predicates (and to show, moreover, if that be necessary, that such identities could not be established quite generally if one started with obviously mental predicates). A different strategy is not ruled out, however. Here one starts with obvious identities, and then works hard to show, what wasn't obvious, that terms on at least one side of such identities are always physical (and to show, moreover, if that is in doubt, that this could not be made out quite generally if the terms had to be found to be mental). Suppose one takes an explanatory, but everyday, account of that portion of the world of events that we talk about without using (intuitively) mental language, then—it might be argued—by introducing vocabulary we regard as mental we can extend that account in such a way that the occurrence of mental events explain and are explained. But if we take an account of the world that we talk about without using (intuitively) physical vocabulary, it cannot be thus extended to explain the occurrence of all physical events.—So the argument might continue.— Combine these, and add the premiss that the occurrence of e explains the occurrence of f only where e and f can be seen as belonging to some common kind, and there would be a reason for thinking that the mental things are physical which could never be a reason for thinking that the physical things are mental.

If this is how an argument for a physicalist ontology proceeds, the sense of 'physical' is given first by the vocabulary which we use to describe the world that we take ourselves to perceive and to act on, and which we use in stating the content of one another's beliefs and desires; and then we seek to show that in that sense of 'physical' the physical things might as well include the happenings of our mental lives. We appeal to explanatory connexions to make this good, but there is no resort to laws or to science. Thus if I were asked, 'Which physical events are mental events?', I should answer, 'Actions, perceptions, pains and so on', believing that there is nothing more obviously physical with which these can be identified; and that there need not be.

Postscript to Part I: The Nomological Character of Causality

Essays 3 and 4 both implicate the thesis of the Nomological Character of Causality in a spurious mereological conception of events. If a proponent of Nomologicality can solve the 'transitivity problem' only by resorting to a mereological conception, and if the needed mereological conception is incompatible with an account of causation that appeals to Nomologicality, then the thesis is discredited.

The thesis was not so much as credited in Rorty's account of Davidson (discussed in the postscript to Essay 2). Recall that there was a lacuna in Rorty's account. Rorty introduced the ontological claim comprised in Davidson's theory by speaking of the 'ontological neutrality *characteristic* of non-reductionism'; but he told us nothing about why ontological neutrality is in non-reductionism's character. Well, the neutrality that Rorty means, by which mental events belong to a 'neutral' domain when recognized to be 'physical', can actually be characteristic of the particular non-reductionist who believes in causation's Nomological Character. The Nomologicality thesis guarantees a domain ruled by laws which includes all causally related things. A correct account of Davidson could be got by placing the thesis into the lacuna in Rorty's account.

It is curious that Rorty did not so much as mention the Nomological Character of Causality in his description of Davidsonian philosophy of mind: it is, after all, a premiss on which anomalous monism is built. Perhaps Rorty himself feels some tug towards ontological neutrality, so that he sees no need for any thesis about causation to take him from the mental's irreducibility to the monism that both he and Davidson accept. It seems possible that there is an outlook which makes a doctrine of ontological neutrality or a doctrine of causation's nomological character seem equally reasonable. Perhaps this is the outlook that gives philosophers their conception of the world in which minds have to be able to operate (cp. Essay 1). It may be that Rorty arrives at ontological neutrality by adopting the outlook, that others arrive at mereological principles by adopting it, and that yet others arrive at the idea of a certain uniformity in accounts of things' doing causal work.

If these different ideas—about neutrality in ontology, about wholes and parts, and about causation—are indeed plausibly the products of the same basic outlook, then we should consider where it comes from. What seems to be common to the different ideas is an assumption that anything we might come across in the world might also have been discernible to someone working at a higher level of abstraction than us. For these different ideas all require us to believe in a vantage point on an item that we pick out using (say) commonsense psychological vocabulary which can be occupied independent of using commonsense psychological concepts, and from which, using mereological or nomological concepts, the item could be picked out. The vantage point would be a 'neutral' one, in Rorty's sense. From the neutral vantage point, it may be supposed, the concepts of *part-whole* and of *cause* can both be applied. (This supposition will support the thought, rejected in Essay 3, that mereological conceptions can always be pressed into service to defend the Nomological Character of Causality.) But then might not the outlook be generated by what Rorty called 'the impulse that leads to reductionism'? This is the impulse felt by those who take themselves to have a conception of an 'uninterpreted world' (see postscript to Essay 2). And is not an 'uninterpreted world' what would—supposedly, but *per impossibile*—be confronted by someone going in for, as it were, the ultimate in abstraction?

At the end of the discussion of Rorty on Davidson (in the postscript to Essay 2), I entertained the suspicion that the pressures that lead to reductionism can also work to sustain a monolithic attitude to what there is. That suspicion would be confirmed if the diagnosis here of Rorty's ontological neutrality is right.

But the 'impulse that leads to reductionism' is the impulse that Rorty told us that *Davidson*, in his attack on 'correspondence truth', has shown us how to avoid. So if the Nomological Character of Causality substitutes for ontological neutrality in the way I have suggested, then it should in fact be no part of the Davidsonian position.

It would take more than these remarks to make out that there really is the tension that I suspect there is between Davidson's rejection of correspondence truth and his position in philosophy of mind. But it is worth noting that none of the advantages of what Rorty calls Davidsonian philosophy of mind is lost if this is right about Davidson. What we gain by avoiding the impulse to reductionism is an attitude towards an irreducible subject matter which ensures that it is in no way deprecated by being revealed to be irreducible. In that case a satisfactory anomalous anti-Cartesianism cannot require a version of monism in which the Nomological Character of Causality is the crux.

II

Agency

5

Introduction: Action and the Mental-Physical Divide

1

I don't think that we shall have a credible philosophy of action until it is freed from wrong assumptions imported from philosophy of mind. This part of the book is about action, but the matters it purports to pronounce on are not the concern of 'action theory' narrowly conceived.

There are enough controversies about the nature of action itself to make the philosophy of action seem like a self-contained area of study. We may be told that 'a theory of action' is 'largely independent of a general account of mental events' (see, e.g., Brand, 1984). Certainly there are some questions about the events of concern to "action theorists" which can be taken on their own. (The principal ones are addressed rather summarily in Essay 6, §2.) But the right answer to these questions will not be given if a faulty assumption from philosophy of mind is stolen in.

The assumption that seems to me to have damaged philosophy of action may be stated generally and rather roughly. It is that we can always draw lines between the mental things in the world and the physical things there. When the assumption is in play, a distinction between mental and physical is not just a distinction based on an intuitive difference that we may recognize between two sorts of properties, but a distinction that actually carves things up in the spatiotemporal world. The mind-body problem can then be thought of as the problem literally of finding a place for mind. The question becomes: how can there be volumes of the spatiotemporal world for the mental to occupy, if the spatiotemporal world is a natural physical world? Essay 2 suggested that such a question inspires a Cartesian idea of a mental-physical divide; and Essay 3 was meant to expose the errors of the neutral spatiotemporal conceptions that the question involves. The assumption works at a less abstract level when it comes into philosophy of action. Those who make the assumption expect to be told a story about human action whose ingredients in particular cases can be articulated around the putative lines between mental and physical. The assumption is at work when actions, but not their antecedents, are taken to be unproblematically physical, and when the antecedents of actions, but not actions themselves, are taken to be problematically unobservable.

Sometimes the assumption is explicitly made. Some philosophers, in defending physicalism, begin from their confidence that *action* is physical. They think that an attack on dualism will take the form of showing that the causal antecedents of action, which *prima facie* are mental, must be shown to be physical too. (Here we have a particular case of the sort of thinking about the 'micro' items which I was concerned with throughout Part I.) Other philosophers begin from a conception of the mental—as hidden from view. People's believing things or desiring things or intending things is not visible (they say); but we can simply observe their actions when we look at the physical world. What is wrong with dualism on their account is that it treats as necessarily hidden something that is really only contingently hidden—as if a closer inspection of a person's insides could assure us that she participates only in physical events and states. We are required then to find the internal states from which actions issue in the bits of the physical world which are ordinarily concealed from sight.

The assumption of a line dividing the mental from the physical is often present implicitly when philosophers think about the processes that constitute human action. If a person has got what she wants because she did something to get it, then a causal story can be told. The picture that many philosophers adopt is one in which the elements of this story are members of a sequence of causally connected states and events, where the surface of the person's body marks a cut-off between the mental states and events and the subsequent physical ones. A theorist's overall view of the nature of *action* is supposed, then, to be determined by her answer to the question 'What event on the sequence is the action to be identified with?' (Brand, 1984). Now there seems to be something rather odd about the question in the first place, even before an answer to it is meant to tell us whether the theorist thinks that action is 'mental' or 'physical'. The theorist surely had to set out thinking that she knew what an action was before she could know which causal sequences she was meant to be locating one on, so that it is not at all clear why the real truth about her view should be uncovered by contemplating the causal sequences as such. But when the assumption about a cut-off point between mental and physical is made, it seems impossible for certain theories to be held. For instance, it is now ruled out that an action should be the cause of a bodily movement yet be properly regarded as something physical; and it is ruled out that an action should be identified with the agent's trying to do something, yet not be taken to be something hidden.

In the philosophy of action, I have claimed that an action (when it has effects beyond the agent) *is* a cause of a bit of the agent's body's moving, and that an action (very nearly always) *is* an event of the agent's trying to do something (see Hornsby, 1980, ch. 3, and Essay 4). As a result, I have been said to hold that actions are not 'overt' (Brand, 1984), to locate 'the essence of action in the will' (Duff, 1990), to identify an action with 'a purely mental act of will' (Brewer, 1993), and I have been called 'a mental action theorist' (Moore, 1993). But until some doctrine about mental-physical difference is introduced, my claims have none of these consequences.[1] I take the fact (as I see it) that we can usually redescribe a person's action as her trying to do something to show that our intuitive distinction between mental and physical does not partition the events that there are. This means that even if it is right to regard some things as physical, and some things as mental, others may best be regarded as *psychophysical*. To take an example: suppose that her hammering of the nail is her trying to fix it in the wall. Then we have (in my view) the identity of her hammering . . . with her trying to . . . The identity has been supposed to lead us to abandon our ordinary view of the nature of someone's wielding a hammer, and to say that the action is 'an act of will' which is 'mental' and not 'overt'. But surely it should be taken rather to show that both mental and physical concepts have application to actions. We have an event which is both someone's trying to do something *and* her actually doing something. This can be a physicalist thesis of sorts: mental things are physical.

The physicalist thesis to which my claims lead is of course different from the one advanced by those who introduce an exacting conception of the *physical*. The exacting conception may get in when mental events are assumed to confront the world at an interface. That assumption, I have suggested, ensures that, in order to make out her title to physicalism, a philosopher has to speculate about the character of what happens on the causal chains leading up to the movements of agents' bodies. Such speculation may be the business of the going naturalism in philosophy of mind, but it is not on the naive naturalist's agenda.

2

In Essay 6, I take on a particular objection to what I had previously argued about action. According to the objection, my account is in difficulty because it renders actions invisible. My response (predictably enough) is that the difficulty comes not from my account of them, but from views brought in by the objector about what it takes to see something or to know something. There is, for instance, the view that motions of body are bits of *behaviour*, and that someone's behaviour is all that we can really observe. The view has to be rejected, along with the idea that we shall understand human agency better by going in for detailed examination of the various events that action theorists distinguish.

The notion of 'behaviour' is put under scrutiny in Essay 7. I suggest there that philosophers equivocate. They may start with a pretheoretical notion got from the idea of people's ordinary, behavioural interventions in the world (people's actions, roughly); but they go on to suppose that bits of behaviour according to this pretheoretical notion have a place in theoretical, or neurophysiological, accounts of the production of bodily movements. I suggest that the equivocation can result from, but also give rise to, the idea that a person's operations are detectable in the operations of her brain. (This equivocation is what a *disjunctive* conception of bodily movements is designed to disallow; see postscript to Essay 6.)

In the terms of Essay 8, a person's operations are known about from the 'personal point of view', those of her brain from an 'impersonal point of view'. The essay's thesis is that actions are not to be identified with any thing that can be latched onto from an impersonal point of view. That might be another way of formulating the anti-physicalist conclusion of Essay 4. But in its new formulation, the thesis evidently puts me in direct opposition to the going philosophical versions of naturalism. If it is true, then there can be no hope of 'naturalizing the mind'. Naturalizing would be a matter of finding objective, norm-free (impersonal) things to say which correspond to the ordinary things that are said when action-explanations are given (see Introduction). My claim, though, is that a different subject matter is treated, not people and their doings, when an impersonal point of view is taken.

3

I started here by indicating that philosophy of action may be damaged by prejudicial assumptions about mind. In fact, I think that philosophy of mind and philosophy of action have done each other no good: there is a reciprocal sort of damage, done when certain ways of talking in philosophy of action come into philosophy of mind. I take the opportunity to say something about this now, because it may help in understanding some of the material on action that follows. Some of my terminology may not be familiar. If it is unfamiliar to readers of the philosophical literature, then that is because the ways of talking that the literature has made familiar lead one astray (in my opinion). In particular, there are ways of talking about action which make it easy to forget that people and their doings are the subject.

In philosophy, talk about action has to be couched at a level of generality that no one needs to achieve in the normal course of events: theorists have to frame generalizations of a kind that do not occur in day-to-day language. Presumably action theorists want their generalizations to have true instances in ordinary English: the theories, after all, concern things that people talk about every day. But their generalized ways of talking can take on a life of their own, and dispose us to accept claims that we should never have made if we had concentrated on the accepted truths about particular cases.

Even apart from its need to speak especially generally, the philosophy of action is bound to go in for some non-everyday ways of putting things right from the start. Ordinarily we do not say things like 'there was an event which was Jane's unlocking of the door'; we say, 'Jane unlocked the door'. But the more extraordinary way of putting things, which explicitly introduces an event, seems inescapable if questions of certain sorts are to be raised. Suppose that Jane tried to unlock the door, but was using the wrong key. Then one may want to know how her trying to do one thing, and her actually doing some other (jiggling the key in the lock, say), are related—by identity? as part to whole? as cause to effect? Questions of this sort, which so much occupy action theorists, cannot be put without talking about the events—about the actual dated occurrences that make sentences like 'She unlocked the door' true. The questions just are questions about connexions between events of certain sorts. (My own answers to such questions are sketched in Essay 6, §2.)

If we are going to talk about events, then we need to keep track of when we are doing so. My policy is to use 'an action' of things in the domain of events: there is an action when there is an event which is someone's intentionally doing something—when, for example, there is Jane's unlocking of the door. Now the policy puts me in line with other philosophers: disputes about 'the individuation of action' have concerned just such particulars. But the policy does not reflect the everyday use of 'action'. (This is hardly surprising, given that events are not *explicitly* talked about every day.) Errors may result when the philosophical use is run together with the everyday one. In the everyday use, actions are things people do. When this use is combined with the philosophical use, it seems as if people did events. But they don't. It is simply wrong to say that an action is something someone does *if* 'action' denotes events. Phrases that speak of an event are phrases such as 'her raising of her arm', or 'Smith's killing of Jones'. And she doesn't do her raising of her arm, and Smith didn't do his killing of Jones. At least if we are in idiomatic English, we do not speak of people as related to events by 'do'. What she did, we say, was [to] raise her arm, and what Smith did was [to] kill Jones. These things—raise one's arm, kill Jones—which people do indeed do, and which are the actions of common parlance, are muddled up with events when 'action' is not confined to a single sort of use. So I use 'action' *only* for things in the domain of events.

The confusion between philosophers' actions and the actions of common parlance is helped along by a further piece of equivocation, now on the word 'particular'. In most philosophers' reckoning, events are in the category of particulars, where the intended contrast is with a category, say, of universals. Someone who wants to emphasize that it is something in the category of particulars that she is talking about—something dated, and unrepeatable, in contrast to something that might happen several times—may then say 'particular event' or 'particular action'. It can come to seem as though writing the word 'particular' before 'event' or before 'action' somehow ensured that one had written a phrase that denotes a particular. But in fact, it does not ensure this at all. For 'particular X' may just mean particular—sc. certain—thing, which is X. And where an X is something in a category of non-particulars (of universals, or whatever), a particular X simply will not be a particular. (Colours, for instance, are not particulars; nor are particular colours.) The step of putting the word 'particular' in, which is meant to make it absolutely certain that a particular is spoken of, often serves to distract us from the fact that the thing spoken of is not a particular at all.[2]

The muddling up of philosophers' actions, which are in the category of particulars, with things not in that category has caused needless dispute about their individuation. Davidson promoted the view that we usually describe actions in terms of their effects; and that since a single action can have many effects, it can have many descriptions (Davidson, 1971a; see also §2.1 of Essay 4 above). His thesis about redescribability holds, for instance, that 'her raising of her arm' and 'her casting her vote' may be alternative descriptions of the same action: they are alternatives for the case where some action of hers was responsible both for her arm's going up and for her vote's being cast. Putting this without ascending to the level of descriptions, we may say that her raising of her arm was her casting of her vote. And if we want something more general, so that we are no longer talking only about the single case, then we may say that her doing one thing was her doing another thing. But this way of putting it would be unavailable if actions got confused with things she does. The Davidsonian view of individuation that we want to advance gives us theses of identity for *actions*. If the things done were in question, then there could hardly be an identity: she did *two* things, raise her arm and cast her vote; *these* are not identical; she did one by doing the *other*. The claimed identity consists not in one of these things being the other of these things (of course not), but in her doing one of them's being her doing the other.

There is another source of the confusion of actions with things people do. The confusion crops up also when phrases standing for actions are not distinguished from phrases standing for things done. This latter confusion sometimes gets in through a sort of shorthand. It is laborious to keep on using the event-denoting nominals like 'her raising of her arm', and it is especially laborious if one is discussing identities and has several such phrases simultaneously in play. So one abbreviates. Instead of asking whether her raising of her arm was her reaching for the book, one asks whether raising her arm was the same as reaching (say). But 'raising her arm', which is now introduced, can serve as a phrase suited for talking about what she did ('Raising her arm was what she was doing'). Shortening the nominals, then, leads to something ambiguous, so that the distinction between actions in the philosopher's sense and the actions of common parlance is eradicated once again.

The shortenings have further consequences, which go beyond action theory proper. The effect of the shortenings is to drop mention of the agent from the nominal phrases. One finds, say, 'signalling' where it would be agreed that the event is *someone's* signalling. Quite often one finds '*the* signalling', which presumably reflects indifference about *which* agent it was, but which may encourage indifference about whether there was an agent at all. And (as I have suggested already) one finds 'something done' when 'her doing of something' is meant. In all these cases, the agent is left out: although we may be meant to be thinking about a person's doing something—Mary's doing this, or John's doing that, as it might be—what we actually encounter are phrases which make no allusion to any person. It is no wonder that it seems as though the events that there are when there are actions can all be thought about impersonally. Philosophy provides ways of making it seem so.

One further effect of a certain shortening is worth mentioning here. In discussions where several event descriptions are in play at once, we find, say, 'Ben's trying to get out of the house by 9 o'clock' abbreviated to 'the trying'. (There is an example of this sort of shorthand in Essay 6, where I use 'the attempt'.) It becomes possible then to forget that to try is always to try to do something. And it may be that forgetfulness about this is what makes philosophers (Duff, 1990, and others) think it obvious that—as they say—'tryings are mental'. The phrase 'trying' sounds as if it named something less robust than her trying to fix it in the wall by wielding a hammer.

To complete the catalogue, I draw attention to one last way of talking that fuels impersonal conceptions of agency. This is talk of bodily movements, of a kind which I regret I may have abetted in the past. Bodily movements come to the fore in philosophy of action, because they are treated as the physical things whose place in an account every theorist must speak to (see above, and Essay 6). But we should be sure that we know what is meant by 'bodily movement'—whether a bit of someone's body's moving is meant, or someone's moving of a bit of her body. Wanting to be able to be sure, at one time (1980) I employed subscripts: 'movement$_I$' was to be short for phrases using the intransitive verb—such-and-such's moving—'movement$_T$' for phrases using the transitive verb—someone's moving such-and-such. The ambiguity in 'move' is surely worth taking care over. For sliding between intransitive and transitive senses is sliding between events in which bits of people's bodies participate and events in which people themselves also do. The trouble is, though, that although the verb 'move' is indeed ambiguous between transitive and intransitive, it is far from clear that the ambiguity carries over to the nominal 'movement'. When 'move$_T$', the transitive verb, occurs in an event-description, we have (say) 'a person's moving of her leg', and it is not at all obvious that 'mov*ement*' in any sense can serve as shorthand for this. If indeed it cannot serve, then writing a subscript will not make 'bodily movement' stand for any event reported by a sentence which has a *person* as its subject. (By allowing 'bodily movement$_T$', I may myself have encouraged confusion about which events they are that people participate in.)

The subscripts do not come into what follows. I have used them here to show up the possible dangers of carefree use of 'movement'. Using 'movement' as if it were short for 'a person's moving something or other' can give rise to an idea that naive naturalism sets itself against—the idea of a person as separated from the events into whose description mention of her properly enters. The idea may lead to accounts of agency that prescind from agents. The argument of Essay 8 is that there can be no such accounts, because we change the subject if we stop talking about people. I hope by now to have conveyed some idea of the many terminological forces that this argument may be up against.

6

Bodily Movements, Actions
and Epistemology

1

In philosophy we find reasons for recognizing events that fall under the generalized description 'a person's body's moving' or 'bodily movement'.

One reason that might be offered for talking about such events—about movements of fingers, or legs, or whatever—is that in doing so we talk about what is overt or in the public and observable realm. If knowledge of people's minds needs to be built upon observable features of people, and if movings of peoples' bodies are all that can be observed, then we should have to focus attention on bodies' movings to understand how people can learn what they do learn about one another. But I shall suggest that we make a mistake if we think that people's bodies' movings must have the special status of being visible alike to a psychologically quite ignorant and a psychologically informed spectator, so that they can serve as a neutral basis for knowledge of mind.

Another reason for concern with people's bodily movements has nothing directly to do with epistemology: we want to understand the relations between the things that happen when there are human actions. Where so-called physical action is in question, it is a necessary condition of someone's doing something that a movement of her body occur;[1] and we can have a clearer picture of what goes on if we are able to say how the event that is her body's moving is related to her doing what she does.

I take the view that the relation between an action of someone's moving her body and her body's moving is a causal one and that a person's body's moving is no part of her action of moving her body. It has been objected that this view has the consequence that we do not see actions and that this consequence is problematic. I hope to fend off this objection in this essay. I shall start by sketching and discussing various views in the philosophy of action; to begin with, I shall avoid any epistemological matters.

2

Three claims about human physical action will have to be taken for granted here. First, when a person intentionally does anything, that person's doing that thing is an action, and this action is her moving her body.[2] Second, if a person moves a part of her body, that part of her body moves. And third, typically at least, when a person intentionally does something, she tries to do that thing.[3] If these three claims are true, then when someone does something and intentionally moves her body,[4] there are events of three sorts: there is an event of that person's moving her body, which is her action; there is an event of her body's moving; and there is an event of her trying to move her body.

These claims are controversial. But even when they are accepted, there is still disagreement about what relations obtain between particular events of the three sorts. (Note that to say that there are events of these three sorts is not yet to say whether there are three events.)

Let us focus on a particular occasion of an action—someone wiggles her finger to attract someone else's attention, say. Call the event of her wiggling her finger *the action*, the event of her finger's wiggling *the movement*, and the event of her trying to wiggle her finger *the attempt*. Then I claim that the action causes the movement; but others claim that the movement is a (proper) part of the action; and others that the movement is the same as the action. Claims about the relation between the action and the movement are not independent of claims about the relation between the action and the attempt. I claim that the attempt is the same as the action. But some of those who hold that the movement is a part of the action or that the movement is the same as the action will deny that. Those who hold that the movement is a part of the action and deny the identity of attempt with action think that the attempt is a part of the action: their picture is one in which actions are "ontologically and conceptually hybrid", composed from events of trying on the one hand and movements of the body on the other.[5] Those who hold that the movement is the same as the action and deny the identity of attempt with action think that the attempt causes the movement: their picture is one in which actions are those movements of the body that are caused by events of trying.

There are so many possible views here (including ones not sketched above) that one must hope to rule out some with a general argument. It is often supposed that we are more or less free to choose whether actions are to be identified with attempts and that we have only to compare the pictures we get of action according as we assume the identity or not.[6] But in fact it is possible to argue in a general way against any view that denies the identity of actions with events of trying (or attempts). For it seems that someone who accepts the account of the individuation of actions presupposed here (which is summed up in the first of the three claims being taken for granted) must already have an argument for such identities. To argue for this account of individuation is to argue for the following schema:[7]

If x φ-s by ψ-ing, then x's φ-ing is the same as x's ψ-ing.

Clearly this yields statements of identity relating actions. But if we can write as an instance of 'φ' or of 'ψ' here 'tries to ———', then we shall reach a statement of identity linking action with attempt. And we can sometimes instantiate 'φ' or 'ψ' with 'tries to ———': we can truly say such things as 'He upset Mary by trying to pacify John' or 'She managed to trill moderately well by trying to move her fingers in the way her teacher had shown her'. It seems then that whatever leads one to say that Jones's killing Smith was the same as his moving his finger (on the gun) will lead one to say that Jones's *trying to* kill Smith was the same as his moving his finger on the gun and (if Jones tried to move his finger) was the same as his *trying to* move his finger.[8] If this is right, the identity of action with attempt may be assumed in determining whether the relationship between movement and action is *part-whole* or *identity* or *cause-effect*.

One motive there has been for thinking that movements and actions are related as *parts to wholes* is that it enables us to give a particular literal sense to the idea that actions are psychophysical.[9] But this motive seems to lapse when we assume the identity of the action with the attempt; then we cannot say that actions are composed both from events that we recognize as psychological (viz. attempts) and from events that we recognize as physical (viz. movements). Given the identity of action with attempt, someone who thinks that movements are parts of actions, when he is asked what it is that along with the movement constitutes the action, apparently has no way to answer except by saying, 'that which is left over when the movement is subtracted from the action'. Of course, someone might find plenty to say about the event that is action-minus-movement residue even though no psychological term straightforwardly latches onto it. But he would now do well to offer an argument specifically for the view that movements are parts of actions.[10]

If the thesis that the movement *is the same as* the action were correct, then the three sorts of events we began from would prove to be such that a single event is of all these three sorts: the action is itself movement and attempt. If we favour a certain uniform account of the nature of trying, however, we have a reason to think that the movement is distinct from the attempt.[11] The difference, we may want to say, between a successful and an unsuccessful attempt to do something (no matter what that something is) is that a successful attempt, but not an unsuccessful one, results in an event whose occurrence then suffices for the thing's having been done. The difference between a successful and an unsuccessful attempt to turn on a light, for instance, is that the former but not the latter results in an event—a light's going on— whose occurrence then suffices for the light's having been turned on.[12] Applying the account to the case of trying to move the body, we find ourselves saying that successful but not unsuccessful attempts to move the body result in bodily movements.[13]

This last argument purports to demonstrate not only that the relation between action and movement is not identity, but also that the relation is in fact a causal one. Doubtless the argument is not definitive.[14] But perhaps it can be allowed that nothing in the sorts of consideration so far adduced suggests that a view of movements as parts of actions, or as the same as actions, is obviously correct if set against a view of movements as caused by actions.[15] At this point, then, I turn to something thought to be definitive against this view: it is said that it has the absurd consequence that actions are invisible.[16]

3

Actions are events. So we might suppose that a question about their visibility would have to be answered by reference to some general account of what it is to see events. Notice that the usual discussions of the perceptual relation do not supply such an account. We are accustomed to thinking of vision as relating persons (or other animals) to things that can be described as being opaque, say, or as having some particular surface facing an observer. Applying this conception of vision in an automatic way to the case of events would appear to have the consequence that all events are strictly invisible. For events presumably do not have the light-reflecting properties that the objects of vision are now conceived as having.

Perhaps something could be learned from a general account of what it is to see an event, as opposed to a material object. But we shall find that there is no need to seek such an account here if we pause to consider the source of our confidence that we see actions. It might be that we felt so confident because we are sometimes so sure of the truth of such simple relational visual claims connecting persons with actions as 'She saw his moving of his finger' (or, generally, 'She saw his doing something'). But this seems unlikely: claims like this are so seldom made that they are unlikely to ground our confidence.[17] It is much more plausible that it is claims such as 'She saw him move his finger' (or, generally, 'She saw him do something')[18] that convince us of the belief expressed when we proclaim the visibility of actions: 'Why are you so sure that actions are visible?' 'Well of course we see people acting'.

What is at issue, then, when it is asked whether some thesis allows for or precludes the visibility of actions, is only whether that thesis accommodates the fact that people see one another doing things. It seems that the visibility of actions can hardly be the crux in determining whether bodily movements are caused by, or partially comprise, or are the same as, actions: the obtaining of any of these relations would presumably present no obstacle to the idea that people can be seen doing things.

4

'This is all very well as far as it goes', it may be said, 'but one leaves something out of account if one is prepared only to address questions about what people can be seen doing. If we want an understanding of how knowledge of others is gained, then we need to be told *how* it is that people can be seen doing the things they intentionally do. After all, it can perfectly well be said that we see people try to do things. ('I saw him trying to catch the chairman's attention.') But in this case, if we assume that events of trying are hidden from view, we surely want to know what sort of thing we directly see, in virtue of which it can be said that we see someone try to do something.'

The objector maintains that literal questions about the direct visibility of particular events have to be pressed. So let us for the moment take him on his own terms and see what might come of pressing such questions. (In §5, we shall consider what his terms are.)

Let us adopt a picture of attempts causing movements. But let us resolve to leave it an open question where actions fit into this picture. (If any conclusions were reached in §2, they are to be ignored here.) We can raise a question now about visibility in respect of certain events that we may call attempt-plus-movements; these we stipulate have as parts an attempt and a movement and nothing else.

Someone who was convinced that attempts themselves are hidden might have his doubts whether an attempt-plus-movement is visible; but perhaps the overtness of movements can somehow persuade even him of the visibility of attempt-plus-movements.[19] So let us take it that our question might be settled in the affirmative: attempt-plus-movements can be seen. Would this be a useful result?

Well, if we thought that our knowledge of other people had to be got from seeing their attempt-plus-movements, then no doubt it would be as well to be sure that these things are indeed visible. But if the visibility of these things were the issue, then the needed result could be secured (if it could) while setting to one side the question whether actions are visible. For we have not said which of the events in the picture the term 'action' applies to. And if someone now introduces the claim that actions are attempt-plus-movements, his claim appears idle when it comes to the questions about other minds which were supposed to turn on issues of visibility.

A similar point may be made in relation to the thesis that actions are movements simply: someone's stand on that thesis apparently need not affect his view about what it is upon whose visibility we rely for our knowledge of other people.

It seems, then, that if we do insist upon raising questions in miniature about what is and is not visible among the events that occur when there is an action, then nothing of moment has to revolve around the specific question whether, among these events, *actions* are visible. And it is arguable that we have no firm intuition on this specific question which is not dependent on some prior view of what actions are.

5

Our objector had some definite ideas about why we should need to determine what is and what is not literally visible among attempts, movements, and actions. He thought that when we look at people, only some of their features—or only some of the events that go on where they are—are open to view, whereas others are hidden; and knowledge of others needs to be based on what is open to view.

It is easy to suppose that these ideas stem from a certain traditional epistemology of "other minds", which makes joint use of a division between physical and mental and a division between what can be present to another's senses and what can be known by another at best less directly.[20] The view is sometimes expressed using a distinction between bodies and persons: only other bodies are unproblematic objects of sense experience; experience of other bodies provides the basis, if anything does, for knowledge of other persons. A similar distinction can be made in the realm of events—between bodily movements available to sight and hearing on the one hand, and mental events occurring inside people on the other. If we attached any serious theoretical status to this distinction, we should feel forced to ask upon which side of the division actions lie, and the visibility of actions would come to seem to be an issue of the sort that our objector suggested it was.

Someone might think not only that the traditional epistemological

outlook prompts particular questions about what is strictly and literally visible, but also that the thesis that actions cause movements en-
genders such an outlook. It is sometimes said that there is a tendency
to use the word 'behaviour' ambiguously: bits of behaviour may (i) be
the colourless, unproblematically visible, "mere" bodily movements of
the behaviourists; or they may (ii) be actions, things coloured by their
own significance.[21] Now what someone might think is that when
movements are distinguished from actions, the distinction made runs
along the lines of this ambiguity in 'behaviour'. In that case, bodily
movements would have to be credited with the special epistemological
status that is assigned, from the traditional outlook, to colourless
"mere" movements.

But here we need to use not one distinction, but two.[22] A distinction
can always be made within the realm of events between those items
there to which a particular predicate applies and those to which it does
not; taking the predicate in question to be 'is an action', and granting
the distinctness of the action and the movement of §2, we obtain a distinction between actions and movements. But this is different from any
distinction between, so to speak, what is colourless and what is not—between different characterizations of events (or whatever), according as
those characterizations do or do not presuppose a subject of mentality.
This latter distinction will be required if the epistemology of other
minds is to be conducted in the traditional way: we have to be able to
separate what is psychologically uncontaminated from what is not; and
such a separation would make a division in the realm of facts, and not in
the realm of events. One cannot say of an event *per se* whether it is a psychologically neutral or a psychologically contaminated thing.

This last point may explain why it seemed impossible (in §4) to tie
questions about the strict and literal visibility of actions to anything of
real epistemological interest. Concerned with epistemology, we might
want to ask, say, whether someone can become acquainted with the
psychological facts about others simply by keeping her eyes and ears
open in their presence. But we should be no further forward with such
a question if we were told only which events are seen. Suppose we
were told that actions are seen. Unless we could say that it was known
that the things seen are actions, we should have made no advance in
ensuring that vision gives us knowledge of "other minds".[23]

If one is guided by an epistemology that uses a division between what takes place strictly before an observer's eyes and what does not, and correlates that with a division between a kind of fact that is immediately accessible to an observer and a kind of fact that is not, then one will want a single line to be defined by both of the two distinctions I have made. But there is nothing in the thesis that actions cause movements which should make us expect to find such a line. And there is nothing there that demonstrates that bodily movements are the behaviourists' colourless items. Once both distinctions are in play, we can insist that bodily movements, even if they are not the same as actions, are not the colourless "mere" movements of the behaviourist: they may participate in all of the colour of the actions that cause them.

The bodies that these movements are the movements of are, after all, the bodies of persons, and not "mere" bodies. Consider now how the relevant class of movements might be specified. A movement, one might say, is something that occurs in any normal case of an unparalyzed person who tries to do something that requires her to move her body. The psychological element in this specification is ineliminable. There need be no suggestion that what we pick out when we pick out bodily movements are events that could occur even if there were no "other minds".[24]

At this point, we can appreciate the proper source of the claim that the ordinary idea of seeing people do things is all that is needed for knowledge of actions. This claim need not spring from thinking that what we ordinarily say is all that ever matters; nor need it be the product of evasion. For there is no urgent question about how we get to know about one another that someone who makes this claim refuses to face up to. Rather, the claim can derive from a reasoned rejection of the outlook from which putative questions about the strict and literal visibility of events are supposed to arise. Wittgenstein (1953) rejected the conception of a body required by the epistemological outlook discussed here.[25] We may reject any related conception of a movement of such a body.

6

Nothing here has been intended to establish the thesis that actions cause movements; I have hoped only to displace one argument against that thesis.[26] I have tried to show that the metaphysical questions in the philosophy of action of §2 can to a large extent be freed from epistemological questions that are posed as questions about the visibility of actions. And I have suggested that the two sorts of questions have wrongly been allowed to impinge upon each other: some people may have been deterred from adopting a particular view of actions for fear that that would require of them an epistemological outlook that they preferred not to take: again, some people may have allowed that same outlook to influence their view in the philosophy of action.[27]

This latter suggestion may seem mischievous. The epistemological outlook I have spoken of is not an attractive one. Has not philosophy learned to abandon it? How could it still influence thought?

Well, there is more prevalent than ever before in the philosophy of mind the idea that people's behaviour can be given an exhaustive, colourless characterization (in the terms, say, in which a functionalist would wish to describe "outputs"), which combines with a characterization of the stimuli impinging upon them (of "inputs") to determine their psychology. This idea often appears to have the status of assumption. It is hard to see how it can seem so obviously correct unless some doctrine that appears evident from the traditional epistemological outlook makes it seem so. But whatever is in fact responsible for the idea about the determinants of people's psychology, the epistemological issues may be worth addressing. If the only escape from the epistemological outlook that I have considered, and that seems so unattractive, were to argue against the reality of the concept of bodily movement that that outlook requires, then the very possibility of colourless characterizations of behaviour, the alleged determinants of psychology, would have to be cast into doubt.

Postscript: a disjunctive conception of bodily movements

I have said that we should resist thinking of the bodily movements caused by actions as the 'colourless' items of the behaviourist. I should like to go further now. Since this essay was written, a certain view in philosophy of perception has gained some currency. This has come to be known as the disjunctive conception of experiences.[28] Connecting up the disjunctive conception of experiences with a related conception of bodily movements leads to a conclusion more radical than any actually advanced in the essay. The conclusion advanced there, on the basis of considerations mainly about knowledge of action, will then be seen to be thoroughly in keeping with the ontological conclusions reached in the essays in Part I.

(I shall carry on speaking as if 'bodily movements' applied [*inter alia*] to such things as Jane's hand's moving, and 'actions' applied [*inter alia*] to the causes of such things, which are distinct, such as Jane's moving of her hand. Much complexity would be introduced if I tried to speak in a manner impartial between the views that bodies' movements are effects of actions, that they are parts of actions, that they are the same as actions. I avoid this complexity.)

The essay began with two reasons philosophers focus on a class of bodily movements. There is another possible reason: bodily movements may be introduced in order that we should be able to maintain a view of actions as 'parts of the ordinary physical world'.[29] The thought here need not be the epistemological one addressed in the essay—that movements are particularly easy to observe—: the thought may be the related metaphysical one—that to call an event a movement is to ensure its 'physical' status. Following up on this thought, we may be meant to turn our attention towards such movements as these: someone's calf's jerking when a doctor is testing her reflexes, someone's hand's moving on an occasion when it is blown in a gale. Lacking any immediate psychological history, such movements have first claim to be 'parts of the ordinary physical world'.

The fact that movements like these are in an obvious sense psychologically neutral does not suffice to establish that all bodily movements are. Call bodily movements that are immediately caused by actions *A-movements*, and movements that are not associated with actions— bodies' being blown about, reflex movements, and so on—*B-movements*. Then we can consider something which is actually a B-movement, say, a knee-jerk reaction, and ask: Could it have been an A-movement? The answer, fairly evidently, is *No*. It is true that it may not be apparent to inspection whether a movement of the calf was one that the doctor's hammer caused or not: a patient who actually shows a knee-jerk reaction might appear indistinguishable from another patient who simulated one. But this shows only that one may be ignorant about whether a movement falls into the category of A-movement or of B-movement; and we cannot argue from the possibility of such ignorance to the real possibility of a B-movement's having been an

A-movement. The claim, then, might be that A-movements are necessarily not B-movements. Such an essentialist thesis lends support to the idea that the concept *bodily movements* subsumes events of significantly different kinds: there is no unitary category to which both the effects of actions and the mere B-movements both belong.

This is the idea which connects with the disjunctive conception of perceptual experiences. Here again it is claimed that a certain putative category is not a unitary one. In the case of vision, the category whose unitariness is put in question by a disjunctive conception is given by 'its seeming to a as if . . .'. When this is introduced, a person's seeing a chair (say) is classified alongside her having a hallucination as of there being a chair. But proponents of the disjunctive conception maintain that the co-classifiability of perceptions and hallucinations reflects no deeper sameness of experiences of the two sorts. It is rather that any experience caught in the class is *either* the manifestation to a of what a sees *or* there being merely an appearance as of something to a. Each of these disjuncts gives a determinate kind of which *its seeming to* a *as if* . . . might be thought of as a determinable. The disjunctivist considers it an error to take the determinable as fundamental.

The disjunctive conception of experiences has been formulated in a variety of ways. And many of the formulations would expose failures of parallel between experiences and bodily movements. I want next to bring out some differences between the two cases, in order to be able to go on to elicit what seems to me the real point of disjunctive conceptions for both.

Philosophers' quest for analytic definitions is partly responsible for the treatment of visual-like experiences as a basic, non-disjunctive category. The analyzing philosopher is struck by the fact that 'its seeming to a as if . . .' specifies a class of events some, but not all, of which are people's seeings of things. If he wants necessary and sufficient conditions for someone's seeing something, then it appears that his task is to find conditions satisfied by only some of the events in the class. The conditions, to be satisfied by perceptions alone, will concern their peculiar genesis: this will be supposed to differentiate veridical perceptual experiences from other things belonging in the supposed underlying class.

If a similar analytic strategy were followed in the case of action, then the class introduced would contain, among other events, actions; and the conditions to be satisfied would concern the upshot, rather than the genesis, of some of the events in the class. The likely basic category here, then, from which actions would be meant to be extracted, is *not* a category of bodily movements (since an action is not a bodily move*ment*, but a person's moving of a bit of her body). Not that it would be impossible for someone to start with a basic category of bodily movements, and then try to demarcate actions by looking for a distinctive kind among the causes of the movements. But the only things one can find to say about actions which differentiate them from different sorts of causes of bodily movements will surely use a concept like *action* itself. And then it seems that circularity threatens, so that a neutral category of bodily movements does not have any role to play in the analytic definitional endeavour.

This difference, in the analytic possibilities, is connected with two other differences between the case of perception and the case of action. The reason a category including the B-movements alongside the action-related A-movements is of no avail in analysis is that neutral B-movements appear not to have much connexion with action at all. That indeed is why a disjunctive conception was so easily made out above. The essentialist thesis used in its support derives some of its plausibility from the fact that, at the physiological level, we suppose that there are very different stories to be told about the movements following on actions and such things as reflex knee jerks. But matters are otherwise when it comes to perceptions and hallucinations: whether someone is actually seeing something or merely hallucinating, we may expect to find some same excited bits of visual cortex. In fact, some philosophers have refused a disjunctive conception of experiences on the grounds that there is (they say) a physiological ingredient common to all visual-like experiences.

The other difference between the cases shows up not in what opponents of the disjunctive conception of visual-like experiences say, but in what its proponents say. A proponent insists that our concept of hallucination is in a certain sense derivative from that of genuine perception: we can understand what a hallucination is by thinking of it as subjectively akin to the real thing. That in fact is why the analytic trail leads nowhere: if the concept of hallucination is got from the concept of perception, then an appreciation of what is involved in perception cannot be gained by thinking up some condition to add on to something which might be a case of hallucination. Well, a proponent of the disjunctive conception of *movements* is unlikely to insist that the idea of a B-movement is similarly got from the idea of an A-movement. It would be absurd to suggest that we understand what it is for someone's hand to be blown in a gale (say) by starting from the movements that occur when someone intentionally moves her hand.

At this stage a disjunctive conception of bodily movements might appear rather uncontroversial. It appears neither to require the arguments which a disjunctivist about visual-like experiences gives, nor to be open to the objections which she confronts. It may seem unfit for comparison with the contested disjunctive conception of visual experiences. But if we are prepared to enter the contest on behalf of the disjunctive conception of experiences, then our reaction now should not be to give up on the disjunctive conception of bodily movements, but to elaborate it further.

We were looking for events that are most obviously 'parts of the ordinary physical world' when we took events such as hands' being blown and knee-jerk reactions as paradigms of B-movements. A philosopher who thinks that it is necessary to make out actions' claim to be physical has a reason to give impartial treatment to such paradigm B-movements and to the movements immediately caused by actions. But then a disjunctivist conception ought not to seem so uncontroversial to *him*. He lumps all bodily movements together because he wants to exploit the evidently non-psychological character of what is bodily. And a point is made against him when the non-unitary character of the class of bodily movements is drawn to attention.

Such a philosopher, though, keeps company with many others. They do not all want to assimilate the bodily movements that actions cause with those we have so far taken as paradigms of B-movements. But nearly every philosopher of action these days seems to assume that describing actions' immediate effects as bodily movements locates them in a non-psychological, or at least a psychologically neutral, class. The disjunctive conception is set against their assumption. Conceiving bodily movements disjunctively, one draws a line between the movements that occur when and because people have reason to do things and the movements of a neutral ontology. The effects of actions do not belong with the movements that an observer with no interest in the agent would articulate.

We may continue to call the effects of actions A-movements and all the rest of the bodily movements B-movements. But there is no call now to focus particularly on what, up to this point, we have been thinking of as paradigm B-movements. Hands' being blown in a gale suit the specific purposes of the behaviouristic reductionist. But the class of B-movements has really to be characterized by reference to whatever physicalist pretensions inform the conception of bodily movements to which the disjunctive conception is opposed. The disjunctive conception partitions the bodily movements into those that are uncovered when psychologically neutral concepts are employed from those that are the effects of actions. Using this conception, then, we must refuse to treat as basic a category which any old 'action-related' movement comes into. We have to allow a picture in which there are movements of two different sorts when there are actions. Some of the movements that occur when actions occur are neutral B-movements, which are not picked out *as* the effects of *actions*.

When the disjunctivist introduces this picture, she can be seen to make a claim which is parallel to that which, in the case of visual-like experiences, led to the idea of the derivativeness of the concept of hallucination. The claim is that the notion of *bodily movement* applicable specifically to effects of actions is intelligible only to someone who uses *action* concepts. Compare: the concept of *visual-like experience* as it applies to veridical experiences is intelligible only to someone who uses *perception* concepts. No deep fact is appreciated when it is seen that a predicate such as 'is an appearance to *a* . . .' spans both veridical perceptions and hallucinations. Similarly, we have to treat it as a shallow fact that the predicate 'is a movement of a body' spans both the effects of actions and the events of a neutral ontology.

A *non*-disjunctivist conception of bodily movements, as this is now to be understood, is the basis of much physicalist doctrine. There is a familiar argument which concludes that people's thinking things, or wanting things, are internal—are brain events or states. The argument relies on supposing that there is, as it were, just one bodily movement when there is an action. It holds that we have to identify the causes of

actions with the causes of bodily movements discovered by neuroscientists, for we should otherwise have to think that bodily movements
are overdetermined (see Essay 4). But there can be no such physicalist
argument if we abandon any systematic identification of the effects of
actions with bodily movements from a neutral domain. If the disjunctive conception of bodily movements is correct, then a premiss of the
argument is false.

The physicalist argument has many variants; but in one or another
version, it is a main source of the idea that there are events in the brain
which can receive both neuroscientific and commonsense psychological descriptions. The pervasiveness of the argument shows that the
supposition of a neutral conception of bodily movements is not in fact
confined to the behaviouristic reductionist who starts from reflex
movements and the like. Bodily movements neutrally conceived are
common stock in contemporary philosophy of mind.

The putative neutral conception of experiences no doubt has many
sources which are special to the case of experience.[30] But one source of
it may be an assumption about what is required by a respectable naturalism; and this is a source equally of the putative neutral conception
of bodily movements. What is assumed is that a respectable naturalism
requires lines to be drawn between the *prima facie* mental things in the
world and the *prima facie* physical things there, in order that the credentials of the *prima facie* mental things to belong in the natural world
can be made out (cp. Essay 5). Working with that assumption, one is
compelled to characterize perceptual experience (presumed to be
mental) in ways which make no commitments about the physical
world inhabited by the perceiving subject. In the case of action, the assumption compels us to look to the causal chains of events that there
are when people do things for reasons, and to find on them something
without mental taint, with faultless physical credentials. Thus may
bodily movements be hit upon. But if the only bodily movements to
which we can be led by contemplating such causal chains are simply
the effects of actions, then we must reject the assumption.

If we refuse the assumption of a line between mental and physical,
then we can take fully seriously the idea that perception and action are
both ineluctably *psychophysical* phenomena. The *psychophysical* character

of vision is made vivid when visual experiences are conceived disjunctively. For on the disjunctive conception, we can treat perception as—in John McDowell's happy phrase—a sort of *openness to the world*.[31] The *psychophysical* character of action is made out in a disjunctive conception of bodily movements. It enables us to treat the facts about the occurrence of those bodily movements which result from actions as—echoing McDowell—a sort of *disclosure of mentality*.[32]

I have given no actual arguments for the disjunctive conception of bodily movements in this Postscript. The point of introducing it has only been to bring out a possible virtue of a possible view by means of an analogy. What a disjunctive conception in fact comes down to, in the case of bodily movements, is the autonomy of two different modes of individuating events. And this is the topic of the next essay. The idea of such autonomy was introduced in Essay 3, where it was grounded in the fundamental difference in psychological and physical explanatory schemes.

This takes us back to Davidson: a disjunctive conception of bodily movements might now be seen as derivable from what Davidson calls the anomalousness of the mental. In fact, however, the disjunctive conception is actually opposed to Davidson's monism. For the bodily movements which are the effects of actions, like all events which are causes or effects, and like the bodily movements which physiologists study, must, in Davidson's book, by the Nomological Character of Causality, satisfy some predicate which features in a law of nature. The disjunctive conception of bodily movements thus exposes a tension between Davidson's anomalousness and his monism. (This is another surfacing of a tension alleged by those who accuse Davidson of epiphenomenalism. See Introduction, §4.)

I have suggested already that this tension can be relieved by abandoning the Nomological Character of Causality; and that when it is so relieved, nothing is lost—a satisfactory monism cannot require a principle about Causality (see postscript to Part I). A particular version of this point applies now. For it can now be seen to be perfectly consistent with an ordinary physicalism to deny that the effects of actions measure up to the demands of the naturalizers' ontology. Anyone who allows that people inhabit 'the ordinary physical world' should never have supposed that it needs to be demonstrated that actions—events, each one of which is a *person*'s doing something—belong there too. Reassurance on this score really does seem unnecessary. One of naive naturalism's aims is to make such reassurance always seem unnecessary.

7

Physicalist Thinking and Conceptions of Behaviour

1

Consider the two pictures that are shown here.

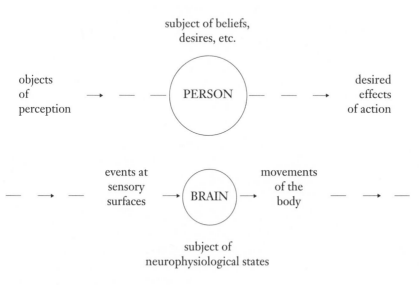

The upper picture presents a view of what is involved when we ascribe propositional attitudes to one another. The lower one presents a view of what is involved when the scientist treats a human being as a physical thing—of what a neurophysiologist sees as going on when he concerns himself with the stimulations of sense organs, with the motor responses in a person's body, and with events and states that intervene between such stimulations and responses.

One has only to look at these two pictures to be tempted to make a superimposition. Two considerations may combine to make the temptation irresistible. First, the brain and central nervous system is a part of a person whose proper functioning is a necessary condition of that person's having the effects on the world she desires to have. Second, the causal chains that lead up to and away from a person's psychological states apparently pass through the events depicted in the area that circumscribes the neurophysiologist's study. If you extend the causal chains of the representation of the brain backwards and forwards, what you reach is the elements standing at the left and right of the representation of the person. The dependence of the person's functioning on the functioning of her brain may make one think of the brain as a mechanism inside the person which is responsible for producing the effects in virtue of which she has her distinctive effects on the world. But then the common properties of the brain's states and of the person's mental states—states of each sort being seen as causal intermediaries—may make one think that in placing the brain inside the person one locates the propositional-attitude states there. Many will therefore feel compelled to say that particular beliefs and desires *are* the neurophysiological states of a person.

This line of thought gives a very quick argument for a version of physicalism. Perhaps no one wishes to acknowledge that he takes such a direct or simple route. But I think that there is a widespread presumption that if beliefs and desires have any place in the physical world, then they are internal states of persons, or of their brains; and I think that this presumption can be created by the sort of high-level comparison of pictures I have just imagined. My project in this essay is to question certain versions of physicalism the quick argument may seem to recommend, by challenging the envisaged superimposition of the two pictures. More particularly, I shall challenge the use to which a certain conception of *behaviour* is put. According to this conception, *behaviour* subsumes both a brain's outputs and a person's outputs, and thus provides an area common to both pictures.

2

Naively we think that we can become informed about people's mental states by receiving right answers to such questions as 'Why did she keep to the edge of the pond?' or 'Why did she turn on the burner?'. And we suppose that such answers give psychological explanations of behaviour. But it is often said nowadays that any account of psychological explanatory states is bound to use a purely bodily notion of behaviour.

Consider, for example, Kim's claims (1982, p. 64):

> [An] action of turning on the burner, insofar as this is thought to involve the burner going on, is not an action that it is the proper business of psychological theory to explain or predict. . . . It is not part of the object of *psychological* explanation to explain why the burner went on. . . . The job of psychological explanation is done once [psychological theory] has explained the bodily action of turning a knob; whether or not this action results in my also turning on the stove, my starting cooking the dinner . . . is dependent on facts quite outside the province of psychology, [which] are not the proper concern of psychological theory.[1]

Kim and others believe, then, that we ought to recognize psychology's proper business to be much narrower than we naively take it to be.

Kim's claim that psychological states cannot serve to explain (for example) why Kim turned on the burner is rested on the premiss that such states do not serve to explain why the burner went on. Both the premiss and the argument here may be questioned. In order to question the premiss, one must take a relaxed view about psychological explanation. Then it will seem that it can be psychologically explained (for example) why a burner went on: 'Why did the burner go on? Is the switch faulty?' 'No: Jane turned it on, she wanted to make some tea.'

To question the argument, one may take a less relaxed view and start with the assumption that any psychological explanation has as its explanandum why some person did what she did. The principle underlying the argument would then seem to be something like this:

> Even if the explanation why p appears to be the fact that z, still if q and r are necessary for p and the fact that z does not explain why q, then the fact that z can only really explain why r.

But such a principle is surely unacceptable. Suppose that we thought we could explain why the window broke by saying that a heavy stone hit it at speed. We then notice that the window's breaking required that the window be situated at p and that p be on the stone's trajectory, and that the stone's hitting the window at speed does not explain why the window is situated at p. We do not conclude that after all the stone's hitting the window at high speed cannot really explain why the window broke.[2]

It is a question how narrow the province of what is psychologically explained would become if one endorsed Kim's argument wholeheartedly. Kim himself speaks as if *turning a knob*, unlike *turning on the burner*, were an admissible object of psychological explanation. Yet *turning a knob* is surely proscribed for him: it seems no more to be 'part of the object of psychological explanation' to explain why a knob turned than it is to explain why the burner went on. And we may wonder whether in fact Kim's principle does not rule out psychological explanations even of 'bodily actions'—of why someone moved her finger, say; for it is by no means obvious that someone's moving her finger is not 'dependent on facts which are not the proper concern of psychological theory'. (I return to this at the end of §3.)

Of course Kim's conclusion about the objects of psychological explanation may not be meant to rely on the principle alone. It may rely on a prior view of psychological states—as internal states of people which are the immediate causal ancestors of movements of their bodies. This view is certainly held by functionalists. And the functionalists' conception of behaviour may be supposed to recommend itself on the merits of functionalism. So it will be worth discovering whether the attractions of functionalism can survive scrutiny of the particular notion of behaviour that that doctrine employs.

3

Functionalists think that the defining feature of any type of mental state is given by describing the causal relations that its instances bear (a) to the environment's effects on a person, (b) to mental states of other types, and (c) to a person's effects on the environment. And they think that mental terms can be simultaneously implicitly defined in a total psychological theory of all the types of mental states. Such a theory contains terms of two sorts, which David Lewis has called the T-terms and the O-terms (1972). The T-terms are, intuitively, mental terms, to be thought of as receiving implicit definition: in a functional theory, their denotations are accorded functional roles that are specified using only the non-mental O-terms. The functionalist thinks of the functional theory (abstracted, as it were, from the psychological theory) as true of, or as realized by, the physical states of individuals: physical states occupy the functional roles of mental states.[3]

Functionalism is to be understood here as a thesis in the philosophy of mind, which treats of those states and events that in the ordinary way we attribute to one another, for example, in explaining action. We can ask then, 'What does the functionalist have to say about the role of the propositional-attitude states in producing action?'. Put in the functionalist's own terms, this is a question about output generalizations ((c) above), which are meant to give an account of the systematic ways in which such states as beliefs lead, as it is said, to behaviour.

We are told that behaviourism is the ancestor of functionalism, and that functionalism inherits the virtues of behaviourism. But the functionalist's notion of behaviour is very much more restrictive than that which some of the behaviourists employed. When functionalists speak of behaviour, they speak, as Kim does, of bodily movements, or else they speak of motor responses.[4] When Ryle spoke about behaviour, he meant such characterizations of people's actions as these: 'telling oneself and others that the ice is thin, skating warily, shuddering, dwelling in imagination on possible disasters, warning other skaters, keeping to the edge of the pond' (1949, p. 129). (It is true that some behaviourists were reductionists, and that they used a narrower conception of behaviour than Ryle. But if one is allowed to think of functionalism as inheriting its attractions from a non-reductionist position, then Ryle's everyday use of 'behaviour' ought not to be legislated into invisibility.)

There are two important differences here between the (Rylean) behaviourist and the functionalist. The behaviourist makes allusion to
things beyond the agent's body in his specifications of behaviour, but
the functionalist does not. And the behaviourist's behavioural items
are actions (that is, events each one of which is a person's doing something such as moving her body), whereas the functionalist's behavioural items are apparently not actions, but movements of people's
bodies (which are either effects of actions, or proper parts of actions,
depending upon your views).[5] We need to understand why the functionalists should depart from the behaviourists in these two ways and
employ the particular conception that they do.

The functionalist's stated objection to behaviourism is familiar
enough: the behaviourist said that to believe something (for instance)
is to be disposed to certain behaviour, whereas the functionalist insists
that belief cannot be defined in terms of behaviour alone, because allowance has to be made for the simultaneous determination of behaviour by many different mental states. In this point alone, however,
there is nothing that evidently constrains one to use a bodily conception of behaviour. And we need to notice something else, which is seldom stated very explicitly by functionalists: the behaviourists' neglect
of the interdependencies between mental things was not in fact the
only defect of behaviourism that the functionalist needed to correct
for. Certainly, if your belief that it is going to rain is to lead you to
take your umbrella, then you need (for example) to want not to get
wet and to believe that umbrellas keep the rain off, and to have no
other countervailing desires or interfering beliefs. But equally certainly, if your belief that it is going to rain is to lead you to take your
umbrella, then you need to believe of something that is your umbrella
that it is your umbrella. Not only can it not be left out of account what
desires a person has (as the behaviourist seemed to suppose), but also
it cannot be taken for granted that what people believe is true. Avoiding taking this for granted, one might say that someone who believes
that p is (very roughly) someone who would, *given that p*, realize such
desires as prevailed given her other desires and beliefs. But there is a
problem about incorporating this into a functionalist psychological
theory as it stands. For this does not tell us, in behavioural terms however broadly construed, what someone with a certain belief would ever
unconditionally *do*.

There are two ways in which the functionalist might try to make allowance for the fact that it is only where other relevant beliefs of the agent are true that behaviour as we naturally and widely conceive it is predictably matched with particular desires and beliefs. First, he might settle for using what one could call a world-conditioned notion of behaviour, saying, at the behavioural end of an output generalization, that a person would do things of this sort: such-and-such-if-the-world-is-as-it-would-be-if-relevant-beliefs-of-the-agent-were-true. (I return to this idea in §5.) Second, he might restrict the notion of behaviour, so that something counts as a description of behaviour only if an agent can be expected to satisfy it irrespective of whether her beliefs are true. In talking about behaviour, he then confines himself to those things that an agent would do no matter whether the world were as she believed it to be—things, one might say, that she is *simply able* to do.

This provides the real explanation of why the functionalist should go back to the body in describing behaviour. And perhaps we can now also understand the functionalist's other deviation from the behaviourist—his not treating actions themselves as behavioural items. Even if a person's beliefs about what it is to φ are false, she will at least *try* to φ if she has overwhelming reason to φ (or so a functionalist may say). It seems, then, that the notion of *trying* or *attempting* can be introduced if one wants a means of saying in 'purely psychological' terms what someone's beliefs and desires in conjunction do produce. One then arrives at a two-stage account of action production, such as can be found in some functionalist writings (e.g., Loar, 1981).[6] At the first stage, one says how beliefs and desires modify one another and mediate the production of attempts; so much is 'pure psychology', in the language of the T-terms. At the second stage, one says what attempts to do things would actually bring about, whatever the truth values of the beliefs that led to those attempts; the idea is that a sufficiently motivated agent who is *simply able* to do something will do that thing. This second stage takes one from the T-terms to the O-terms, and it is here that one is constrained to use the bodily movement vocabulary for describing behaviour, and to speak (not of actions themselves, but) only of things that are the most immediate, bodily effects of a person's attempts.

Something like this functionalist view of action production is presumably shared by Kim (§2). But what one now gets at the second stage of the account of action production will be instances of:

a tries to φ & *a* is *simply able* to φ → there occurs a φ-type movement

(where to be a 'φ-type movement' is, intuitively, to be a movement of the type associated with actions of φ-ing). And this means that, unless we are prepared to say that an agent's being *simply able* to do something is a 'proper concern of psychological theory', the argument that Kim gave in order to encourage us to suppose that only 'bodily action' is genuinely psychologically explicable could be used again now to show that even movements of bodies are not things 'that it is the proper business of psychological theory to explain or predict'. But an agent's being *simply able* to move a part of her body is constituted by the integrity and functioning of the relevant bits of her motor system and the absence of constraints on her body itself, and such things are in no obvious or intuitive sense psychological and would seem to be quite on a par with (for instance) the burner's being such as to light when the knob is turned. Following through on Kim's argument, then, the province of psychological explanation would become even more circumscribed than Kim allowed: the proper objects of psychological explanation could only be events described as agents' *trying* to do things.[7]

4

Functionalists for their part will probably be happy to allow that conditions relating to agents' *simple abilities* have to be specified using T-terms and be caught up with psychological theory. Their aim is to show how some of the brain's complexity can be seen to mirror the complexity of the propositional-attitude scheme. And it might seem that the use of purely bodily O-terms for describing people's outputs is in no way inimical to that aim. Although a bodily motion of behaviour is more restricted than an everyday one, there is much that can be said about people's bodies' movements, and it may seem that functionalists can avail themselves of anything that can be said about them and proceed to an interesting psychological theory.

But it must not be forgotten that functionalist output generalizations are still meant to be got from what we all know about action-explanation in knowing commonsense psychology. One thing that we know is that φ-ing is a proper explanandum of the commonsense psychological scheme only if agents have some beliefs in the ascription of which φ-ing could be mentioned. So functionalists are not in fact entitled to use whichever bodily movement terms they like; their resources can include only such terms as could be used in giving the contents of agents' mental states. It seems, then, that they must refrain from using any very detailed bodily movement terms.

In fact, it will be controversial exactly how much detail can enter into the bodily movement descriptions of commonsense psychology. If someone turns on a light (say), how detailed can a bodily description be of what she intentionally does, or tries to do? What beliefs about the movements of their bodies do people in practice employ? My own view is that hardly any detail can enter. When we engage in the practice of skills that require the manipulation of objects, for instance, it is unclear that we employ any beliefs which concern purely and simply the movements of our hands. It seems that a person can act as a result of having beliefs and desires, while having next to nothing in the way of beliefs about how her body moves when she acts.[8] And if this is right, then the functionalist, in confining himself to bodily movements, confines himself to an extremely impoverished notion of behaviour indeed.

What is certain is that functionalists don't in fact envisage using a notion of behaviour that would strike us as at all impoverished. Even if commonsense bodily movement descriptions can be richer than I have just suggested, we may still doubt that they can be as rich as those that functionalists actually want to employ. In functionalist writings, one often finds what appear to be gestures towards great complication in accounts of behaviour. Armstrong spoke of 'making certain motions with the hand and so on'; he remarked that this was vague, and said that 'the matter might be investigated in a time-and-motion study for instance' (1968, p. 147). Lewis speaks of 'Karl's fingers moving on certain trajectories and exerting certain forces' (1974, at p. 114 in 1983). It can seem as if the functionalists, feeling that the complexity of the propositional-attitude scheme must indeed demand some richness in the specification of behaviour, simply ignore the commonsense character of the truths about propositional attitudes that they represent themselves as beginning from.

It will be no good saying that, since every bodily movement does have some detailed description of which a student of time-and-motion or a physiologist could become apprised, any detail that the functionalist's aims require can always be introduced into functionalist theories. For one thing, the student of time-and-motion may discover that the sorts of bodily movements that agents think of themselves as going in for are not connected in systematic ways with the sorts of motions his studies concern.[9] And even if it were right that there are, occasion by occasion, identities between the (coarse) bodily movement effects of actions and the (refined) bodily movement effects of finely discriminated states of the nervous system, it is unclear that this could help the functionalist who is trying to avoid a notion of behaviour that strikes him as too crude for the use to which he wants to put it. Someone who hoped to use physiological knowledge occasion by occasion to pin down the neurophysiological states that caused some effect of some action would have lost sight of one of the functionalists' aspirations—to use our knowledge of interpersonal psychology to define types of mental states.

5

I suggest that some of the allure of functionalism has resulted from failure to keep track of the use of the simple term 'behaviour'. The elements of common sense that give rise to the idea of a psychological theory seem correct when 'behaviour' is understood in Ryle's way, as including all the many things an agent does. The idea of a functional theory realized in neurophysiological states seems correct when 'behaviour' is understood in (say) the physiologist's way, as an agent's moving her body in all kinds of complex fashions. These two notions of behaviour overlap, and when 'bodily movements' is used to catch them both, they are made to appear to coincide. But the two notions do not coincide. And if one wants to preserve both common sense and the idea about functional theories, then one can only conclude that there is a complexity in propositional-attitude psychology that does not derive from any complexity in people's bodily movements conceived in ways available to commonsense psychology.[10]

No doubt many functionalists will say that theoretical psychology has to be enlisted in the service of commonsense psychology. They would make proposals about how theoretical psychological findings could be brought to bear on commonsense psychological states, and they would claim that the proposals will enable us to discover states that must be counted as beliefs and desires even though commonsense psychology unaided would never have recognized them as such.[11] It is as if commonsense psychology had a hidden complexity that the theoretical psychologist could uncover experimentally; as if the superimposition of the picture of the person on the picture of the brain could reveal a sort of complexity in the picture of the person which ordinarily goes unheeded. But why should we think that commonsense psychology, in order to achieve what we can all achieve using it, must really be capable of achieving a great deal more that non-theoreticians will never know about? If commonsense psychology has no concern with how exactly we move our fingers when we turn on lights (say), then this is because we do not have to try to move our fingers in the exact way in which we actually move them in order to turn on a light when we want to. But where the details of bodily movements are not within commonsense psychology's province, how can that which bears on the details have a bearing on commonsense psychological states? How can theoretical psychology dictate to common sense answers to questions that it is in the nature of common sense not to ask?

Instead of resorting to theoretical psychology, we could suppose that the picture of the brain cannot be superimposed on the picture of the person because the picture of the person has its own fine points which are not such as to be exposed in the structure of the brain. What we should then have to exploit in understanding the felt complexity of propositional-attitude psychology is not the brain's complexity, but our knowledge that commonsense psychology enables us to explain so much more than why there are the movements of people's bodies that there are. The step from a Rylean sort of behaviourism to functionalism will then seem to have been, in a way, a retrograde step. If mental states are to be thought of as dispositions of any sort (or, if you prefer, as states that are parts of systems that exhibit an overall structure), then, to the extent that they are dispositions to behave (or states connected systematically with ways of behaving), the relevant notion of behaviour is the broad one that the philosopher-behaviourists used and the functionalists left behind.

If we do employ the ordinary and richer conception of behaviour in specifying the upshots of mental states, we cannot hope to circum-

scribe mental states in anything like the way the functionalist envisages. Recall what was wrong with the old behaviourist's conception
from the functionalist's point of view. Using that conception, one cannot leave the truth or falsity of agents' beliefs out of account. We
imagined that this point might be accommodated by using a 'world-
conditioned' notion of behaviour, but left this suggestion rather vague
(§3). Now the ramified character of the interdependencies between
mental states, which the functionalist is so anxious to take account of,
ensures that any worldly conditions incorporated in a notion of behaviour would ramify in any theory that attempted to accommodate that
notion. A person can be expected to do what she tries to do on occasion only if certain beliefs that explain her then trying to do that are
true. But the interdependencies between mental things ensure that for
any desire or belief whose causal role we might think to define, it is
possible that almost any belief might interact with it in the production
of some possible event of trying.[12] Thus if the world-conditioned notion of behaviour is introduced by the functionalist, and from case to
case he makes it explicit which beliefs are such that their truth or falsity on occasion is relevant to what behaviour is produced, his task
turns into the project of giving an account of the structure of rational
thought and practice, any exemplification of which is conditioned by a
simultaneous view of the world as a subject confronts it. This is not
the project of providing descriptions, however abstract, of the brain.

6

It is not a novel claim that explanation in the rational mode cannot be
converted into science. As Davidson has said (1971b, at p. 231 in
1980):

> Any effort at increasing the accuracy and power of a theory of behav-
> iour forces us to bring more and more of the whole system of the
> agent's beliefs and motives directly into account. But in inferring this
> system from the evidence, we necessarily impose conditions of co-
> herence, rationality, and consistency. These conditions have no echo
> in physical theory.

I take the mismatch Davidson sees between the mental and the scientific physical to show up in the fact that an attempt to incorporate

conditions of rationality in a physicalist theory, using a conception of behaviour that is bodily but constrained by commonsense psychology, seems to leave something out. Even to its proponents it seems to leave something out, and they proceed by injecting some extra detail into bodily behavioural descriptions (cf. Armstrong and Lewis). But there is no warrant for the extra detail.[13]

Davidson himself thinks that the mismatch between the mental and the scientific physical shows up in two particular ways at the level of what can be said about people's 'outputs'. First, 'Practical reasoning . . . may simply fail to occur'. Second, 'Wanting to do something . . . may cause someone to do [the] thing, and yet the causal chain may operate in such a manner that the act is not intentional' (1973b, at pp. 77 and 78 in 1980). These two claims surely reveal an immediate and insuperable obstacle to constructing functionalists' output generalizations. But I have allowed the argument to progress, believing that the superficial plausibility of the functionalists' contrary claims derives in large part from their free use of a quite schematic notion of *behaviour*.

The idea upon which the arguments here have traded is present in Davidson too, of course—in the claim that the mental is not a closed system. The felt complexity of propositional-attitude psychology will be accommodated only when 'the constitutive role of rationality' is properly acknowledged, and the attempt to see the patterns in a person's mental states embodied in the states of physical science is duly abandoned.[14]

7

The fundamental assumption that has been in dispute is that, in stating the causal powers of mental states, one can prescind from all but the most immediate effects of the actions they produce, and ignore almost everything under the head of 'desired effects of actions' in the picture of the person (§1). This assumption underlay the physicalist line of thought sketched at the outset. And we shall see now that it is the same assumption which leads people to accept the supervenience of the mental on the neurophysiological, and which gives rise to another physicalist view of intentional states of mind.

To many it seems (a) that a difference of mental state between two people requires some difference in their behavioural dispositions, and (b) that a difference in the behavioural dispositions of two animal bodies requires some difference in their internal physical machinery. They think, then, that if one were to allow that there could be a mental difference without a difference in brain state, one would be denying that the brain was responsible for the production of behaviour.[15]

Their argument is guilty of the same equivocation on 'behaviour' as the functionalists rely on. Premiss (a) requires for its truth a broad and everyday conception of a behavioural disposition, whereas (b) requires a narrow one; (a) is true if we take it to mean that a change in mental state affects the proper explananda of psychological explanations, whereas (b) is true if we take it to mean that only a change in brain state could affect how a creature moves itself. Nothing in the argument holds these two conceptions of a behavioural disposition together.[16]

Of course it is well known that there are counterexamples to a thesis of the supervenience of the psychological on the neurophysiological. Putnam's Twin Earth examples show that there can be variations in the objects of *de re* states of mind that are not reflected in any dispositions to move the body one way rather than another (1975). Some proponents of the supervenience thesis try to show that these examples do their thesis only negligible damage, as if the existence of *de re* states posed some special, local problem. But we saw that the so-called holism of the mental is apt to embrace all of those worldly facts which a person's attitudes concern and which her bodily movements confront: the problem for supervenience is not a problem specifically about *de re* states of mind.

In some physicalist writings, this last point is acknowledged, and it is agreed that propositional-attitude states cannot be characterized as the functionalist envisages; but it is then said that these states must nevertheless have causal-explanatory *components*, which components may be seen to coincide with brain states. According to this new view, the picture of a person from which we begin is not itself something upon which any picture of the brain can be superimposed; but the picture of the person can, as it were, be split into two, and one of the resultant parts—the 'internal side' of a person, which is supposed to incorporate explanatory states—is suited to having some picture of the brain fitted on to it.[17]

Yet it is hard to see how anyone is in a position to claim that there are states whose ascription to people is explanatory of their behaviour unless he can demonstrate that the ascription of such states does, or would, cast light upon behaviour. We know of course that such states as we ascribe—beliefs having contents, for instance—do cast light. But it is no help then to be told that there must be states which lurk behind the states we ascribe and which carry their explanatory force. It is a strange idea that the satisfaction yielded by commonsense explanations has its source in something of which the parties to the explanation are quite ignorant—as if light had been cast through a medium that we cannot yet see through. But it would be a quite baffling idea that the explanatory force of an explanation resides in something that is not capable of illuminating anything for us—as if we could be sure that light will one day pass through a medium that is always opaque.

Not only can the picture of the brain not be superimposed upon the person, then; we have no reason to believe in any picture of a person's non-worldly aspect for it to be superimposed upon instead.

8

These conclusions ought not to surprise anyone who accepts that our reason for believing that mental states are occupants of causal roles is given by pointing to the place of mental states in causal explanation. For nothing in the argument here is hostile to the thought that causal roles are constitutive of at least some mental concepts. It can be true that the explanatory task that propositional-attitude ascription serves is a causal one; and it can be true that we cast all the light we can on propositional-attitude concepts by saying (not in functionalist theories, but in the available ways) what explanatory task their ascriptions serve.

It will be said that there is a puzzle here, however. How can the propositional-attitude states be thought of as mediating causally between inputs to and outputs from persons, although nothing with the appropriate causal powers of mental states can be found by scrutiny of a person's interior? Does not our conception of causality compel us to see the states which are cited in causal explanations of (*inter alia*) movements of a body as states which are located on causal chains that can be traced through space and time and that run through space-time volumes incorporating movements of that body? But then are we not obliged to see bodily movements as somehow primary among the explananda of action explanations? (Some line of thought such as this must be what lends plausibility to arguments like Kim's in §2.)

One will feel tremendous pressure to accept this if one adopts a paradigm of causal explanations, got (say) from the picture of the brain, and takes it that the causal explanations obtained in viewing a person as a person must also conform to that paradigm. But if the causal-explanatory powers of mental states cannot be specified in such a way that a scientist could be led to recognize states that are the subjects of his studies as having those powers, then the belief that commonsense psychological states conform to the paradigm is undermined. The impossibility of specifying the causal-explanatory powers of mental states in ways that would suit a scientist is revealed in the difficulty of finding a notion of behaviour which is both available to commonsense psychology and rich enough to define states that are explanatory according to the paradigm even while they share in the complexities of commonsense psychological states.

9

Why is the idea that propositional-attitude states can be fitted to the scientific paradigm so compelling? I suspect that an unacknowledged allegiance to principles of positivist epistemology must take a share of the blame.

If one begins with a distinction between psychological terms and non-psychological terms, and dresses this up in a distinction between T-terms and O-terms such as Lewis's (§3), then one comes to think of the O-terms as conveying all the data from which psychological theories could be constructed. Application of the O-terms seems, then, to be independent of anything one knows about people (*per se*), and commonsense psychology begins to seem to be a theory of such observables as the O-terms describe, a theory distinctive only in its particular concepts.

But reflection on the practice of psychological explanation shows what an extraordinary myth this is.[18] Someone required to explain why some agent has done something has to show how the psychological facts about the agent are consistent with what she ostensibly did. This may require him to become clearer about what went on in the world even as he speculates about her mental states. (Equally, of course, he may learn about the world by learning of her states of mind.[19]) It is not, as the model of theory and observation might suggest, that he has to arrive at a view about what went on in the agent's head which coheres with some prior account of what happened at the place where her body meets the world.

We ought not, then, to expect to find any notion of behaviour ('the observable') that is suited to reductionist claims. Certainly Rylean talk of skaters' dispositions to warn other skaters seems laughable if it is read as offering any reduction of believing that the ice is thin. And there is reason to suppose that the features of Ryle's behavioural terms which contaminate them psychologically must in fact be present equally in any terms that figure in any account of mental things. There are two (related) ways in which the application of everyday behavioural terms is caught up with the application of psychological terms. First, bits, or items, of behaviour, as described by behavioural concepts, are the effects of mental states; but it is impossible to divide behaviour up into bits in such a way that the bits correspond to things that have a psychological history unless we know something about the mental states that actually produce the behaviour. Second, Ryle's descriptions tell us of things that the agent intentionally did; and one is not in a position to take a view of which things are intentionally done by people unless one has some view of their mental states. These two features are bound to be inherited by any behavioural descriptions that are fit for inclusion in an account of mental states: their application must presuppose (a) a psychologically informed method for articulating the events that flow from a person, and (b) a sense of what is psychologically relevant among the events thus articulated.[20]

If one rests content with a naive conception of psychology's province, one cannot then construe 'observable' in positivist spirit and think of behaviour, the objects of psychological explanation, as 'observable'. Helping oneself to 'observable' behaviour is only a way of ensuring that one ignores the truth about psychological explanation.

This is no doubt inadequate as a diagnosis of the attractions of present-day physicalist accounts of intentional phenomena. But here I suspect that the whole history of the subject is to the point. Philosophers of mind have come to see Cartesian Dualism as the great enemy, but have underestimated what they have to contend with. Taking the putatively immaterial character of minds to create the only problem that there is for Descartes's account, they marry up the picture of the person with the picture of her brain, and settle for a view of mind which, though material in its (cranial) substance, is Cartesian in its essence.[21] Of course the acceptance of immaterial substance *was* one of Descartes's errors. But it does not take a scientific materialism to remedy that error. After all, it has been said not that there are elements of the person picture that science fails to deal with because they are ethereal and unnatural, but only that we have to look for the source of commonsense psychology's complexity elsewhere than at the junction between the central nervous system and the world.

8

Agency and Causal Explanation

1. Introduction

Some philosophical problems about agency can be put in terms of *two points of view*. From the *personal* point of view, an action is a person's doing something for a reason, and her doing it is found intelligible when we know the reason that led her to it. From the *impersonal* point of view, an action would be a link in a causal chain that could be viewed without paying any attention to people, the links being understood by reference to the world's causal workings. We might take it for granted that there are truths available to be discovered from each of these points of view. The problems about agency surface when we start to wonder whether the impersonal point of view does not threaten the personal one.

We might think that a full understanding of everything that happens when there is an action could be had without anyone's knowing who did what thing for what reasons. But then, if the whole truth about an action and its causal past and future can be given in viewing it as a manifestation of the world's causal workings, the impersonal point of view can seem to displace the personal one. Of course the personal point of view might still be adopted, even if it seemed redundant from another point of view. But two lines of thought may be used to make it seem redundant *tout court*. First, there is the thought, which Thomas Nagel has made especially vivid, that it is essential to our conceiving of our ourselves as agents that we take our actions to be completely accounted for in the terms that we use as agents; the possibility of treating actions from the impersonal point of view would then subvert our ordinary conception of ourselves.[1] Second, there is the thought, which is familiar in contemporary philosophy of mind, that the impersonal point of view is more 'objective', or for some other reason has better credentials, than the personal one. In order for the personal point of view to be metaphysically sound, then, it would need to be subsumed under the other one; but the possibility of such subsumption may be doubted.[2]

Both these lines of thought introduce rivalry between the two points of view, and suggest that the impersonal one may triumph. Either the personal point of view is supposed to be undermined, by being revealed to rest on an assumption that the possibility of taking an impersonal view shows to be false; or it is supposed to be refuted by the impersonal view, which is meant to be better placed for seeing the truth.

In this essay I attempt to block the idea that the two points of view are in competition. My suggestion will be that actions are not in fact accessible from the impersonal point of view.

Two fairly immediate routes to my suggestion might be taken. One starts from denying that actions are events; the other, from denying that the explanation of action is causal explanation. Each of these denials would enable one to deny, in turn, what I do deny—that actions can be located in the impersonal world of causes. But I shall not follow either route. Indeed, I start by saying why I think that actions are events (§2), and that reason explanation is causal explanation (§3). This will enable me to assemble materials for an argument that makes my suggestion plausible (§4). I offer some further support for it (§5) before I treat the two problems about agency (§§6 and 7).

2. Actions as events

We know something about the causal past of some water's boiling if we know that the water is in the kettle that Peter switched on because he wanted to make a cup of tea. Something has happened because someone wanted it to. If we see the water's boiling as an event, then we may think of an action also as an event: an action is an event that causes another, where the occurrence of the other typically amounts to the agent's having something she wanted.

Someone might allow that there is causality here, but say that only a philosopher bent upon forcing causality into the event-event model would introduce 'an action'. It is Peter with whom we credit the switching on of the kettle, it may be said; and if something about him is relevant, then it is only his wanting boiling water. This response is correct insofar as it looks back to Peter and what he wanted, and recognizes that these are not events. But it ignores the fact that Peter had to do something if the water was to boil, that wanting it to boil was not enough. There is no need to invent an item to bridge the gap between Peter's states of mind and the event of his want's being satisfied: when his want was satisfied, the gap was bridged—he switched on the kettle. Or, in an alternative idiom, there was an event—his switching on the kettle.

When it is accepted that there are actions, and that they are events, questions arise about which events they are, and how many of them there are. Not every event in whose description the name of a person features is an action; there is only an action when someone does something intentionally.[3] But since a person's intentionally doing something may be the same as her doing something else (intentionally or unintentionally), there is more to be said about the individuation of actions. For my part, I accept the view that (nearly enough) if someone did one thing by doing another then her doing the one thing was the same as her doing the other: when Peter boiled the water by switching on the kettle, his boiling the water was his switching on the kettle. On this account of individuation, the various things that people do are, many of them, the bringing about of effects of various sorts. And of course a single action can bring about a series of effects: an action of Peter's was the initiation of a series that contained both the kettle's being on and the water's coming to the boil.

Even when this view of individuation is accepted, it may still be asked to what extremes we should take the idea that things people do allude to effects of their actions. Elsewhere I have argued that *causation* is implicit whenever we impute agency (see chaps. 1–3 of my 1980 book). Our conception of a person as an agent is a conception of something with a causal power; whether we think of a person's having brought about a movement of a bit of her body or a bomb's exploding in a distant field, we should see her action as her causing something—as causing the movement, or the explosion, or whatever. This view has been challenged, because it is thought that movements of bodies must be more intimately connected with actions than is suggested by calling them effects. But the view may not be incompatible with the idea that bodily movements are parts of actions—as David Lewis has pointed out in defending *piecemeal causation* (Lewis, 1986, p. 173). And bodily movements need not be denied a special status in relation to agency. For we may think that our ability to make bodily movements is constitutive of our having the power that we have as agents—to initiate series of events containing some we want. An action is the exercise of such a power, and a person's actions are the events at the start of those series she initiates.

3. Reason explanation as causal explanation

The previous section has been concerned for the most part with the causal future of actions. But it takes something for granted also about the causal past of a person's intentionally doing something: it assumes that in finding out what Peter wanted, we learned something about the causal history of some events. It may seem, then, that the claim which it is the purpose of the present section to defend—that action explanation is causal explanation—has already been presupposed, and that nothing is in dispute here. But the matter is not so straightforward.

What makes it complicated is that there have been thought to be two different issues about causal explanation. We are told that there are philosophers who accept that the items alluded to in giving a reason explanation play a part in the causal past of an action, but who nevertheless deny that rational explanation is itself causal explanation.[4] Supposedly these philosophers think that if you cross the road because you want to get to the other side, then there is an explanation of your crossing in terms of where you want to get to, and there is a causal connexion between the fact of your wanting to be there and your crossing, but the existence of an explanation and the existence of a causal connexion are separate matters. What I mean to defend is the claim that reason explanation is causal in a sense that rules out this idea of causality and explanatoriness coming apart—the claim that reason explanation is causal-explanation (where the hyphen signals that causality and explanatoriness enter the scene together, as it were).

On the face of it, it is a strange position that these philosophers are said to occupy. For one might have thought that the best way to persuade someone that a person's having the reasons she does bears causally on what she does was to show that explanations that give people's reasons are causal-explanations. There is an argument that asks us to consider a case in which someone did something and had a reason for doing it, yet did not do it as a result of having that reason. We are asked to contrast this with the case in which we can explain her action by mentioning her reason—where she did it because she had the reason. The difference between the two cases suggests that *causation* and *explanation* are inextricable: both are introduced when we are told why someone did something—when we find the word 'because' between a statement saying what she did and a statement saying what her reason for doing it was.[5]

Why, then, should claims about causal connexions have been thought to be separable from claims about the causal-explanatory nature of reason explanation? Presumably the answer is that we have to make allowance for those philosophers who deny that reason explanation is causal *tout court*.[6] They do not deny that reason explanation is explanation; so it might seem that in order to be able to contradict them, we have to isolate some 'purely causal' statements about mental states and actions which we, but not they, assent to. A prominent candidate for our endorsement is 'The primary reason for an action is its cause'.[7] Since someone might hold this without assuming any particular account of how the explanation of action works, there seems to arise the possibility of isolating it from any thesis about explanation, and thus of adopting the position that reason explanation, though it mentions causes, it not itself causal-explanation.

Well, we have seen already that support for the thesis of causal-explanatoriness may be given without assuming the availability of any 'purely causal' statements. What we should realize now is that a defense of causal-explanation need have no involvement at all with 'purely causal' statements. Indeed, consideration of what goes on when action explanations are sought and found should make us very sceptical about them.

When we seek an 'action explanation', one question we usually want answered is 'Why did she do such and such thing?'. We may agree that actions are events without supposing that this question is equivalent to 'Why was there an event of such-and-such kind?'. Asking why a ϕ-d, we hope to learn something about a, the person; but if we asked why a's ϕ-ing occurred, a might not be a subject of concern at all. To a question about why someone did something, an expected answer usually is: 'She thought ———', or 'She wanted ———'. Philosophers' official version of an answer is: 'She thought ——— *and* she wanted ———'. The official version is appropriate, because someone who intentionally did something had a reason for doing it, and, having a reason, she must have believed something about what would be conducive to the satisfaction of some desire she had. When a relevantly connected belief and desire are both mentioned (e.g., 'She thought she could get to the other side by crossing and she wanted to get to the other side'), the explanation is successful inasmuch as it brings us to realize that what mattered, so far as her doing what she did is concerned, is her having had the reason she did.

It may seem only a short step from this point to speaking of reasons as 'belief-desire pairs', and to saying, 'The primary reason is the cause'. But if we take this step we arrive on much less firm ground. What sort of thing is the primary reason now supposed to be? It cannot be what an agent has when she has a reason; for you may have the same reason to do something as someone else, but we are surely not to suppose that your believing and desiring something causes someone else's action. If we are to make sense of it as 'the cause', then the primary reason must be an item that there is if and only if the relevant agent believes some particular thing and desires some other (related) thing. But why should we think that there is any such item as this? Why should acknowledgement that we say something about what she believed and desired in causally explaining why she did what she did lead us to accept the existence of anything that 'the cause of her action' stands for?

We are encouraged to believe in the things at issue when we are told that the agent's belief and her desire are each 'token states'. Then her reason (the candidate denotation of 'the cause') is meant to be the fusion, or perhaps the intersection, of two token-states. But even if we think we know what it is for a token-state to be a cause, can we be sure that we know what it would be for this sort of thing—composed some-how from two states of the same person—to be the cause?[8] And if such a fusion (or pair, or whatever) were indeed the cause of an agent's doing what she did, how would it relate to all the other causal truths about the situation? Suppose we could explain why Jane had done something by pointing out that she didn't think that *p*. Is there in that case a token state of her not believing that *p* that was also some part of the cause?

I do not know how one should answer these questions. The point is that we do not have to answer them if we deny that the causal-explanation view relies on the idea of discrete things combining (interacting?) in the pro-duction of action. What we rely on is only a network of intelligible de-pendencies between the facts about what an agent thinks, what she wants, and what she does. When we know why she did something, the fact that she did it may be seen as depending crucially on the fact that she wanted some particular thing and thought some particular thing. And the depen-dence is of a causal sort, of course.

Accepting that *belief* and *desire* are causal-explanatory notions, we cannot but suppose that people really do think things and want things, and that whether or not someone thinks a particular thing, or wants a particular thing, may make a genuine difference to what she does and says. But if the causal reality of *belief* and *desire* is just their causal-explanatory reality, then it need make no use of a further idea—of items inside people that we latch on to when we give action explana-tions.[9] Once this further idea is in place, it can come to seem that the explanatory value of *belief* and *desire* is quite unconnected with the value of those concepts in causal understanding—as if the particular contents of a particular person's beliefs and desires had nothing to do with her tendencies to do one thing rather than another. It is then that one may be led to the curious claim that 'the rational explanation of action mentions causes but is not *itself* causal explanation'.

4. Anomalousness

The philosopher most often said to be committed to this claim is Donald Davidson. The argument that he gave for monism is the focus in the present section. So far as the alleged commitment is concerned, I shall take Davidson's part: he told us why we should think that reason explanation is causal-explanation, and he has never gone back on that.[10] Another thing I shall take over from him is the thesis of the mental's irreducibility. Nevertheless, Davidson's argument runs contrary to my suggestion that actions are not accessible from the impersonal point of view. And it is by questioning it, and attempting to diagnose a widely felt dissatisfaction with it, that I hope to make my suggestion plausible.

Davidson's famous argument uses three premisses: (1) of causal dependence, (2) of causation's nomological character, and (3) of the mental's anomalousness (see, e.g., Davidson, 1970 in 1980, p. 208). Someone who wanted to demonstrate that actions (among other mental events) are present to the impersonal point of view might use only the first two premisses. Premiss (2) says that 'events related as cause and effect fall under strict deterministic laws'; premiss (1) acknowledges (among much else[11]) that actions are related causally to other things. When the operation of strict deterministic laws is thought of as something impersonally described, then the premisses combine to secure a place for actions in an impersonal account. In this argument the presence of actions to an impersonal point of view purports to be demonstrated in the same way as the physical nature of actions purported to be demonstrated by Davidson—through their location in a law-governed world.

Davidson's own argument was different. His route to monism had to be less direct: the nomological character of causality would be of no help to him in showing that mental events are physical if it were possible to see them as law-governed even while they were conceived of as belonging to mental kinds; premiss (3), of the anomalousness of the mental, is ineliminable. This premiss relies on a 'categorial difference between the mental and the physical' which ensures that mental kinds cannot themselves be nomological kinds. In Davidson, then, the application of nomological (and thus physical) vocabulary to mental particulars is shown indirectly—through the involvement of the mental with causality (premiss 1) and the involvement of causality with Nomologicality (premiss 2). But the argument is like the more direct one: in finding mental items to have properties of each of two sorts, where possession of one sort (mental, personal) is the ground of an argument for possession of the other sort (physical, impersonal). In Davidson, there are the properties that mental items have in virtue of which we can treat their possessors as rational, and there are those they have in virtue of which they can be seen as situated in the nomological causal network, and which ensure that they are physical.

Davidson believes that properties of both sorts—rational and nomological—can be used in explanations. And this belief is one source of the widespread supposition that Davidson ought really to deny that rational explanation is causal-explanation. There is thought to be a difficulty about a single thing's possessing two causal-explanatory properties. If there were a genuine difficulty, then a nomological story about an action's occurrence would rule out the possibility of a rational explanatory story that was also causal, so that Davidson would have to reject the causal-explanation thesis. Many have said that Davidson is in truth an epiphenomenalist: that for him, mental events are, *qua* mental, inert, since it is in virtue of their physical, nomological properties that they are causally efficacious (see n. 10). But when the matter is put like this, a reply on Davidson's behalf is easily found. He can simply deny that an item can have only one causal-explanatory property. And he has explained why we should deny this: we are often in the position of taking ourselves both to know one explanation of an event's occurrence, and to be justified in believing that there is another explanatory story about it of whose details we are actually quite ignorant (see Davidson, 1967a). Could it not be like this where actions are concerned?[12] Perhaps the fact that there is a causal-explanatory story that we cannot tell need not interfere with the idea that we can give a rational causal-explanation.

Nonetheless, the feeling that it does interfere is widespread. If we want to understand why nomological and rational explanation, as Davidson interprets them, should be thought to conflict, then we need to remember that his conception of rational explanation was supported by considerations that are quite unaffected when the argument for monism is given. This means that the problem that so many people think they see about his retaining the causal-explanatory thesis may really be a problem about accepting the conclusion that Davidson wants us to add to the thesis. The feeling that Davidson's theses conflict may be based in a sense of conflict between two pictures—the picture one gets of the operation of mental events if one accepts Davidson's version of monism, and a picture of how we understand people. And if that is so, then the supposed difficulty for Davidson corresponds to a more general difficulty: that in attempting to view the mental impersonally, one finds that its causal efficacy is lost.

In Davidson's case, what we have to ask is why it should be accepted that there is a nomological, causal story even about the events that are actions. The Nomological Character of Causality, as it is used in Davidson's argument, says that a law lurks in any case where it is possible to rely on causal notions to make something intelligible. Can we support this even while we assume that finding people causally intelligible is a 'categorially different' matter from understanding physical causal goings on? What are the grounds for believing that rational explanations themselves mention items that can be picked out in nomological vocabulary? Well, Davidson thinks that we regularly have evidence of laws covering particular cases, and that this gives us evidence that some full-fledged causal law exists covering each and every explanation. He has said that the evidence for the operation of laws is summarized in such generalizations as 'Windows are fragile, and fragile things tend to break when struck hard enough, other conditions being right'. And he likened behavioural generalizations to generalizations like this one (see Davidson, 1963 in 1980, p. 16). So his idea must be that our ability to frame rough-and-ready generalizations about pieces of behaviour is to be taken as a symptom that they too are governed by law. But the trouble now is that the thesis of the mental's anomalousness will seem to obstruct any full assimilation of 'behavioural generalizations' to generalizations about the breakings of windows.

The distinctive thing about rational explanations—which points to the mental's anomalousness—is that our acceptance of them relies on the 'discovery of a coherent and plausible pattern in the attitudes and actions' of a person; they are 'governed by an ideal'. In that case the special character of the mental sets answers to *Why?* questions about what people have done apart from answers to questions about why, for example, windows break. Davidson once said that 'our justification for accepting a singular causal statement is that we have reason to believe an appropriate causal law exists though we do not know what it is' (Davidson, 1967a in 1980, p. 160). Well, perhaps we do take ourselves to witness the operation of physical law when we see the window break, and perhaps that is our justification for thinking that the ball's hitting it caused the window's breaking. But our justification for accepting an account of why someone did something would seem to have nothing to do with any reason we might have for believing in the world's nomological workings—not if discovery of a rational pattern is what we actually rely on, and if our aim is conformity with a rational ideal.

Even if a fully general link between 'singular causal statements' and laws could be established, it is unclear that that would help very much in an argumentative strategy for bringing mental particulars inside the scope of laws. For when an action explanation is given, it may be that there is no item said to stand to an action in the relation of 'cause' (see §3). If that is so, then the possibility of a single state or event's possessing two causal-explanatory properties is not something that Davidson can exploit in the present connexion; if we are trying to accommodate the causal efficacy of the mental, we cannot now think of ourselves as seeking another causal-explanatory property possessed by some item already possessed of a nomological one. This point also may be seen as connected with the special explanatory character of the mental, in virtue of which it is irreducible and, in Davidson's sense, anomalous. An action explanation is not a reply to a question about why some event occurred, and, in revealing what an agent thought and what she wanted, it does not introduce any singular term for 'the cause'. Rather, it shows a person's doing something to make sense by seeing her as (at least approximately) rational—as conforming (more or less) to norms of consistency and coherence in her thought and practice. Since its focus is how things were with *her*, it is no wonder that no 'purely causal' statement can be extracted from the explanation. The objective is to see a causally complex whole—a person—in a certain, intelligible light; and this fits ill with the idea of locating an item on which an event that happens to be an action may be seen to follow in the way things do, nomologically speaking.[13]

Of course Davidson himself would be the first to acknowledge that accounts of action are outside the direct reach of physical law. The present question is why physical law should be thought to reach them at all, however indirectly. In order to use the notion of a law to forge a connexion between the causal-explanatory nature of a concept and the physical nature of the things it applies to, Davidson relies on a transition from the causal-explanatory to the 'purely causal'. But the connexion is one that the irreducibility of the mental stands in the way of, and our inability to make the transition may be seen as a symptom of that.

My argument here can be sketchily stated by setting out the steps that Davidson needs to take:

mental → causal-explanatory → 'purely causal' → nomological → physical

Someone might start from a conception of the nomological, and look backwards, insisting that some property that the *nomological* encompasses applies to anything that has some causal-explanatory property. But then she would precisely have disregarded the special causal-explanatory character of the *mental* whose concepts have application to people; and it would be unsurprising if she seemed to reach the position that the mental is epiphenomenal. Someone else might start with a conception of the mental and try to move forwards. But the conception of the causal-explanatory she reaches at the first step provides her with no way of moving to the 'purely causal' that would take her on.

The quicker argument we considered earlier is equally affected if it aspires to bring mental states within the compass of an impersonal view. In order to see the two arguments as alike, we thought of the impersonal point of view as that from which the search for nomological explanation is appropriate. The nature of causation itself was then supposed to take us straight from a personal to an impersonal point of view:

personal → causal → impersonal

Again, there is no way to take the necessary steps. For what constitutes the irreducibility of the mental-personal is the operation of a particular standard of causal intelligibility. But if the causal features of concepts used in action explanation are just their causal-explanatory features, then they are precisely what are missing from the impersonal point of view where a different standard of causal intelligibility is in place.

We now lack any argument for subsuming actions in the impersonal world of causes. When we start from a rational explanation, no conception of the nomological can be brought into sight. It seems that the particular character of action explanation prevents actions from being present to the impersonal point of view.

5. Actions impersonally conceived?

Before relating this conclusion to the problems about agency we began with, I want to draw attention to what I see as a sign of its correctness, and also to some habits of thought that may obscure its correctness.

Seeing something as an action requires the identification of a person and the exercise of concepts that we put to work in understanding people. This on its own does not show that an event that is an action might not also be picked out by someone operating without such concepts as *belief*, *desire*, and *intention*. But I suggest now that someone not operating with these concepts would not in fact be able to identify an action.

Consider a particular case. Bring on to the scene not only Peter's action, and the series of events which he initiated and which the action caused, but also such events as one is likely to think of as causal antecedents of an action—neuronal firings, signals going out to the nerves, muscles contracting. In the picture is a whole collection of events leading from some happening in the depth of Peter's brain all the way to an event beyond his body in which his desire's being satisfied consists. The question to ask is: 'how much of all that we have brought on to the scene does the action consist of?'. About some things, we feel certain: events in the brain quite remote from the motor system are no part of the action; events in the world quite remote from Peter's body are no part of the action. But certainty about these things gives us no exact answer where to draw the lines. Looking at the picture, we have no opinion in some cases whether this or that is a part of the action.

Of course we do know exactly what the action is: it is Peter's switching on the kettle (or whatever). But having a determinate answer from the perspective form which Peter is apparent does not give us anything determinate to say in the terms of the picture. Nor, it seems, do we lose anything by resisting the thought that there ought to be some exact answer from this point of view, or that the answer we give from our and Peter's point of view is somehow inadequate. If we are content to accept that no answer to our question can be forced upon us, that may be because there is no answer: as the picture is drawn, we start to adopt an impersonal point of view, from which it is impossible to locate actions.

A reductionist might say that scientists would be capable of returning the answer, and that it is no surprise to find that we cannot do so without further investigation.[14] But, though it is true that a reductionist is likely to have confidence that there is a definite brain-event at the beginning of the action, when it comes to a question about the end—about the action's finishing-point, as it were—even her confidence will evaporate. For the question in this case concerns the line between an action and its effect, which has always seemed to everyone to be a philosophical question—not a question for further empirical investigation, but one about how common sense and talk operate. Yet it still does not seem that there is a definite answer to it which we have immediate intuitions about.

Thoughts about actions are much less the product of intuitions than philosophers have come by habit to suppose. Of course the thought that there are actions is, in one sense, something that no one would dream of denying. But it is not in this sense that I argued, and tried to make it seem obvious, that there are actions. What a non-philosopher means when she accepts that there are actions is that the phenomenon of action is exemplified: people do things (for reasons). But she does not mean (even if it can be made obvious) that there are events each one of which is a person's doing something. The word 'action' is ambiguous. Where it has a plural: in ordinary usage what it denotes, nearly always, are the things people do; in philosophical usage, what it denotes, very often, are events, each one of them some person's doing something. We may find ourselves with views which we can readily express in the language of action, and then, finding it obvious that there are actions, we (philosophers) assume that we have views which we can readily express in the language of events. Explanation of action is a case in point. We may move from knowing that we have an instance of 'action explanation' straight to thinking that we have an explanation of an action (event).[15]

Our picture may provide another case. If our opinions about *action* do not immediately yield anything definite to say about actions (events), then we should not have expected it to seem evident where the line comes between the action and its effects. Earlier I mentioned the view that movements of people's bodies must be more intimately connected to actions than is suggested when they are thought of as effects, and Lewis's claim that a movement of someone's body is both an effect and a part of her action (§2). It is supposed to be quite plain to common sense that a bodily movement is a part of an action.[16] But is this really something we are justified in feeling we are apt to be right about straight off? (Never mind for the moment whether we are right about it or not.) Certainly we know that no one moves her finger unless her finger moves; and we know that we can tell by observation what people do, and that we could not observe someone move her finger unless we saw her finger move. But we also know that these considerations alone could not suffice to show that her finger's moving is a part of her action—no more than similar considerations could suffice to show that Jones's death was a part of Smith's killing him. Again we know that typically when there is an action, an agent moves her body and thereby initiates a series of events, so that something she wants comes to happen. But this consideration does not circumscribe an action, beyond showing it to be where the agent is. It is not at all clear what would definitively settle the question as to which things are parts of actions. This will not seem worrying if we are aware that there need be no more plain truths about the events that are actions than there are plain truths about action (about agency, and things people do).

The events that are actions are understandably a focus of philosophical debate; but they are not ordinary objects of scrutiny. It is important to appreciate this, because the supposition on the part of philosophers that all our naive opinions in the area of action readily come to us stated in the language of events is one source of the presumption that actions are impersonally apparent.

6. Agency undermined?

Thomas Nagel takes it to be evident that actions can be impersonally apparent. I turn now to the first of the two problems about agency—the one that he introduces. In his *View from Nowhere*, he assumes that we know that there is a possible picture from an 'external perspective' which includes actions in it; the 'external perspective' is supposed to provide 'an objective view of a particular person with his viewpoint [which is an internal one] included' (1986, p. 3). (I hope that it will be enough for the time being to say that the external perspective of Nagel's assumption is thus an impersonal one. I leave it to the next section to relate Nagel's external/internal or objective/subjective distinction more exactly to the impersonal/personal one.)

Nagel thinks that the threat to autonomy—to the idea that 'we are authors of our actions' (1986, p. 114)—arises when we find that our conception of ourselves as agents is ambitious: 'our capacity to view ourselves from outside . . . gives us the sense that we ought to become the absolute source of what we do' (1986, p. 118). This sense 'is not just a feeling but a belief', he says, although he suspects that it may be 'no intelligible belief at all' (1986, p. 114). But Nagel does not think that our inability to make the belief fully intelligible diminishes the threat to agency: we can have aspirations without knowing how they might be met.

There is no doubt that it can be disturbing to try to think about ourselves in the manner that Nagel suggests. And it may seem evasive, even unphilosophical, to insist that we turn from our thoughts to their verbal expression. Nevertheless, I suggest that we have to look carefully at Nagel's words, and to ask in the first instance what he means by 'action'. There are two possibilities. If 'actions' stands for the things we do, then, evidently enough, we do them; but they are not particulars, and we are not their authors or sources. If 'actions' stands for a class of events, then there seems to be no better way to say how an agent relates to her action than to say that it is hers. The relation between agent and action is signalled by the genitive in phrases for actions—'*her* speaking'; '*a*'s opening the door'. We find here a sort of ownership; but it does not seem to be authorship. Perhaps the thought that we are authors, or sources, of our actions need not be taken literally at all.

I think we know what Nagel means, however. An agent is the source, or the author, of the events that she causes. Earlier I called actions the initiatings of series of events—as a way of trying to place them on the causal scene. Our sense of ourselves as authors is then the sense that we are responsible for the events in those series that we initiate; to hold ourselves responsible for an event is to take responsibility for initiating the series it belongs to. But our responsibility consists in the action's being ours, and not in its having been caused, or done, by us. Nagel makes it sound as if we might locate an agent and find her action set apart from her. But though we may separate the events she causes from the agent, we cannot separate her from the event that starts the series—which is her causing them.

When Nagel says that 'everything I do or that anyone else does is part of a larger course of events that no one "does", but that happens' (1986, p. 114), he entices us into thinking that we have located actions from an external viewpoint. But what a person does is not an event, and it is therefore not a 'component of the flux of events in the world'. Nagel's ways of putting things suggest that we always have aspirations, which, in fact, we come to seem to have only when the event language is used as if it expressed things that cannot be said. Perhaps Nagel is only too right when he holds that the 'difficulty' is that 'it is impossible to give a coherent account of the internal view of action which is under threat', and that we 'cannot say what would . . . support our sense that our free actions originate with us' (1986, pp. 112–113, 117). Perhaps we have said everything that we need to say when we have understood what it is to be responsible for our actions' effects.

But Nagel things that our conception of ourselves as agents is revealed more fully when we consider the explanation of action. 'The final explanation . . . is given by the intentional explanation of my action, which is comprehensible only through my point of view. My reason for doing it is the *whole* reason why it happened, and no further explanation is necessary or possible.' And now, thinks Nagel, the trouble is that this sort of explanation, on which our sense of agency is based, is shown to be unsustainable when we take account of the possibility of an objective view; for that view 'admits only one kind of explanation of why something happened . . . and equates its absence with the absence of any explanation at all'.[17] Intentional explanations are shown up as inadequate, Nagel says, when we see that they 'cannot explain *why I did what I did rather than the alternative that was causally open to me*' (1986, p. 116).

Intentional explanation may in fact be more powerful than Nagel allows here. At least it seems to be more powerful if we take it to be the kind of explanation in which concepts such as *belief* and *desire* are used to make sense of people and what they do and don't do—rather than as consisting in a series of once-off occasions on which 'the' reason for something actually done is given. I might tell you why she refused the job, but leave you realizing that there is more you could learn to help you to see why accepting it was something she didn't do. It is true that there could come a point at which there is no more for anyone to say about why she did one thing rather than another, and I have to resort to 'Those were the reasons she saw in favour and against, and the reasons in favour weighed more heavily with her'. But it is not as if you would then suppose that you would understand better if only you could see that the event which is her action 'or a range of possibilities within which it falls, was necessitated by prior conditions and events' (1986, p. 115). It seems that up to a point we can meet the demands that Nagel puts on action explanation, and that beyond that point, they are of a sort that it is simply not susceptible to.[18]

The pressure of these demands is supposed to be felt when the internal and external perspectives come together. In Nagel they are brought together through an equation of his reason for doing something with the explanation why 'it' happened. ('My reason for doing it is the whole reason why it happened.') But really Nagel's reason for doing something is not an explanation of any happening. (His reason does not explain anything, although the fact that he had it may explain why he did something.) Nor is the explanation why Nagel did something itself a reason for anything. (The explanation gives his reason.) It seems that a threat to our sense of agency has been created by an illusion that we are trying to explain an event's occurrence when in fact we are trying to make sense of a person and what she did.

I may seem to be suggesting that the barrier between the external and the internal explanatory schemes is a merely terminological one. The obstacles to thinking what Nagel wants us to think are created by differences of category—between actions and things done, between reasons and explanations. But I think that these obstacles mark the presence of a genuine barrier. Accounts in terms of what a person thinks and wants are fitted to provide explanations for those who share with that person a point of view on the world. When the ideal of rationality can be brought to bear on explaining something she has done, that can be seen as something delivered from the contents of her thoughts and wants. Those who seek and give 'action explanations' do not regard the matter impersonally or externally, any more than the agent herself does when she deliberates about what to do.

7. Agency refuted?

Nagel's problem is engendered in the first instance from within the personal view—when it seems to need to rise above itself and take on the ambitions of an impersonal view. The second problem about agency is engendered from outside—when the impersonal view seems to swamp the personal one.

The ambitions of the impersonal view are not usually seen as a problem for agency. But there must be acknowledged to be potential problems here. For there are philosophers who think that any real phenomenon, however we may actually understand it, is intelligible from an impersonal point of view. And if it could be demonstrated both that the whole truth can be told from there, and that it leaves out of account everything that is personal, then the effects would be quite devastating: at stake is the idea that anyone ever really means to do anything, or wants anything, or believes anything. These truly devastating effects are seldom contemplated, because they cannot seriously be entertained, and because those who hold the threatening metaphysical doctrine for the most part believe that it actually holds no threats—that actions and their explanation can in fact be accommodated in an impersonal view. But something slightly less devastating is more frequently contemplated, as we have seen in reactions to Davidson. His anomalous monism is thought to deprive the mental of causal efficacy: the intrusion of the impersonal view is supposed to render people's being in states of mind causally quite idle, yet somehow to leave people intelligible.

The problematic effects on our conception of ourselves would be the same whether agency was undermined, from the inside, or refuted, from without. And the idea that I am suggesting stops those effects, and ensures that there is no real threat, is the same. But different considerations show how the threat is prevented from arising in the two cases. In discussing Nagel, the strategy was to deny to the personal view the pretensions he accords to it: I tried to show its explanatory scheme as insulated from that of the impersonal view. When agency seems to face refutation, though, the ambitions of an impersonal view are called directly into question. I finish with some further explanation and defense of the idea that we may resist them.

To be satisfied with saying that actions are apparent only from what I have called the personal view we need in the first place to be clear that this is not a view confined to a particular self. We cannot explain what someone has done unless we know whether she has been successful in achieving what she wanted. So the point of view from which she is understood must not only be one from which she can be seen to be in states of mind representing things beyond her, but also one from which those same states of mind can be evaluated, as correct or incorrect representations. The personal point of view, then, may differ from the most 'internal' view of Nagel, of 'a particular person inside the world'.

In Nagel, it is a matter of degree to which a point of view is objective or external: 'to acquire a more objective understanding of some aspect of life or the world, we step back from our initial view of it and form a new conception which has that view and its relation to the world as object' (1986, p. 5.) Now the notion of an impersonal point of view as I have used it is related to Nagel's internal-external (or subjective-objective) dimension: when we step back sufficiently that we have detached from everything contingent to our human subjectivity, we have reached a point of view that is external enough to be impersonal. Two of Nagel's ideas, then, need not be in dispute. First, we can allow that one point of view may incorporate another: a state of affairs might impinge upon a point of view, but it be possible to take up a more external one from which that state of affairs and that point of view were both represented. (Perhaps this is what happens when, from my point of view, I understand another person's.) Second, we can allow that there is such a thing as an impersonal view: we have a conception of an objective world whose nature is independent of whatever conscious beings occupy it, and our own capacity to stand back entitles us to this. But to allow these things—that one view may subsume another, and that some things can be viewed quite impersonally—is not to grant that we can always step away from any phenomenon and retain a view of it.[19]

Some people are persuaded that we can step back from actions when they are told that we have 'a view of persons and their actions as part of the order of nature'. The idea that actions are 'components of the flux of events of the world of which the agent is a part' combines with the idea that the flux of events in nature constitutes how things objectively are to make it seem that an impersonal view of actions is not only possible but appropriate. But we need to consider carefully this thought that persons and their actions are part of nature. It seems right when we point out that nothing supernatural needed to happen for human beings to evolve, and that it is a natural fact about people that, for instance, they have the abilities they do, and thus a natural fact that there are actions. Such considerations ensure that a naturalistic view of ourselves is in order, and indeed that the personal point of view is itself a naturalistic one. But they do not help to place our actions in a world 'of nature' if a world 'of nature' is to be thought of as constituted independent of the conscious beings that occupy it. It is (as Kantians might say) an empirical question whether an event is such that it would exist whether or not we were present in the world. If the event is an action, the answer is 'No'. So where the world 'of nature' is not the naturalistic world in which we find ourselves, but the world as it might be anyway—whether there were any people, or whatever any person's states of mind might be—actions are no part of it. This is not a particularly shocking conclusion: our conception of the world independent of us is not a conception of the world including us.

The conclusion evidently fits with the Davidsonian thesis of the disparateness of two conceptual frameworks—that by which we render ourselves intelligible to one another, and that by which we understand what goes on as the operation of physical law. But the conclusion is equally evidently at odds with Davidson's monism. For it would be a very strange idea that, from the impersonal point of view, we employ conceptual resources which describe the world 'of nature' and which are not such as to identify actions, which, however, for all that, can be used to identify actions. We saw in §4 that we were left without any reason to believe in the identities that Davidson asserts. Without such reason, we have no inclination to use the quicker argument that we considered there for bringing the mental inside the scope of law. Arguments like that one simply assume that whatever principles govern our account of a world 'of nature' have universal application, in any area where we can use causal notions to make sense of something. And the suspicion arises that Davidson himself, in invoking the Nomological Character of Causality, has simply imported his own universalizing assumption about 'nature'.[20]

So we have to say that there are events that are not in the world 'of nature'. Perhaps this ontological doctrine is the stumbling block. In addition to the feeling that it is a naturalistic world that we inhabit, there is the belief that the world 'of nature' is complete; and would it not be incomplete if it did not contain us and all the events we participate in? Someone who objects at this point may think that the cost of saying that we and our actions are not in the world 'of nature' is to render that a gappy world—with pieces missing where people and their actions should be. But she would be mistaken if she supposed that because people and their actions are absent from the impersonal point of view, the portions of space and time occupied by persons are missing too. We have to distinguish between an aspect of reality and a portion of reality. The claim about the completeness of what is accessible from the impersonal point of view is ruled out if it is the claim that every aspect of reality is present to it. But if it is a claim to survey the whole of space and time and deal with every portion of what it surveys, then nothing stands in its way. A correct account of an impersonal conception brings 'the whole world of nature' within its scope. Some portions of space-time are occupied by the bits of matter that people are composed from, and the account will deal with them, with flesh and blood, and nervous systems.[21]

There must, of course, be things to be said about how it can be that people are the sorts of being that we are, given that they are composed only from what can be scrutinized impersonally. It is in virtue not only of our occupying the position that we do in the world on which we act, but also of our being constructed as we are that we can have the cognitive and practical capacities that we do, and can, for instance, initiate series of events containing some of kinds we want. So there are questions about how nervous systems can subserve the phenomena of mentality and agency.[22] But these questions are not made easier by the assumption that, to everything we speak of from the personal point of view, there attaches a piece of vocabulary apt for describing things impersonally. This assumption after all is the source of the thought that actions are swallowed up from an external perspective, and of the thought that the mental is epiphenomenal. And it is not as if the assumption on its own could do anything to integrate the personal with an impersonal point of view. Davidson himself has made this clear: in the sphere of reason-explanations, causality is 'connected with the normative demands of rationality' (Davidson, 1985, p. 246).

There is, then, no new problem about integration when the assumption is abandoned, and actions are thought neither to be swallowed up nor deprived of genuinely causal explanations, but absent simply, from the impersonal point of view. When we see an action as a person's initiating a series of events, we recognize a type of event whose causal ancestry is understood from a personal, rational point of view, and whose causal successors come to be understood from an impersonal, perhaps scientific one. And we appreciate that causality is a concept that we may operate with from both points of view: people make a difference, and do so because their actions are events which make a difference.

Appendix

In emphasizing my real agreement with Davidson (on the causal-explanatoriness *and* irreducibility of the mental), I have ridden over some areas of disagreement. In this Appendix, I attempt to clarify these, taking in turn: *(A)* 'purely causal' statements, *(B)* the Nomological Character of Causality, *(C)* the relation between *(A)* and *(B)*.

(A) It is assumed nowadays that we find claims such as 'Reasons are causes' or 'Beliefs and desires causally interact with one another to produce actions' to be at least as obvious as the causal-explanation thesis. Davidson's influential simultaneous defense of both the claims and the thesis (1963) has probably contributed as much as anything else to the prevalence of this assumption. And in §3 I may have let it seem to be more surprising than it really is that separate explanatory and causal elements have been supposed to be extricable from Davidson's causal-explanation thesis. I hoped to make it clear *(a)* that the claims are in fact more dubious than the thesis, and *(b)* that if we attend to Davidson's arguments, we shall give the thesis priority. The consequence is that I have ignored Davidson's own support for claims to the effect that 'purely causal' statements about actions are available.

It is worth noting that, although 'The primary reason is the cause' is one of Davidson's own formulations, it is not obvious that he endorses actual statements that would count as instances of it. All the same, Davidson certainly does believe that we are entitled to more in the way of causal statements than the everyday 'because' ones. Whereas for some philosophers the purpose of making out our entitlement is served by talk of token states (and I addressed them in §3), for Davidson, it is served by arguing for the pervasiveness of events. Two of the things he said to this end seem to me inadequate. (1) He said that we may associate with a person's being in any mental state an event that is her coming to be in that state. But so long as we realize that an event that is the onslaught of someone's being in a state must plausibly be (identified with) a precisely datable event, there will not appear to be many of them. (2) He said that where we cannot find any candidate for the immediate cause of an action using psychological language, we are still 'sure that there was an event or sequence of events' (1963 in 1980, p. 13). But we might accept this because we know that there is an impersonal story to be told whenever a bit of someone's body moves; in that case our acceptance again lends no support to a causal statement of the kind to which entitlement was sought—such that statements of that kind go hand in hand with truths stated when action explanations are given.

(B) In §4 I questioned whether our belief in laws can ground our belief in psychological causal-explanatory statements. Davidson never asserts that it can. What he does assert is that our ability to generalize—including our ability to generalize psychologically—grounds our belief in the operation of laws. (General statements linking mental and physical are said to be heteronomic (Davidson, 1970 in 1980, p. 222), and the instantiations of heteronomic statements are said to 'give us reason to believe that there is a precise law at work' (1970 in 1980, p. 219).) Of course I should question this also: if explanations using 'believe' and 'desire' are credible even when they are not seen as nomologically grounded, why should these generalizations be thought to provide evidence for the operation of laws?

Evidently, raising these questions does not prove the falsity of the Nomological Character of Causality. But it may make us wonder whether we could have a case for it where Davidson needs one most. I let the argument with Davidson rest here, because I think that we shall resist the motivation for the Nomological Character of Causality when we see the sort of principle that it is, in the context, for example, of the quicker argument which I contrasted with Davidson's in §4.

(C) In the schema in which the quicker argument was summed up (at the end of §4), personal, and impersonal, and causal might be taken as properties of facts (if one is prepared to talk in that way). Thus in thinking about that argument, one need not assume an account of causation with the specific ontological presuppositions of an account that is grounded in 'purely causal' statements. Though it is formulated in terms that make it comparable with Davidson's own, then, the quicker argument is an instance of a more general style of argument: namely, an argument from a conception 'of nature', which I address in §7. It rests on a universalizing assumption, that there are principles governing any area where we can use causal notions to make sense of something (see n. 20).

In the schema in which Davidson's own argument was summed up, nomological, causal-explanatory, and mental can be understood as second-order properties. Such an understanding may reveal the indispensability of the items (states or events) to Davidson's way of thinking: these are the particulars having the properties that have the (second-order) properties. Certainly 'purely causal' statements are needed for a monistic argument like Davidson's. For unless rational-explanatory statements are seen to be concerned with the same things as laws are concerned with—with states or events or whatever—the Nomological Principle cannot do its work. (Nor can we find heteronomic generalizations of such a form as could provide us with reason for belief in laws.)

The two schematic arguments show us, then, that a universalizing assumption may be held in the absence of belief in 'purely causal' statements, although a conception of the 'purely causal' is needed for Davidson's own particular universal principle to be put to work. We should also notice that belief in the ubiquity of 'purely causal' statements does not introduce any universalizing assumption all by itself: someone might think that wherever there is (as we say) an action explanation, there are statements having the form but not the import of the statements needed for an argument that actions are present from the impersonal point of view. This dialectical situation explains a certain tentativeness on my part about whether we should hold that discrete items interact in the production of action. My own opinion is that we should not hold this; but, for the purposes of the argument here, it may be enough to cast the tenet in doubt. A reader is then free to accept the principle of the Nomological Character of Causality provided that its domain is restricted so that we are outside it in the rational realm (and psychological heteronomic generalizations can then lend it no support). Alternatively, she is free to carry on asserting the usual 'purely causal' statements about beliefs and desires and/or associated events, provided that she now denies that there is any principle of Nomologicality having application wherever statements of a 'purely causal' kind can be asserted (and psychological heteronomic generalizations then require a different attitude from that which Davidson takes towards all heteronomic generalizations).

III

Mind, Causation and Explanation

9

Introduction: Personal and Subpersonal Levels

1

Reading contemporary philosophy of mind, one is often distracted from personal-level explanation. I have mentioned ways of talking about action which make it easy to forget that people and their doings are the subject: in philosophers' writings, we encounter phrases which make no allusion to any person, even when we are meant to be thinking about a person's doing something (see Essay 5, §3, and Essay 8, §6). In their next breath, these philosophers may tell us that the things referred to by such phrases (which had been meant to be actions) are 'caused by beliefs and desires'. It is then as if a person's believing something were an impersonal state, something brutely there, as it were. The impersonal language, which has no use for the idea of rational motivation or of a sentient being, takes over. So we find 'two beliefs produce a third' standing for a person's arriving at a conclusion. We find 'an experience causes a belief' in place of the idea that a person believes something because things look to her to be a certain way. We find 'pains result in avoidance/reactions' substituting for a conception of a person's behaviour as intelligible in the light of the fact that she suffers pain. In all of these examples, suppression of mention of a person works like a bit of invisible scene-shifting. The change may go unnoticed, but understanding of a certain kind has been excluded.[1]

The excluded understanding is of a kind that is constantly relied upon. We constantly treat one another as sentient and rationally motivated: we use commonsense psychology. The thesis that reason explanation is causal explanation has application outside the domain of action; it is not only where human beings are agents that reason is at work. Action explanation, one might say, is one species of reason explanation, where reason explanation is something of which we find examples not only when we ask, 'Why did she set out then?', but also when we ask, 'What made her think that the lecture began at 6 o'clock?'. In much of the philosophical discussion of "mental causation", the concern has been explanation of people's doing things, not explanation of their thinking things (for instance); and Part II had the same narrow focus as such discussion. But if one wishes to investigate the repercussions for the philosophy of mind generally of the idea of reason explanation as causal, then one must take account of the pervasiveness of rational-causal-explanation. In whatever sense we expect to see someone as rational in learning why she did what she did, we expect to see her as rational again in learning why she thought what she did.

Naive naturalism, in accepting commonsense psychological subjects as belonging to a natural world, vouches for the probity of explanation in terms of reasons. But this would be threatened if commonsense psychological explanations had to be assimilated to explanations of another kind, in which the idea of something sentient and rationally motivated had no part. Of course there are explanations of other kinds; some of these can yield an understanding of how there can be beings having some of the properties which sentient, rationally motivated ones have. Naive naturalism, then, requires a distinction between two sorts of explanation where human beings are concerned.

The needed distinction corresponds to the distinction between the two pictures of Essay 7—the picture of the person and the picture of her brain. (But we should now include in the world inhabited by the person much more than the desired effects of her actions.) It is a distinction that Daniel Dennett made twenty-five years ago, between the explanatory level of people and their sensations and activities and 'the subpersonal level of brains and events in the nervous system' (Dennett, 1969; see also Essay 10). Ryle and Wittgenstein inspired Dennett: both of them thought that philosophers were prone to misconceive certain questions—questions which use commonsense psychological vocabulary essentially, but which, when misconceived, are supposed to be answered by speaking about internal machinery. In their different ways, both held there to be a range of personal-level facts no further illumination of which can be got by digging deeper.

At the time that Ryle and Wittgenstein wrote, impersonal explanations were apt all to be conceived mechanistically, and there was no such subject as Cognitive Psychology. It is possible to think that the last thirty or forty years have shown that Ryle's and Wittgenstein's insistence on a self-standing level of explanation which is a personal level depended upon their ignorance. Computers have provided us with new ways of understanding things, both by serving as models, and by enabling previously impossible calculations; and in physics itself a Newtonian materialist mechanism has been gradually relinquished. There is no longer any need to choose between accounts of things that run like clockwork and accounts of the kind that Ryle and Wittgenstein accepted at the personal level. But the existence of new kinds of explanation could hardly undermine the idea of a distinctive kind of understanding indigenous to the personal level. By making a personal-subpersonal distinction, one keeps Ryle's and Wittgenstein's point, but allows that there are other explanations. These other explanations—at the subpersonal level—can, in their turn, be in many and various styles, and they may help to make the possibility of explanations at the personal level unmysterious.

By keeping subpersonal questions apart from questions at the personal level, we can understand the negative ontological claims of Part I better. There need be no fusion of micro-states in the brain constituting someone's being in a mental state. But this is not to say that the micro-events and states are irrelevant to the possession of commonsense psychological properties: an account of them can satisfy curiosity about those of our capacities and abilities upon which our being commonsense psychological subjects depends. People would not be able to recognize faces, to catch balls, to do long multiplication, to hear people saying things, to keep track of time, to see where arguments lead, and so on, unless there were structures inside them of immense complexity.

But it is not enough for me to say, as anyone blithely can, that by making a distinction one ensures that one set of conclusions (about commonsense psychology) does not interfere with another set (reached by scientists). For one cannot mean just anything one wants by 'subpersonal' and suppose that a personal-subpersonal distinction does the particular work I want of it—of preserving intact both commonsense psychology as it is here conceived and the findings of scientists. So there is more to be said about the use, and possible abuse, of the distinction. (There is actually a great deal more that might be said. In §3 below, I confine myself to a few points about its possible abuse.)

2

The personal-subpersonal distinction is seen at work in Dennett in Essay 10. One of the essay's aims is to give a sharper sense of what naive naturalism amounts to by contrasting it with Dennett's own position. I suggest that Dennett's use of intentional systems as a surrogate for persons is a consequence of his belief in the orthodox kind of naturalism. The inadequacy of intentional systems to do duty for persons then counts in favour of naive naturalism, and of locating commonsense psychology at a properly personal level—in a sense of 'personal level' corresponding to Dennett's original (1969) understanding of that.

Essay 11 connects personal-level psychology with other subject matters, and now not just with 'science'. It was written for a conference at which developmental psychologists were present, and it brings to philosophers' problems a different perspective from the usual one by considering children's acquisition of a world view. The considerations are meant to encourage the idea of a seamless connexion between commonsense psychology and intuitive physics. And I explore the possibility that the problems of relating commonsense psychology to the scientific sort may not be very different from the problems of relating intuitive physics to high science.

Essay 12, in its present setting, can be conceived of as a response to a challenge. The challenge is to give some positive account of the irreducible subject matter of the personal level. The account offered in the essay places a theory of meaning—in a particular sense—at the centre of an account of personal-level psychological understanding. The idea of such a theory was by no means new at the time the essay was written. What was meant to be new was the suggestion that the proposed overall account, in which such a theory plays its part, can be a genuine rival to the naturalizing accounts which were increasingly popular then, and whose descendants have since held their place in approval ratings. It is probably no accident that such an idea of a theory of meaning has fallen from favour even as the philosophy of mind has developed in the way it has. But however that may be, questions about the nature of linguistic meaning, introduced only in the final essay, are intimately bound up with questions about the nature of persons' states of mind, which have been of concern throughout.

3

Suppose that the personal level is a level at which mention of persons is essential, and that commonsense psychological explanations are indigenous to that level. What should we then mean by 'subpersonal'?

As they are countenanced by the naive naturalist, subpersonal accounts are accounts which stand to the personal level in a certain relation but which are nevertheless impersonal in a certain sense. They are impersonal in the sense of Essay 8—knowing what they say is not a matter of finding a person intelligible as rationally motivated. But they connect with personal-level facts in that they have a place in a story of how it can be that something has the various capacities without which nothing could be the sort of intelligible being that a person is.

Sometimes the subpersonal is characterized using *parthood*. Then the idea is that at a personal level, one speaks of whole persons, and at the subpersonal level, one speaks of proper parts of persons. There need be nothing wrong with this idea itself: our being constructed as we are is surely what enables us to be the kinds of beings that we are. But troubles come with some of the ideas that may be introduced along with *parthood*. When *parthood* is used to characterize the subpersonal, one can easily be led to an understanding of 'subpersonal' which is different from that which a naive naturalist countenances. This may happen in various ways.

In the first place, an erroneous mereological conception may be imported. (We met this in Essay 3.) Philosophers who work with such a conception readily assume that when accounts of Xs are accounts of parts of a whole W, a complete account of W can be got by compiling the accounts of the *X*s. (One use of the saying that 'the whole is more than the sum of its parts' is to draw attention to the falsity of this assumption.) If the assumption were made in the case where *X*s are subpersonal items, then it would come to seem as if a treatment of the subpersonal enabled an account of the personal level to be given in what are actually impersonal terms.

In the second place, those who bring in the notion of parthood may suppose that parthood has a role to play in actually defining the idea of the subpersonal. With this supposition in place, it seems as if the distinction between subpersonal and personal could be made out in part-whole terms (and not merely that subpersonal accounts in fact treated proper parts of persons). Well, if a part-whole distinction did define a division between two levels, then the personal level would be the level at which one spoke so long as one made predications to (whole) persons. But this gives a different usage of 'personal level' from that which Dennett originally intended (in 1969), in which the personal level is the level at which one speaks only so long as one's concern is with commonsensically tractable explananda. Using 'personal level' as Dennett first did, there can be facts about (whole) persons which, because they lack explanations from the commonsense standpoint of commonsense psychology, are not personal-level facts. If a subpersonal-personal distinction is made out in part-whole terms, it will be a distinction between subjects of predication: it would be a mistake to think that such a distinction could provide the distinction which talk of 'levels' is supposed to record—between kinds of explanation.

Even those who do not aim for the distinction of levels of explanation, which Dennett originally wanted, must acknowledge that it is not enough to gesture towards the part-whole relation to say what is meant by 'subpersonal'. Or at least, if there is a subject called 'subpersonal *Psychology*', then invoking a part-whole relation will not be enough to mark it out. The reason for this is simply that there are parts of persons (kidneys, say) which usually have no relevance at all to people's psychological properties. It may be said that subpersonal accounts add up to an account of a person's *behaviour*, 'behaviour' being used to catch the missing idea that what is subpersonal bears specifically on the psychological. But when this is said, there is a danger of forgetting that there are accounts of human 'behaviour' which rely upon thinking of human beings as sentient and rationally motivated, and accounts of human 'behaviour' which do not rely upon this. (See Essay 7 on behaviour, where it is claimed that neurophysiology and propositional attitude psychology each has its own kind of complexity.)

A final way in which *parthood* can lead one astray in thinking about the subpersonal arises from the fact that there are two different notions of parthood which may be relevant. Speaking very broadly, one might distinguish between two sorts of subpersonal Psychology—the neuroscientific and the functional. Some scientists study what are literally, spatially, parts of people. A visual system, for instance, composed from the eye's retinae, optic nerve, and so on, can be investigated neurophysiologically; and knowing what goes on there can surely contribute to understanding people's capacity to see things. In the terms of the broad distinction, such investigation falls within *neuroscientific* subpersonal Psychology. But much of subpersonal Psychology pays no direct attention to what happens in the brain: there is a kind of relatively abstract theorizing, removed from any lower-level science such as neurophysiology. (Some Cognitive Psychologists say that neuroscience does not merit the title of 'Psychology'.) If one wants to account for the fact that people can recognize one another's faces (say), then one may consider how a device might be capable of discriminating one human face from another on the basis of the kind of information that can be present at the surface of the eyes. The device may be described computationally, so that something which ran through its procedures would be a simulation of a face-recognizer. We have here an example of a *functional* subpersonal Psychology. Now a kind of part-whole thinking comes into this, because the device will be described as having a certain internal organization; the various subtasks carried out when it operates must be so related to one another that different outputs of the device correspond to different faces. But in giving such an organized description, there is no need to think of the parts of the device, which carry out the subtasks, as having any necessary correspondence with actual volumes of matter, with bits of the brain in a person who can recognize faces. The transitions between states of the device are transitions between functionally characterized states, not between neural states. Of course it may be proposed that a human brain, or a part of it, is an actual implementation of a device studied in subpersonal Psychology; and then aspects of the brain's arrangement will be taken to mirror the device's organization. But one does not have to go in for any hypotheses about actual implementation in order to theorize fruitfully in the manner which leads to theories in Cognitive Psychology. So it would be wrong to think that the part-whole relation which comes naturally in Cognitive Psychology ensures that any subpersonal account is to be treated as an account of (literally) part of a person.[2]

Our brains are parts of us, of course. And some subpersonal Psychology is concerned directly with parts of persons. It may be an eventual goal of cognitive science to understand all subpersonal tasks in such a way that structures in brains can be seen to carry them out. In that case, we could think of the whole of a finished subpersonal Psychology as concerned with what are parts of persons. But it would engender an illusion to conflate the neuroscientist's notion of a part with the functionalist's proprietary organizational notion. The conflation would have the effect of making it seem that progress in subpersonal Cognitive Psychology counted as evidence for a micro-reductionist view of psychological subjects.

In philosophy of mind, Functionalism (with a capital 'F' now) is put forward as a doctrine about *commonsense* psychology. Functionalism tells us that (roughly) commonsense psychological states are to be understood in terms of the things that cause them or that they cause, so that states such as belief and desire are treated in the manner in which the states of a subpersonal Psychology are treated. The personal-subpersonal distinction then works differently from the distinction made here. My distinction is meant to show how subpersonal explanations can fittingly be kept apart from commonsense psychological ones. But when commonsense psychological states are treated by the Functionalist, psychological explanations at the personal level seem to be continuous with subpersonal ones; it comes to seem to be the purpose of subpersonal Psychology to explain over again the things commonsense psychology can be used to explain.

The fact that so much philosophy of mind is written by people of Functionalist persuasion can be an obstacle to keeping hold of a personal-subpersonal distinction such as naive naturalism recommends. But even without Functionalism, the study of subpersonal Cognitive Psychology itself can lead to kinds of thinking that go against the grain of such a distinction. I have already tried to show

how ill-considered play with the idea of 'part' gives rise to unwarranted ideas about the subpersonal. I shall conclude with consideration of two kinds of thinking that may be introduced by reflection on the practice of Psychologists.

First, there is some subpersonal Psychology which involves itself with states of great informational, or 'cognitive', sophistication. If such states can help us to understand how people are able to do things, then, it may be thought, *belief* and *desire* must receive similar treatment.

An example here would be an account of catching balls—something that children may learn to do at about the age of four. In personal-level terms, one watches the ball and adjusts one's position so that there should be a moment when one's hands can clasp the ball; one then clasps it. But how does one do that? By noting the ball's place at a particular time, keeping track of it, and moving one's legs and body at such a speed and in such a direction and manner that there can be a later time when a possible place for one's hands coincides with the ball's trajectory. We have already left behind anything that any four-year-old intentionally does. The calculations we have to envisage next, if we are to see a reliable method for a ball-catcher's hands' coming to be in the right place at the right time, will require a batch of formulae which effect correlations of motions of objects through air with motor signals issued, the computations all being updatable in a matter of milliseconds.

The transitions between states which we envisage in this example are intelligible to us insofar as we ourselves can calculate. But we do not postulate a person doing calculations when we imagine the calculations carried out as someone comes to catch a ball. A ball-catcher lacks any knowledge about balls' trajectories as these enter into calculations, whereas a person who does a calculation usually takes herself to know the result, and, at least roughly, how she obtained it. The ball-catcher in fact not only obviously does not, but actually cannot, do the calculations that figure in the subpersonal account: only those mathematicians who have learned the formulae know how to do them. We can understand how a person is able to catch balls by supposing that certain calculations are carried out. But they are carried out inside her; and not *by* her.

When students of subpersonal Psychology speak of states possessing kinds of content which obviously do not feature in our thought, we may not be much inclined to think that *our* states have these contents: it could not even sensibly be said that we (for instance) believed them. But when the Psychologists speak of states whose contents are of the right sort to be contents of states of ourselves, it is possible to forget that their concern is with the subpersonal level. And when the Psychologists go in for homuncular functionalism, treating the parts of a functionalist Cognitive Psychology as if they had beliefs or knowledge, it becomes easy to assimilate the subpersonal states to the states of sentient, rationally motivated subjects by reference to which they have to be understood. We have no difficulty in resisting the assimilation in the case of the ball-catcher: we simply remember that until very recently no one knew the formulae which those states concern. Once it is sufficiently appreciated that, as they figure in subpersonal Psychology, these are not states of people at all (even where they are modelled on states of people, and where one's grasp of them depends upon their coming to be one's own states) the different explanatory role for commonsense psychological states can be preserved.

Now for a second obstacle to retaining the idea of the subpersonal meant here. Sometimes it is impossible even to start to understand how a person could possess commonsense psychological properties unless one has a conception of her capacities which goes beyond the everyday conception of them brought to bear in commonsense psychology itself. We saw an example of this above, when ball-catching was redescribed in terms that would be hard for a four-year-old. But there are many other sorts of examples. Much of Experimental Psychology is concerned to discover more about what people can and can't do; and hypotheses in subpersonal Psychology may be based upon such discoveries. Realizing that the account of a person is developed as subpersonal Psychology moves forward, some people think that the subpersonal is introduced in order to fill out commonsense psychology and thereby legitimize its explanations.

Given that a commonsense psychological subject has properties of all the kinds we expect to be had by any inhabitant of the material world, and given that a subpersonal account shows how it can be that something has the various capacities without which nothing could be the sort of commonsense psychological subject that a person is, it is only to be expected that investigations in Experimental Psychology are needed if subpersonal Psychology is to proceed. But subpersonal accounts which are introduced to explain the results of investigations are not to be thought of as providing a new kind of understanding of that which commonsense psychology previously explained. The questions that laboratory Psychologists answer when they do the kinds of experiments that lead to subpersonal theories are not the questions which we can know the answers to by interacting, as commonsense psychological subjects, with others.[3] There is no need, then, to think of it as any part of subpersonal Psychology's job to recapitulate the explanations given in commonsense psychology.[4] Indeed, it is because the everyday *Why?*-questions which are answered using commonsense psychology require one to operate with a conception of a subject as rationally motivated as one is oneself that the accounts of subpersonal Psychology must be addressed to a different set of explananda.

10

Dennett's Naturalism

In 'Fodor's Guide to Mental Representations' (1985), Jerry Fodor presented a decision tree on which to locate various possible philosophical views about the propositional attitudes. Further branches could no doubt be added to it to accommodate views that have come onto the scene recently. But I have always taken exception to the choice which is supposed to be forced at the very first node of Fodor's tree. Fodor thinks that one must *either* treat the attitudes as states 'whose occurrences and interactions cause behaviour' and then adopt one or another view of them, *or* be irrealist about the attitudes. I refuse to allow that irrealism is the price of avoiding all the views Fodor outlines. The reason is that I reject the conception of mental states introduced by Fodor at the start (Essay 7, §7, Essay 8, §§3 and 7, Essay 9, §1), and I believe that a certain simple-minded realism is appropriate (see postscripts to Essay 2 and to Part 1).

Naive naturalism is the result of rejecting Fodor's conception of mental states and allowing a simple-minded realism to prevail. Here I hope to shed light both on naive naturalism and on Daniel Dennett's position in philosophy of mind, by contrasting the two. Dennett's position, unlike naive naturalism, had a place in Fodor's Guide. But it dropped out of the picture early on. For Fodor classified Dennett as a sort of irrealist—as an Instrumentalist. Instrumentalism, Fodor said, is a way of avoiding 'the hard questions about what the attitudes *are*' (p. 6). And he would surely say something similar about naive naturalism.

A response to Fodor may be made on Dennett's behalf, and on my own. The response is that an account of what the attitudes are is a personal-level account, to be given without broaching the questions which are 'hard' in Fodor's reckoning—questions about how a computational psychology may be conducted. The 'hard' questions are subpersonal, to be answered at their own level.

A genuine similarity between naive naturalism and the position of Dennett addressed by Fodor shows up in this response. But what about the difference between them? How should one explain the irrealist tendency in Dennett, which Fodor, in company with many others, finds so perplexing? I suggest that it is explained by Dennett's brand of *naturalism*. Adoption of naturalism of Fodor's non-naive sort leads Dennett to his kind of irrealism, because (like the naive naturalist) he finds the various naturalistic views that Fodor sketches to be out of keeping with their supposed subject matter.

Dennett's naturalism is implicit in his declared starting point, which is 'the objective, materialistic, third-person world of the physical sciences' (1987b, p. 5). Starting from here, one will find sentient rationally motivated beings who can think about themselves to be a suitable case for treatment. I argue below that the treatment accorded to them by Dennett is unsustainable. If that is right, then Dennett cannot go along with what he calls 'the orthodox choice today in the English-speaking world' (1987b, p. 5)—the choice which has been made already both at his starting point and at Fodor's (before the first node in Fodor's decision tree).

I shall begin by trying to show that the seeds of naive naturalism are to be found in Dennett's own writings. That will put me in a position to say why, it seems to me, these seeds must be allowed to grow, and why the 'objective materialistic third-person standpoint' which destroys them cannot be sustained. So the first part of what follows (§§1.1–1.3) is irenic: I touch on three areas in which I take Dennett to be on the side of naive naturalism. In the next part (§§2.1–2.2), Dennett and the naive naturalist part company over their different uses of the personal-subpersonal distinction. The argument against Dennett's treatment of persons comes in the third part (§§3.1–3.2), and I present its consequences in a final part (§§4.1–4.2). My aim here is not to give an overall unprejudiced review of Dennett's writing of the last twenty-five years. I consider his contribution selectively, hoping to show that naive naturalism survives when the untenable concessions to orthodox naturalism are retracted.

1.1

Within a certain (admittedly rather local) tradition, Dennett was the first to draw attention to the significance for philosophy of mind of the fact that persons are living things. We are biological creatures who would not exist but for an evolutionary process, of natural selection. This is the initial point on which Dennett's naturalism and naive naturalism agree.

It might be thought to need support to proclaim that we ourselves, psychologically constituted as we take ourselves to be, are contained in the natural world. But this has all the support it needs from a certain biological view of ourselves. Support for the thought that the world containing us is a *natural* one is got from the idea that the natural world is the actual home of natural selection, and that biology is one of the natural sciences. And support for the thought that persons specifically, as opposed to bits of matter comprising persons, are contained in such a natural world is got from the idea that whole organisms have been visible to natural selection: whole organisms, such as persons are, have been better or worse adapted and thus more or less likely to have left offspring.

Dennett himself favours a much more ambitious biologism than anything introduced by these points. He is attracted to the lofty perspective which Richard Dawkins adopts when he argues that genes, not organisms, are the units of natural selection; from this perspective, the organism has to be rediscovered. And Dennett believes in a version of adaptationism in biology which, if correct, would ensure that the scope of explanation from the design stance of biology extends well beyond what is admitted when a person is acknowledged to be a member of an evolved species. But these features of Dennett's view are not made compulsory by the idea that the rationally motivated subjects with which the philosophy of mind has been concerned are animals among others.[1]

1.2

A second affinity between Dennett and naive naturalism shows up in their shared opposition to Cartesianism. Dennett's anti-Cartesianism leads not only to his outright denial of Cartesian minds, but also to his less than thorough endorsement of certain other putative bits of mental ontology. Dennett's views are slippery here, because he doubts whether we should get steamed up about questions of ontology. (Where my arguments of Part I were meant to show that we should deny various ontological claims, Dennett thinks that it must be enough to refrain from asserting them.) Dennett used to represent himself as an eliminative materialist with respect to all so-called mental things (1979, p.xx); but he has come to countenance some such things, at least as products of an idealizing abstract method (1981).

In order to find an ontological point on which Dennett and the naive naturalist certainly agree, Dennett's eliminativist claims have to be seen as having arisen from his opposition to a certain Cartesian account of first-person knowledge. On that account, the knowledge a person has about herself mentally speaking is arrived at by a faculty deserving the name, literally, of introspection: a person who satisfies some mental predicate and who knows that she does has perceived some object within herself. The mental then may come to be thought of as constituted by tracts of inner objects onto which the owners of which can turn their attention. Insofar as Dennett's eliminativism was fuelled by rejection of Cartesianism of this sort, nothing revisionary is involved in taking his part. When Dennett described himself as an 'eliminative materialist', that might have suggested that he was someone who, save for his materialism, might have allowed talk of certain objects, which objects, however, his materialism leads him to banish. But if the account of self-knowledge that gives rise to the view of the mental as inner is in error, then the objects in question are only figments of a piece of misconstruction, so that there never was anything for the materialist to eliminate, and Dennett's anti-Cartesianism is not yet materialistic.

But this much anti-Cartesianism provides part of the explanation of why Dennett disowns the usual mental-physical *identities* that his fellow sophisticated naturalists have been so keen to endorse. Talking about ourselves as persons is not a matter of talking of objects that we find inside ourselves, which a materialistic account of our inner workings could be thought to talk about too, in different terms.

1.3

Of course many defenders of the contemporary naturalist faith will deny that objects introduced by a *Cartesian* view of first-person knowledge are the mental things that they identify materialistically: their candidates for identities are items supposedly recognized not when people introspect, but when they are seen to participate *causally* in the world. Dennett does not go along with them. And it is here that we come upon the article of orthodox naturalist faith that Dennett renounces. Whereas the modest biologism and the anti-Cartesianism that he shares with the naive naturalist are not often found contentious, what we find in Dennett now is, by the going standards, a piece of actual heresy.

The usual arguments for materialistic identities start out with some claim about a unitary causal world, which is physical, and in which mental things can have a place only as they coincide with physical things. According to the usual train of thought, if m which is mental caused p which is physical, then, since p, because physical, was caused by a physical thing, we must identify m with the physical, causing thing. It is often a part of this thinking that the real causal workings go on at the physical level, so that many materialists not only identify m with the physically described cause of p, but also make the claim that m's causal powers are those physical causal powers which are revealed in the identification. This additional claim can seem unexceptionable once a homogeneously materialistic causal world is assumed. But it is this which has given rise in the recent literature to the expression of a range of epiphenomenalist anxieties. The mental, we are told, may be inefficacious causally, strictly speaking, it having come to seem as though a mental state, as such, never really makes any difference to anything that happens. Where there is (say) the desire of a conscious subject, the real difference to what happens is made by the causal powers of this state, which, according to the materialistic story, is a physical power. No counterpart of practical rational motivation gets into their causal story.

Dennett will have none of this. Charged with epiphenomenalism, he responds that 'if one finds a predictive power [of a certain sort] one has *ipso facto* discovered a causal power'. When his opponents accuse him of epiphenomenalism, they have used a 'simplistic notion of causation', he says (1991b, n. 22, p. 43). The simplistic notion in question is just what is used by the materialistically minded to unify the mental and physical worlds. According to the simplistic notion, a real causal claim is made only if a genuine relation is asserted, so that where there is causation, there must be two items—cause and effect—each with a range of alternative descriptions that can be intersubstituted without affecting the truth of the asserted relation. Once such relations are in place, it is a relatively easy task to convince someone of mental-physical identities. And the versions of realism to which Dennett is opposed come into their own.

By refusing a simplistic notion of causation, one allows that there can be real instances of causality's operation without genuine relations obtaining between items. A statement of the form '*P* because *Q*' can, just as it stands, be a causal statement. Such a statement does not evidently make mention of any items: '*P*' and '*Q*' are replaced by sentences, each of them saying, perhaps, that a person had some or other property, one of them, perhaps, revealing her agency. Such a statement may provide an explanation, and it can record a causal power of a person. Dennett uses the example of a sign saying 'Free Lunch' (1991b, p. 44). The sign may induce people to form a queue. It appears obvious that the level at which materialistic accounts of causal processes are given is not the level at which to understand such a causal power of such a sign. As with the sign, so with the fact of someone's noticing it, or of someone's saying what it means, or of someone's wanting to have lunch and preferring a free one. Suppose that we can understand why Jane turned away from the sign by mentioning that Jane had often been told that there's no such thing as a free lunch. We may then think of a property of Jane as relevant (causally) to her reaction. But only if we bring the simplistic notion of causation to bear will we feel any need to treat Jane's thinking that there's no such thing as a free lunch as an item (usually called a belief) which is related to another item—Jane's turning away—such that someone with no interest whatever in Jane might latch onto these items.

To see that commonsense psychology itself introduces no such items, we have to attend to that subject itself, not to what philosophers typically say about it. And Dennett has offered a wide range of considerations to help us get away from thinking that someone's believing something is actually treated as a matter of the presence within her of an individually causally potent state. There is, then, no need to demonstrate that commonsense psychological explanations are in good order causally. Like the naive naturalist, Dennett takes those causal claims which yield understanding of people to be at least as firmly grounded as the simplistic notion of causation. The simplistic notion is what his fellow naturalists use sometimes to try to vindicate the explanations, sometimes to show us that we should be rid of them.

2.1

From both Dennett's position and the naive naturalist's, one can see persons as biologically recognizable things (1.1). Both positions emphasize the need to avoid the errors of Cartesianism (1.2). And both take causal explanations at face value, refusing to reconstruct them so that a simplistic notion of causation may be deployed (1.3). These pieces can be assembled to provide a coherent view of sentient, rationally motivated beings—a view which, in order to remain with Dennett, one may state 'third-personally'. It goes as follows. There are biological beings of whom certain psychological predications can be made. Such predications introduce no special realm of things, but they enable special sorts of explanations to be given. These explanations give causal understanding in saying why such a being had one or another property, but they do not require there to be items participating in causal relations of their own.

No materialistic properties of persons are introduced here: the presence of mind or mentality in the world consists in the presence there of certain natural beings, acted upon, and acting, and thus with certain intelligible properties. But although there is no materialism about persons, there need be nothing anti-materialist. Persons are composed entirely from matter, and are surrounded by things likewise composed; no doubt persons would not have the properties they do unless the various bits of matter that make them up had some of the properties that they do. Materialistic accounts can surely be given of all the collections of bits of matter that persons are made up of; and we know that inside people there are structures and their states participating in causal relations of their own.

Such a combination of non-materialism about persons and non-anti-materialism about their constitution cries out for the distinction Dennett made between personal and subpersonal levels of explanation. This is how he first introduced it in *Content and Consciousness:*

> When we've said that a person's in pain, that she knows which bit of her hurts and that this is what's made her react in a certain way, we've said all that there is to say within the scope of the personal vocabulary. We CAN demand further explanation of how a person happens to withdraw her hand from the hot stove, but we cannot demand further explanations in terms of "mental processes". If we look for alternative modes of explanation, we must abandon the explanatory level of people and their sensations and activities and turn to the subpersonal level of brains and events in the nervous system. But when we abandon the personal level in a very real sense we abandon the subject matter of pains as well. (1969, p. 93)

'The subject matter of pains' can only mean the facts about people's being in pain. For, as we have seen, if pains are supposed to be introspectible items, then Dennett's anti-Cartesianism forbids him to think that there are pains at any level; and Dennett rejects *states* of pain except insofar as these may be thought to enter into explanation of a certain sort. Part of the reason we must abandon the personal level when we turn to saying how a hand happened to move is that a person's feeling pain is not identifiable over again at the level at which anything *happens* to move.

If the motive for introducing the personal level was to ensure that psychological predications are true of beings in the natural world which lend themselves to a distinctive kind of explanatory account, then the items imported with a simplistic notion of causation will seem now to have something in common with the objects invented by a Cartesian story about first-person knowledge. For things of both sorts are supposed to be capable of a self-standing conception, so that they can be thought about at a different level from that at which a person is interpreted. Cartesian pains ('objects' here) are what something is alleged to stand in relation to when there is introspection and a pain is discovered; whereas materialistic pains ('items' here) are allegedly there for finding from a scientist's impersonal point of view. So neither the Cartesian pains nor the materialistic pains will be admissible if the personal level is correctly thought of as a level at which common-sense psychological subjects, which are whole persons, are not only present but ineliminable. Dennett himself used to speak of problems that are common to dualists and certain materialists. On this reading of his early work, it seems that the key to a solution is to provide for the autonomy of a kind of explanation at the personal level. That is what enables us to see that a mental life is not constituted of inner happenings, neither of objects recognized by an individual mind nor of items accessible to an arbitrary scientist. A mental life consists, rather, of a person's being some way, then, intelligibly, some others.

What goes for the subject matter of pain goes for the subject matter of the intentional states. For just as a certain sort of biological being is something that may understandably move its hand because it feels pain, so it may understandably move its hand because that is a good way to do something it has a reason to do. Those who introduce so-called beliefs and desires at this point are moved by the consideration about causation, which leads them to treat questions about the understanding of people in the world as questions about putative 'token states'. We foreclose on all of these questions when we take a different view of causation, and attribute to the personal level the degree of autonomy which Dennett's distinction seems to accord to it. Persons are what are understandable as avoiding pain, reaching conclusions, acting on reasons. The things at this level are not indifferently identifiable, but things (if these are things) such as 'a's having a toothache', 'b's thinking that p' or 'c's trying to ϕ'. None of these can be latched onto otherwise than by taking account of how it is with a or b or c.

2.2

This attitude to the personal-subpersonal distinction leaves out of account Dennett's choice of orthodox naturalism. A different attitude, now influenced by that choice, perhaps, shows up in what Dennett wrote ten years later, when he said: 'Sub-personal theories proceed by analyzing a person into an organization of sub-systems . . . and attempting to explain the behaviour of the whole person as the outcome of the interaction of these sub-systems' (1978, at p. 153 in 1979). Dennett appears to have changed his mind. For that which was to have been accounted for only at the personal level is now to be seen as explained by a combination of accounts given at the subpersonal level. Personal-level subject matter is to be reconstructed when subpersonal psychology is pursued. And we can no longer think that 'when we abandon the personal level . . . we abandon the subject matter of [commonsense psychology] as well'.

Dennett seems to have come to allow that subpersonal psychology can approach those 'hard questions' which Fodor thought of him as avoiding.[2] But whatever exactly the change of mind that this quotation records, Dennett still does not line up with those philosophers who take the subpersonal level to be the level at which the real truth about the aetiology of personal-level behaviour is uncovered. For Dennett's view of those subpersonal theories which analyze persons into systems is no less instrumentalist, no more realist, than his view of commonsense psychology itself. Dennett thinks that a student of subpersonal systems has to take a certain stance. This is the intentional stance, from which commonsense psychology and subpersonal psychology alike proceed. In accepting what we learn from the intentional stance, we provide ourselves with predictions that we can confirm, but we add nothing to knowledge which can be got from the best starting point.[3] Statements made from the intentional stance can be treated as 'true only if we exempt them from a certain familiar standard of literality' (1987b, p. 72).

Seeing the irrealist strand in Dennett running through the subpersonal and personal levels exposes two features of his position. First, Dennett does not regard the personal level as explanatorily autonomous. But, second, the continuity between the two levels that he sees is not the product of a quest for 'realism' such as may be instigated by the 'naturalizers'. The first of these points puts Dennett in opposition to naive naturalism; the second, on the face of it, puts him in opposition to orthodox naturalism. So how is Dennett led to his position?

Well, if one sticks to 'the objective, materialistic, third-person world of the physical sciences', as orthodox naturalists do, but if, like Dennett, one refuses to introduce a simplistic notion of causation in order to accommodate personal-level psychological explanation, then explanation which makes use of commonsense psychological categories is bound to strike one as aberrant. There has to be some accounting of it. An intentional systems account of it will seem to have the merit of requiring no very great departure from the standpoint of the physical sciences. For when persons are looked on as intentional systems, they are thought of as one among a great number of sorts of systems towards whose behaviour a certain attitude enables prediction. It is true that such an account of persons may not be very 'materialistic'; but it can at least be a view as 'objective and third-personal' as the view which is taken towards a thing that may be treated as an intentional system.

An intentional system is defined as something to which intentional states can predictively be attributed, something towards which a certain stance is useful. Subpersonal systems, animals of all sorts, and even thermostats, are intentional systems in Dennett's sense. What I shall argue now, against Dennett, is that the objective and third-personal character of the intentional stance cannot be preserved in the case where the system towards such a stance is taken is a person.

3.1

Dennett thinks that the success of the predictions made when something is treated as if it had intentional states relies upon finding patterns, on seeing what order there is out there. The relevant patterns are discernible in systems' behaviour subjected to 'radical interpretation' (1991b).

Now given Dennett's starting point, one might suppose that Dennett would want the patterns discerned from the intentional stance to be imposed onto what is brutely materialistically there—onto displacements of matter, say. But it is surely utterly incredible that distinctive patterns of displacements of matter could be associated with particular beliefs or desires of people.[4] It is fairly incredible that beliefs and desires might be associated even with distinctive patterns of locomotion and vocalization corresponding to the things that people do and say—to commonsensically conceptualized *kinds* of locomotions and vocalizations. Even this is fairly incredible, because we know that for almost anything a person might believe, endlessly many things that might be done could be revelatory of someone's believing it; and that for almost anything a person might do, endlessly many beliefs are such that having them might be revealed in someone's doing the thing.

In order to avoid the utterly incredible idea (of beliefs as patterns among what is materialistically there), it must be allowed that discerning the patterns associated with a system's being in some intentional state is part of the project of discerning patterns in the world in which the system behaves. The patterns imposed in taking the intentional stance enable one to see, for instance, what leads to what when a system does something, so that what are evident from the intentional stance will not be raw data, but such locomotions and vocalizations as have relevance to interpretation. This means that in taking the intentional stance, one has to exercise all those concepts that are attributed to a system towards which the stance is taken.

Think now about the *taker* of the intentional stance. And assume that the system it looks onto is found where we should say a person is. Consider that the stance taker must then operate with all those concepts that figure in contentful ascriptions to a person, and that it has somehow acquired the concepts of belief and desire.[5] We can raise the question whether the stance taker is in a position to ascribe to itself those intentional concepts that it has learned to ascribe to others. These are concepts which, if it is doing at all well, it will treat those others as seeming to ascribe to *them*-selves. But what about it? Does it know what it thinks—what it *itself* thinks, that is? The answer appears to be *Yes*. For how could there be something able to interpret people as doing the things that they interpret one another as doing, which fully understands 'believes' and 'desires', which knows what it is for those others to use 'believe' and 'desire' in self-ascription, and yet which has no conception of itself?

It is not meant to be the conclusion of these considerations that *any* use of an intentional concept from the intentional stance requires the ascription of that concept to the stance taker. If the argument were meant to have application whatever sort of system the stance was taken towards, then it would have no plausibility. But the considerations are meant to suggest that a genuinely first-personal view is assured for something that is in a position to recognize the intentional states of people. It would miss the point to suggest that a stance taker which applies the concept of belief to itself has simply turned the stance towards where it is, rather than towards something out there. The considerations do not invite us to find it incredible that something taking the intentional stance towards persons might fail to notice that it, too, was a case of something that it might set about observing—as if, having a view, it might then be drawn into noticing its behaviour to see whether it could fathom what its view was. What is meant to seem incredible is that there should be something capable of taking a view of the world, of recognizing another person's actions in the world, of using the concept of belief, yet not in a position to have such a thought as 'I believe that *p*'.

Dennett sometimes responds to critics who stress the *explanatoriness* of intentional concepts, and say that Dennett exaggerates their predictiveness. His answer is that we tend not fully to appreciate the predictive value of the intentional stance, because we rely on it continually and unreflectively. But the answer fails to speak to the real source of the critics' disquiet, which is surely the fact that the intentional concepts can be illuminatingly applied to oneself. Towards oneself, of course, one's point of view is not that of a stance-taking predictor: one does not have to set about finding patterns in those of one's own locomotions and vocalizations that others may be taken to observe.

3.2

From the naive naturalist's standpoint, it was only to be expected that first-personal points of view are introduced along with a third-personal one. The category of persons is a category of natural beings, and it is characteristic of some of the predicates that characteristically apply to such beings that they can be both self-ascribed and other-ascribed. The predicate 'believes' is a P-predicate in Strawson's sense: it is 'unambiguously and adequately ascribable *both* on the basis of observation of the subject *and* not on this basis'; 'to learn the use [of a P-predicate] is to learn both aspects of [its] use' (1959, pp. 109 and 110).

Once a class of P-predicates is recognized, it must be counted a mistake to postulate something which can use a concept like belief in relation to persons, but which lacks any capacity to ascribe the concept to itself. Our reluctance to make this mistake is what I hoped to rely on to persuade you that, in trying to tell the story of an interpretable intentional system in Dennett's way, we come upon a first-person view.

Granting that first-person thought is present where beings of a certain sort are interpretable, we shall find a Cartesian conception of such thought inappropriate. And indeed, Strawson's account of P-predicates was designed to steer clear of the Cartesianism that we saw Dennett anxious to avoid. If Dennett rejects Strawson's account, then it is because he is not similarly anxious to avoid the behaviourism that it was designed also to steer clear of. It is true that Dennett allowed that the deliverances of an intentional stance may be taken at face value and need not be made 'materialistic'. But when he introduced the intentional stance, he wanted to show how certain of the commonsense psychological predicates could have application from the 'objective, third-person' standpoint from which behaving things are on view. His attempted substitution for persons of mere behaving beings must now be counted a sort of behaviourism—the sort that is evidently untenable when the intentional state concepts that *a* applies to *b* are seen to get no purchase until there is the possibility of *a*'s applying them to him or herself.

There should never have been supposed to be any need to make intentional systems serve as surrogates for persons. When persons are accepted in the spirit of naive naturalism, there is no call to reconstruct a position from which the P-predicates might have been introduced. Dennett's instrumentalism can then be seen to be unmotivated (4.1), and we may take a different attitude from his to consciousness (4.2).

4.1

For Dennett, the point of treating persons as intentional systems was to acknowledge the impossibility of accommodating the propositional attitude states in a homogeneously materialistic causal world, while continuing to view the beings in those states from the perspective of something that might be a part of that world. Possession of the propositional attitude states came to be regarded as a matter of the success of a certain stance—the stance taken when the patterns which attributions of those states are based on were discerned. We were to think of the property of (say) *being a believer* as grounded in the property of *being interpretable as a believer*. This is Dennett's instrumentalism: it is appropriate to treat persons *as if* they had intentional states, but only as if.

Now if we can imagine a creature possessing the property of *being interpretable as a believer* only as the intentional stance is taken, but if, in imagining the stance taken, we must already have introduced something entitled to say what it believes, then we can no longer suppose that it is *only* because people are interpretable as believing things that they do believe things. An intentional stance taker capable of making sense of persons has beliefs. Its believing something can be a reason for it to believe some other thing, and its endorsing certain considerations can be a reason for it to do something. Finding commonsense psychological language explanatory, it sees reason at work in others; but if it were only as if it saw reason at work, and it were not itself moved by reason, then we could never have imagined it taking its stance in the first place.

When they are human beings towards which the intentional stance is taken, it has to be accepted that it is not *only* as if they had intentional states. The autonomy of personal-level explanation is then assured. And persons' intentionality having been recognized as underived (as 'original', or literal, or real) stories can then be told of intentional systems of other sorts than persons which show the derivativeness of *their* 'intentionality'. The possibility of taking an intentional stance towards thermostats and other such things may be explained by the fact that these are persons' artifacts. The possibility of taking the intentional stance towards subpersonal systems may be explained by the fact that it can cast light on human beings' possession of commonsense psychological properties to suppose that there are clever-seeming mechanisms inside them. (Instrumentalist thinking can then be quite appropriate at the subpersonal level.) The possibility of taking the intentional stance towards non-human animals may be explained by the fact that it is, as Darwin taught, as if they had been designed.[6] In all of these cases, then, it may be *as if* there were intentional states.

Dennett wants us to think that finding something intelligible as a rationally motivated being is a condition of finding a being that is rationally motivated. To this there need be no objection. But if the existence of a rationally motivated being (rather than just a discerner of patterns among locomotions and vocalizations) is a condition of the relevant sort of intelligibility, then no instrumentalist consequences can follow. Dennett's concession to naive naturalism not only rules out naturalism of the orthodox sort; it removes the grounds of his irrealism.[7]

4.2

When the intentional stance is taken towards a person, we have the view of a being which has a basis for ascribing P-predicates to itself otherwise than by observation of itself. This is a conscious being. Strawson introduced the P-predicates as those which 'imply the possession of consciousness in that to which they are ascribed' (p. 107). Consciousness is introduced, then, as we think of something which takes the intentional stance towards persons.[8]

Consciousness may seem to have been stolen in. But Dennett himself is friendly to the idea that we need not work very hard to ensure that we are treating conscious beings. Dennett has no sympathy for the fiction of the philosophers' zombie: he thinks that we deceive ourselves if we suppose that we can imagine something with all the manifest properties of a human being, which yet lacks consciousness. My claim has been that we deceive ourselves if we suppose that we can imagine something exercising all the intentional state concepts of persons, which yet lacks any capacity for first-personal ascription.

If consciousness enters the picture at the same time as the intentional stance towards a person, there can be no need for the divide-and-conquer strategy that Dennett favours. 'First content, then consciousness', as he puts it (1991a, p. 457). 'Content' is Dennett's label for all the facts about people's being thinking, acting beings, which are supposed to be relatively tractable; consciousness is to be accounted for after they have been dealt with. The notion of an intentional system, then, is the basis for the first stage of Dennett's overall account of commonsense psychology; at the second stage, with content on the scene, one goes on to say why it should be reasonable to suppose that these beings, in contentful states, should seem to think that there are conscious states which they are apt to call their own.

Consciousness is commonly treated as if it were some super-added phenomenon of mind, deserving of separate accounting in contemporary philosophy of mind (see Essay 1). Many philosophers are brought to treat it so by their acceptance of states of mind that might have been encountered otherwise than through encountering a person. If no person is in view when a question about consciousness is raised, then a conscious state cannot be reckoned a particular sort of state of a conscious being; instead, consciousness has to characterize the putative internal items that are brought in through consideration of causation. Dennett, I have said, rejects the items. But Dennett can seem sometimes to forgo the anti-materialistic features of his view of persons. For he thinks that we can understand consciousness to the extent that we can account for the productions of fictional texts describing heterophenomenological worlds. And what brings the process of understanding to a conclusion, as I understand him, is an identification—albeit a strained identification—of neural events with causes of such productions (1991a). To this extent, Dennett strives to locate consciousness at the inside, by introducing internal items such as might have been supposed to have been got rid of when a simplistic notion of causation was repudiated.

At any rate, the personal-subpersonal distinction plays hardly any part in Dennett's latest work. When Dennett's original distinction between levels was admitted, we were encouraged to see consciousness in the natural world where persons are—not as a phenomenon *sui generis*, but as a property of certain beings and their states. Viewing it in this way, we do not suppose that consciousness might be understood otherwise than by relying on the fact that we ourselves are conscious beings. Philosophers who think that consciousness might be explained from some different perspective from our own usually try to locate it at the level of people's materialistic innards—as Dennett (sort of) does—[9]; or they tell us that it is quite mysterious.

Sometimes philosophers incite us to puzzle over the mysteries of consciousness by invoking a distinction between subjective and objective which is meant to cut across the personal level[10]—rather as Dennett seems sometimes to want to find at the personal level both the meaningful behaviour with which beliefs can be associated *and* some more materialistic data. Theirs is another attempt to introduce the orthodox naturalist's conceptions at a level at which, according to a naive naturalist, they can have no application. However this may be, Dennett told us that his own accounts would provide a way of avoiding the mysteries (1987b, p. 6). What naive naturalism offers is an alternative way of avoiding them, to which certain features of Dennett's early views are crucial.

11

Causation in Intuitive Physics and in Commonsense Psychology

A contrast is sometimes made in developmental psychology, in thinking about children's development of causal concepts and their acquisition of a so-called theory of mind—a contrast between causation in intuitive physics and causation in psychology.[1] To this can be added another contrast—between causation outside science (everyday causation) and causation in science.

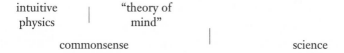

I shall take it for granted that people operate with causal concepts in the areas of intuitive physics, commonsense psychology, and science. The question I want to raise concerns which of these three areas we should expect to go together with one another if we are drawing metaphysically significant boundaries. My suggestion is that causal concepts are to be seen as doing the same job whether the subject matter is intuitive physical or commonsense psychological, so that one important boundary brings together these two everyday subject matters.

I can explain why this idea is worth encouraging, by looking at a quotation from Davidson: 'Cause is the cement of the universe; the concept of cause is what holds together our picture of the universe, a picture that would otherwise disintegrate into a diptych of the mental and the physical' (1980, p. 7). This might be understood in two ways. On the first interpretation, 'our picture of the universe' means simply the world that is present to us when we take an ordinary perspective on the things we interact with every day. Many of the things we interact with are unquestionably *physical* things. So the claim about cement can be the claim that there are causal pathways connecting us, psychological beings who perceive things and do things intentionally, with the things we perceive and which we intentionally act on. A different interpretation is promoted by those who think that an ordinary perspective disposes us to dualism, and has to be replaced. On this other interpretation, 'our picture of the universe' means something got by stepping back from our view of the world with which we ordinarily interact. The claim about cement is then the claim that causation enables us (human beings) to be stuck into a universalistic picture. We are to come to see ourselves inside a physical universe in which we might never have existed, by realizing that bits of cranial matter composing us interact causally with other bits of matter inside just such a universe.

What I shall defend is the idea that the everyday physical and the everyday mental are equally parts of a single causal world view. This is to interpret 'picture of the universe' in the Davidson quotation in the first, worldly way. The idea may seem rather obvious. If it is worth defending even if it is obvious, that is because it contrasts with the idea got when 'picture of the universe' is given the other, universalistic interpretation. Perhaps this other idea can be made to seem less attractive in contrast with the real attractions of the idea I want to encourage. At any rate, I hope not only to promote the idea of the mind as not needing integration into an intuitive physical world, but also to demote the idea of the mind as needing to be integrated into a scientifically conceived universe. I consider both the relation between commonsense psychology and intuitive physics (§1) and the relation between science and each of these things (§2).

1

In taking it for granted that people operate with causal concepts in the areas of intuitive physics, folk psychology, and science, one takes it for granted that there are causal dependencies between us as psychological beings on the one hand and non-psychological things on the other hand. So, for instance, when someone sees particular objects because they are there outside the window through which her gaze is directed, one thing (her seeing what she does) depends causally on another (the presence there of those objects). Again, when someone's hand moves her teacup towards her mouth because she wants to take in some tea, one thing (a motion of her hand) depends causally on another (the fact of her wanting some tea).

This has been denied, and not only by the scientifically minded. Some philosophers influenced by Wittgenstein, recognizing that a distinctive sort of explanation is offered when psychological terms are used, have wanted to distinguish between causal explanation and another sort which they say is non-causal—namely, rational explanation. Nowadays, relatively few people are persuaded of this view. But it may have an unfortunate influence nevertheless. These philosophers never denied that rational explanation is explanation, only that it is causal. And it can then seem as though in order to make allowance for their view, in order to say what the difference is between them and us (who do think that rational explanation is causal), we need to discover a kind of causal truth which they deny but we accept. This leads to the idea that associated with each rational explanation is, as it were, some purely causal truth. So in place of the thesis that rational explanation is a species of causal explanation, we are enticed into thinking that rational explanation has to go hand in hand with a certain sort of causal truth—that alongside any rational explanation there is a causal statement which is not itself a familiar explanatory statement at all (see Essay 8, §2). Except for this philosophical current, we might find it obvious that rational explanations simply are causal ones just as they stand.

When one takes a developmental perspective, the view of rational explanations as themselves causal explanations can be made to seem not so much obvious as inevitable. Developmental psychologists have been concerned both with how a child comes by a conception of a coherent, more or less predictable physical world, and with how a child comes by a theory of mind (as they say). Their empirical work deals with these two areas separately. And there is surely something right and important about thinking of two separable skills that the child has to learn. Thinking in this way, one acknowledges that rational explanation is a distinctive sort of explanation. A child's coming to see that there are people, and that she is a person among others, is not to be assimilated to a child's getting to see that there are televisions (say) and that these are machines among others. A child who comes to know that people think things and do things, and that they may think things that aren't true and do things for reasons, has not learned about any old sort of entity present in the spatiotemporal world where things interact causally. This is what makes possession of a theory of mind a skill in its own right. The skill is autonomous insofar as it requires mastery of concepts which apply to people, and insofar as these concepts form an interconnected group. The special group of concepts are those that are learned in acquiring a conception of a conscious being motivated by reasons.

But the fact that 'a theory of mind' provides a separate skill from the skill of the intuitive physicist does not mean that there is any special sort of causal dependency that has to be learned about in acquiring one skill and not the other. On the face of it, we find the same 'because' in 'The window broke because the stone hit it', and in 'He left because what you said was upsetting' or 'Mary didn't find the tea because she thought it was in the other cupboard'. On the face of it, then, the child's coming to know (for instance) that someone's false belief can explain something she did need not involve the child in latching onto some new sort of causal relation. Of course, we have not only the word 'because': there are numerous causative verbs whose understanding cannot be freed from a conception of causal dependence; and there are, as well as 'because', all of the words 'causes', 'result', 'by', 'effect', 'consequently', which record dependencies, often of a causal kind. We might attempt to categorize the various species of relation that our understanding of all these causal terms involves. And if we did, we might discover that some of those species were used specifically in contexts where rational explanations were given, so that they could not be grasped in the acquisition of the skill of the intuitive physicist. But even if it were true (which seems doubtful) that some of our causal conceptions were got in learning 'the theory of mind' and could not be learned in learning intuitive physics, that would not interfere with the thought that a single notion of causal dependency has application both in the rational and in the intuitive physical realm.

One thing the child may come to grasp, for instance, is that whether or not Mary thinks some particular thing may make all the difference to what Mary does. From the point of view of the causal notions involved, there is no reason this fact should be any more difficult to grasp than that whether or not a balloon is filled with a light gas may make all the difference to what happens to it when you let go of it. Of course there is a kind of understanding that we gain when we learn why Mary went in through the back door which we don't gain when we learn why the balloon rose. But this is no obstacle to thinking that in both cases having an explanation requires recognizing a causal dependency.

Perhaps the best way to see that there is (to put it loosely) only one sort of causal dependence at issue in the commonsense world— whether psychological or physical—is to consider cases where psychological and physical explanation go hand in hand. Suppose that Jane's pressing a button causally depends on her wanting to watch BBC1. And suppose that the television's coming to be tuned to BBC1 causally depends on this button's being depressed. These two facts about causal dependence—the first psychophysical, the second intuitive physical—can be combined, in a perfectly natural way. When combined they ensure (in the most usual case, other things being equal) that Jane intentionally switched the channel. The example suggests that it is not appropriate to speak of physical causation and psychological causation: the simplest explanation of why we find transitivity is that there is, as it were, only one sort of causation at work.

Here Jane's believing in a certain external causal dependency is something upon which both the realization of that very dependency and Jane's getting what she wants depends. In understanding Jane, we have to recognize the causal connexion between the TV channels and the buttons, as well as her belief about that causal connexion. This is just an example of a central feature of the application of propositional attitudes. We advert to how the world may be in saying how people's minds are. The propositions that are the contents of the attitudes that are attributed to people are understood and evaluated by those who attribute them. Thus: you are not in a position to know that someone thinks that p unless you know what it would be for it to be the case that p. And you won't usually be in a position to think that someone did something because she believed that p without taking a view yourself of whether or not it is the case that p. It is no wonder that the theory of mind (which describes people as thinking things and wanting things) is inextricable from the theory of the world about which they think things and in which they want things. When the child gradually grasps increasingly complex causal concepts, it is part both of an increasing understanding of her environment and of an increasing understanding of how she herself and the people around her relate (through the psychological facts about them) to that environment.

This leaves out language. But of course the use of language must be on the scene here implicitly. However much the child is an experimenter, and to whatever extent her own interactions with objects are a condition of her learning of some dependencies, knowledge of how things work must in large part be got through her being *told* things. If we take account of the fact that the child's gradually emerging conceptions both of people and of the quotidian physical world that people live in go hand in hand with her gradual acquisition of language, then the actual interconnectedness of the two kinds of understanding will be re-emphasized. As language is mastered, the child recognizes people not only as beings whose properties causally depend upon the world and upon whose properties local bits of the world to some extent depend, but also as sources of knowledge of that world. They are such sources because of dependencies in their turn—now dependencies (in both directions) between thinkings of thoughts and audible expressions of them. Hearing someone say that p can serve just as well as a way of getting to know that p as taking steps to observe the world to determine whether p (and usually it is much quicker). Social interaction, then, is quite on a par with looking and seeing, and moving things about, as a way of adding to a developing conception of how things are.

By now it should be clear that the presence in the causal world of both the mental and the physical is a condition of that world's being something of which the human infant gains a picture. We can return to the Davidson quotation at this point, and ask: How could there be a threat of the picture of the world falling apart into a diptych of the mental and the physical? What we have all acquired is precisely a unified picture. The cement of causation can hardly be needed to stick two pictures together if our understanding of causality straddles the two pictures, and if neither picture is one that we would have come by unless it were already a part of the other.

These considerations might give some comfort to someone accustomed to problematizing the mind in the usual way. When we are being brought to raise questions in the philosophy of mind, we turn our attention to commonsense psychology and latch onto something treated as a self-contained subject matter about whose status questions have to be asked. It is easily forgotten that we never learned to operate with this subject matter in independence from everything else we have learned, so that we come to entertain the thought that we could be wrong about this, but be right about everything else.

Nothing here speaks to the universalistic interpretation of the Davidson quotation, however. Any reassurance got from appreciating how everyday psychology is caught up with other things which we take quite for granted depends upon thinking that it is admissible to interpret 'the universe' in the Davidson quotation in the first, worldly way. And if the second, universalistic picture does not go away, then it will not be enough to seek comfort in the worldly one. It may help, then, to see that everyday psychology is not the only subject matter that may be supposed to need to be brought into relation with serious science. So I turn to the relations to science of both intuitive physics and everyday psychology.

2

In the 1920s, a debate was started which might, retrospectively, be called a debate about the status of intuitive physics. Those on one side of the debate pointed out that atomic theory tells us that where there is a table, there is really a cloud of particles containing more space than matter. They allowed that we think of the table as solid, but said that given that nothing is really solid, we should recognize that there is no table. More generally, they might have said: since the truths we accept about the macrophysical world are incompatible with truths that physical scientists have discovered, we must take them to be false. Their attitude to the everyday physical world was a sort of counterpart to the more recent doctrine of neuroscientific eliminativism, which tells us that commonsense psychology is false.

The debate about tables has subsided, and the question whether people can really believe anything has come to seem much more pressing than the question whether there really are tables. But in fact, if either question—about everyday psychological facts, and about everyday physical facts—were really a pressing question, then the other could be made to seem to be so too. A proposal to eliminate tables (and so on) and a proposal to eliminate commonsense psychological subjects may receive the same sort of defense, and they are vulnerable to simultaneous attack. The interconnexions we have seen between our views of ourselves and our views of the intuitively physical world that we inhabit suggest that they stand or fall together.

If there really were a need to extract 'purely causal' truths from any causal explanation, then everyday physical causal explanations using 'because', as well as the rational ones, would be found wanting. Whatever cement might be thought to be needed 'to prevent our picture of the universe disintegrating into a diptych' would then be needed also to keep the physical part of it intact. Certainly there are special features of rational causal explanation which have made those explanations seem to be in special need of reconstruction.[2] But it is not as though everyday physical causal explanations presented us with the sort of 'purely causal truths' to which all causal explanation is sometimes supposed to aspire.[3] It may be difficult then to argue that commonsense psychology is rotten, but to take an everyday account of the physical world to be in good order.

In fact, it would require a quite extraordinary narrowness of vision to convict intuitive physics and 'theory of mind' of gross error, one at a time. Given that the propositions that characterize people's states of mind are understood and evaluated by those who use the 'theory of mind', a child's acquisition of usable concepts for describing 'physical things' and for describing people must be thought of as proceeding in parallel. If one has learned nothing in just one of the two areas, when did one go wrong?

Those who urged us to deny the existence of tables presumably thought that all phenomena are intelligible by reference to the best scientific theory. And it is no doubt part of the reason the debate about tables has subsided that physicists, seeking overall theories with the greatest depth, have come to abandon the idea that atomic physics might be a 'Theory of Everything'. The more progress is made in fundamental physics, the less bearing it seems to have on the kinds of everyday physical explanations that are regularly caught up with those given in 'theory of mind'. Certainly the explanations that physicists provide are broad as well as deep; but their breadth, we may now think, has more to do with their touching the outer reaches of the universe than with their covering the same ground as everyday explanations.

The development of physics reminds us of the diversity of explanations even within science. The molecular theory of matter is often held up as an example of a scientific theory which made many macrophysical phenomena intelligible. But there are many things about the ordinary interactions of ordinary objects which are fully intelligible without resort to thinking about their composition. And the scope for casting light at all directly on ordinary things by thinking about their invisible parts' interactions is rather limited.

When it is acknowledged that science is not designed to explain ordinary macrophysical phenomena over again, there is an easy answer to the atomic physicist who didn't believe in tables. The standpoint from which atoms are studied is not one from which to legislate tables out of existence, because it is not one from which to talk about *tables* at all. The atomic physicist changed the subject when he spoke of the particles composing tables: he failed to bring the concept *table* to bear when he said that nothing in a certain region was solid. Now given that common sense recommends a world view with physical and psychological elements, the neuroscientific eliminativist about everyday psychology may perhaps receive the same sort of answer. The standpoint from which neuroscience proceeds is not one from which to legislate against the 'theory of mind', because it is not one from which rationally motivated subjects can be talked about at all. The neuroscientist changes the subject when he speaks of states of the brain: he fails to bring a concept of *person* to bear when he says that commonsense psychology merits elimination.

There are of course important differences between the two cases. In the psychological case, there are introspective ways of thinking. These may distract us from the unified outlook which reflection on some simple empirical facts about children's development can help us to retain. (Distinctively philosophical ways of thinking may be an even worse distraction.) And in the psychological case, the everyday facts about ourselves are facts which we think that science must in some sense account for. We may want to know, for instance, how people's possession of visual systems makes it possible for them to become informed of the particular features of their environment which they can learn about when they keep their eyes open; and knowledge of the structure and workings of our visual systems may show how this is possible. In the case of the table, although we take it for granted that there is an account of the microscopic, ordinarily unobserved particles which are present where the table is, we do not think that this scientific account is to be arrived at by raising questions about how it can be that the table has its observable properties. (In the case of artifacts more complicated than tables, knowledge of internal workings may well cast light on observable properties; but the questions about how these artifacts can possibly have their observable properties does not arise, because knowledge of the answer was required for their creation.)

The difference between the project of neuroscience in relation to us (psychophysical beings) and the project of physical science as it may connect with macrophysical things (such as tables) means that it is easy in the psychological case to be under the illusion that we are not changing the subject when we ask the scientific questions. It is very evident that someone using the language of atomic physics is not talking about tables. But because so much of computational psychology and neuroscience is provoked by interesting questions precisely about our own capacities, it is harder not to treat it as if it competed with, and attempted to improve upon, our understanding of ourselves.

There is no need to reject the scientific questions even when the outlook that has led to neuroscientific eliminativism is rejected—any more than there is any need to reject physicists' questions when the argument that said that tables aren't solid is rejected. To retain one's faith in commonsense psychology, it is only necessary to deny that the universalistic perspective is appropriate to it. Someone who rejects the outlook that has led to neuroscientific eliminativism can retain her faith in commonsense psychology without seeing it as founded in the answers to the scientists' questions; she may see it as standing with the ordinary beliefs about the world upon which it depends.

12

Semantic Innocence
and Psychological Understanding

1. Introduction

1.1 Semantics and psychology

Philosophers' views about meaning and mind, about semantics and psychology and their relations, have proliferated in recent years: if one is looking for an account of these matters, then there are more and more in the philosophical literature to choose from. But reviewing that literature, one may be struck more by an idea that is common to a majority of the new accounts than by any of their subtle differences. The idea is roughly this. That if we are to give an account, of the sort that philosophers do, of intentional mental states, then we have two tasks. One is the task of dealing with the features of such states as beliefs and desire in virtue of which they play the role they do in causal explanation; the other is the task of saying how such states, and how the sentences of human language, relate to the world at large. Allow that semantics is a subject that makes mention of things in the world external to a subject, and let psychology be what we use to make sense of one another, then the idea is that psychology is one thing, semantics another. This essay attempts to do something to dislodge this 'two-task idea'.

I take the two-task idea to be central in some of the work of at least

Block, Field, Fodor, Harman, Loar, McGinn, Putnam and Schiffer (and one could name more).[1] There are too many variations on the theme for my descriptions of the two tasks to be acceptable as they stand to all those whose views I have in mind.[2] And among those whom I take to share the two-task idea, there are differences of opinion as to how separate these two tasks can, or should, be kept, and as to how their connexion is to be conceived.

Something that unites all the philosophers I mentioned, and which is symptomatic of the two-task idea, is their confrontation of the question 'Why truth?'.[3] According to their idea, we can and should give an account of mental states which treats their attribution as having explanatory force and which includes the role of the states in linguistic productions and perceptions; but the account is separate from any which mentions connexions between those mental states and things in the world, or between bits of language and things in the world. Why, then, do genuinely semantic notions such as *truth* and *reference* loom so large when it comes to language and mind? Why, for instance, do we think of names as referring, and of a person as related to, the objects that we name in saying what she thinks? Why should truth-conditional accounts of meaning have been so pervasive in philosophy and linguistics? Semantics can't be made to go away, because we know that we are not in error when we say (speaking about our own language) such things as 'Everest refers to Everest', or 'An object satisfies "is a mountain" iff it is a mountain'. But if psychology is what we use to make sense of ourselves, and if the task of explicating psychology has no need of semantics, but uses only a notion of 'conceptual role',[4] then why doesn't the subject of semantics simply lapse?

I find such a question strange. Or at least I find it strange that some philosophers seem to have become unwilling to contemplate the possibility that the reason semantic notions persist in seeming ineliminable from accounts of the explanatory function of psychological and linguistic content is that they are ineliminable. I shall present a case for the view that accounts of content incorporating accounts of meaning given in the truth-conditional way constitute the foundational level of psychology. If that is right, it will seem that there is no *awkward* question 'Why truth?' to face up to.

The interpretational truth theories which I shall defend have often been claimed by their adherents to be or to serve as theories of meaning, and to help us to say or to show what knowledge of language consists in.[5] These claims are not at issue here. I want to place the emphasis slightly differently, however, and to suggest that interpretational truth-theories are illuminatingly seen in the context of providing an elucidation of the phenomenon of intentionality quite generally. In §2 I present a unitary account of content, which is in competition with the two-task idea; and I do this in an attempt to make the two-task idea seem as superfluous as it seems to me to be strange. The point of the presentation is dialectical: I do not pretend to refute the two-task idea; but when I come to discuss it in §3, I shall be in a position to suggest that its advocates have given a wrong impression of what the alternative to it might be.

1.2 Psychological understanding and semantic innocence

People's having and gaining psychological understanding (as I shall speak of it) is a matter of their finding and coming to find one another intelligible. In particular cases, we find a person intelligible in knowing why she does what she does. And the concepts that we use when we manifest our possession of psychological understanding are the concepts that an account of mind and meaning are concerned with—such concepts as belief, desire and saying. They are concepts whose attribution in particular cases specifies a state of mind or a speech act using a 'that' clause, a state of mind or a speech act with a content.[6]

An example shows that the notion of content relevant here may attach both to psychological states and to uses of language. Assume that (1) is correct. Then the content of a speaking of (2) is the same as a content of a belief of Bill's.

(1) Bill thinks that the sky is blue.
(2) The sky is blue.

If a person came out with both (1) and (2), then there would be something she had done twice, namely, utter English words having the content that the sky is blue. Most likely there would also be things that she did only once—namely, (a) state that the sky is blue (which she will have done in uttering (2) but not in uttering (1)), and (b) tell something of what Bill thinks (which she will have done in uttering (1) but not in uttering (2)). The content she states in uttering (2) is the content she states-that-Bill-thinks in uttering (1).

Davidson encouraged us to see this point as crucial to a correct account of the construction of speech reports when he insisted on what has been called the Principle of Semantic Innocence. This is the principle that the words which are used in saying what someone has said (or, more generally, words in 'that' clauses following propositional attitude terms) mean and refer to what they ordinarily mean and refer to. Davidson himself used the principle to support his paratactic account of indirect discourse (1968). But the present point, encapsulated in the Principle of Semantic Innocence, may be less controversial than any claim about the logical form of sentences containing 'that' clauses. It is simply that specifications of what people think or want or hope or fear rely on the use of words as meaning what they do when it is, for example, stated how things are. An account of linguistic meaning has to be able to deal with utterances of both (1) and (2) (along with all the other possible utterances); and an account of psychological states presumably has to rely on a correct understanding of how utterances like (1) work.[7]

2. A unitary account of content

2.1 Interpretational truth theories

Accepting the Principle of Semantic Innocence, one may hope that an account of content will be suited to the treatment of the use of language both to speak of the world at large and in making psychological attributions. If there is a role which indicative sentences play both as used by speakers assertorically, and as used in specifying the contents of people's states of mind, then seeing what it is for them to play that role ought to illuminate our understanding of both linguistic and non-linguistic action. An account of content, then, should be fitted to the idea that a recurrent thing done with words, a thing which is typically done whatever else is done, is: producing sequences of sounds as having the content that they do.

Such an account recommends itself even if the use of words in psychological attributions is not explicitly considered. Language users have a stock of words whose relatively stable properties enable them to convey their thoughts in a changing world. In the case of non-context-dependent words, the stable thing is what the words would be uttered as contributing to content, and in the case of context-dependent words the stable thing is something that contextually determines what those words would be uttered as contributing to content. Ineliminable from an account of the use of a particular language, then, will be some theory on the basis of which one could say, in the case of whatever sentence *s* any speaker of the language came out with:

> At *t* she produced *s* as having the content that *p*.

And in any particular case, the (relatively) stable properties of individual words contained in *s*'s instance must be relied on in getting the correct thing to write in at the place of *p*.

Now the claim that a truth-conditional theory could serve as a theory of meaning for a language may be put by saying that it could be that a theory of truth, by virtue of its containing axioms stating properties of individual words, was such as to be targeted on theorems of this form: 'An utterance of *s* as uttered by *X* at *t* would be true iff *p*', *and* was such as to deliver such a theorem only where *X* would produce *s* at *t* as having the content that *p*. By 'interpretational truth-theory', I mean such a theory.

A distinction often made in discussion of theories of meaning is crucial here. On the one hand, there are theories which treat particular languages, each of which can put one in a position to say what content any of the well-formed sentences of the particular language it deals with would be uttered as having. On the other hand, there is an account (probably best not credited with the title of 'theory') which, as it is said, locates the concept of *meaning* in relation to other concepts, and which does so in part by seeing what a theory of meaning treating a particular language has to do, and how it might do that. In fact, a further distinction might be made within this latter account between its statement of principles that would guide any actual empirical description of what speakers do, and a philosophical gloss which says how such principles would work together with a theory for a particular language. Here I shall think of the account as incorporating the principles about language use as well as the philosophical gloss on the whole. When thought of in this way, the account evidently goes beyond what anyone who started out looking for a philosophical analysis of linguistic meaning might have sought: it is an account of much besides meaning.

It is obvious that a theory of meaning (for a particular language, as opposed to the account requiring some settled conception of such a theory) does not describe the *use* even of the particular language productions of whose sounds by speakers it enables one to redescribe. For it is clearly not enough, if one is to say how a language is used, to be able to say, 'She used sounds as having the content that ———'; one must be in a position to say also, 'She said that ———', 'She asserted that ———', 'She warned that ———', 'She ordered that ———', 'She conveyed that ———'. These further things that are done when speakers produce sounds are things which aren't seen to be done until the theory of meaning is embedded within an account of force.

The division between a theory of meaning and a theory of force is a division within an account of language between what is specific to a particular language and what is not. What a speaker does with words depends on the content which those words have, and which, as a user of the language, she utters those words as having. But once the content has been made determinate, there is nothing further which is specific to her language and which determines what she does.[8] The non-language-specific character of the account in which a theory of meaning is seen to be embedded gives it its claim to serve as locating the concept of linguistic meaning quite generally. But to locate that concept generally is to see how it plays a role in conjunction with other concepts in making sense of people.

An interpretational truth-theory enables one to see speakers' productions of noises as contentful utterances by way of assisting in the task of seeing those productions as intelligible speech actions, having some purpose. But any hypothesis about the purpose of a person who used words on an occasion goes hand in hand not only with a hypothesis about the content of her utterance but also with a hypothesis about her mental states. Any such hypothesis is thus potentially confirmable or disconfirmable by reference at least to linguistic actions of that person and others who use the language on other occasions, and also to actions of any kind of that person on other occasions. We cannot understand people on the basis of what they do with words considered separately from all the other things they and others do. An account of the use of a language is just one part of a total account of the lives and minds of the people who speak it. If a theory of meaning is embedded in an account of force, an account of force is embedded in an account of mind, where an account of mind, if made explicit, would spell out (insofar as that is possible) everything that we effortlessly use in gaining psychological understanding. The principles I spoke of the account as incorporating must say everything that can be said to introduce our conception of a rational mind.

2.2 Saying

It is sometimes held that a theory of meaning should be targeted towards a theorem of the form *s* is true iff *p* just in case *s* can be used to *say* that *p*. But if one wants to keep in mind that it is not only with *linguistic* actions that an interpretational theory is concerned, then formulations like this, using 'say', serve less well than the formulation using 'content'.

And there is another reason to avoid the 'say' formulation: it is simply false that only a sentence having the content that *p* can be used to say that *p*.[9] Take the English sentence 'It seems to have been raining all summer'. If the notion of content is connected with recurrent properties of words, then the content that an interpretational theory of truth should show that sentence to be used as having is that it seems to have been raining all summer. But someone who utters that sentence might perfectly well be said to have said (say) that the weather hasn't been very good this summer. The former report, towards which an interpretational truth-theory is targeted, pays maximum respect to the fact of particular words having been used in a particular construction; but the latter report, which is typical enough of an everyday report of what someone did using words, does not pay particular attention to that fact. There is no definite answer to the question how far a non-quotational report of speech even by someone who uses the same language as the person reported can deviate from the use of her words over again (see Quine, 1960, p. 218). And as the present example can illustrate, this is a highly context-dependent matter. Exactly which words can truly and fairly be used to say what was said by someone who came out with 'It seems to have been raining all summer' will depend, for instance, on what beliefs about the usual weather in the summer are shared by the original speaker, the reporter and the audience to the report. (That will depend in its turn, for instance, on where they live.) We usually accept far fewer substitutions in the slot in

s would be used by X at t as having the content that ——

(which has been introduced for the purposes of theorizing) than we should accept in the slot in

X; if she used s at t, would have said that ——

(which uses the everyday 'say').[10]

2.3 Content

Acceptable substitutions inside the slot in 'used as having the content that ——' are guided (we have seen) by a conception of a theory of meaning as a theory that takes account of the recurrent features of individual words. The notion of content, then, is determined in part by the need to recognize syntactic structure in a language, and contents are accordingly finely discriminated. But exactly how finely they should be discriminated is revealed only in the broader framework where interpretational truth-theories have been located.

Frege held that it is a sufficient condition of the difference of two thoughts that it be possible for a person to have some attitude towards one and not the other. This is evidently the right criterion of difference for contents as conceived here. We cannot be indifferent to whether we attribute (say) the belief that p or the belief that q to a person if we know that that person might believe that p and not believe that q; and we must use a notion of content which, like Frege's, precludes such indifference. Frege's principle is implicitly accepted in most discussions of opacity where it is acknowledged to be a sufficient condition of its being a non sequitur to move from 'a believes that p' to 'a believes that q' that words that contribute differently to thoughts (in Frege's sense) be intersubstituted in the sentences that occur at the places of 'p' and 'q'.

Of course in practice we often feel justified in moving from ascriptions of a belief with one content to ascriptions of a belief with what has to be counted another content. It may be in a strict sense a *non sequitur*, but nonetheless a safe bet, to move from 'Harriet believes that the present British Prime Minister is uncompromising' to 'Harriet believes that Margaret Thatcher is uncompromising'. Treating content in the Fregean way, it can often be taken for granted that if someone believes one thing she believes another. That this can be taken for granted is reflected in our reports of speech, as we have seen: we allow that someone's saying one thing is her (actually) saying what, according to the Fregean (modally defined) notion of content, is another thing.[11]

When we appreciate how the Fregean psychological idea of a content has to work hand in hand with an account of linguistic content derived from facts about recurrent properties of words, we see that an interpretational truth-theory is sensitized to, and thus sensitive to, precisely the Fregean sense of words (or, in another idiom, to the conceptual repertoires of psychological subjects). For Frege, the sense of a word is what it contributes to a thought; and thoughts are the contents that the project of elucidating the propositional attitude concepts requires.

2.4 Indexicality

The presence in natural languages of indexicals has seemed to some people to stand in the way of the idea that one can simultaneously elucidate the role of *meaning* and the role of the concepts for intentional mental states generally. Evidently, meaning and content cannot be equated if a single sentence (which "has some one meaning") can be used now with one content now with another. But there has been no equation of linguistic meaning and content here. Indexicals are words that contribute differently to the contents of utterances of sentences they occur in, though in contextually more or less predictable ways.

It needs to be acknowledged that not all thoughts are available to be entertained in all contexts. Suppose I overheard someone talking, and I tell you something of what she said. There are two ways in which my reports of her utterances will deviate from those that assign contents according to the Fregean notion. First, wanting to be understood as well as may be, I shall avoid expressing thoughts which aren't available to you, for example, because you don't know the person spoken of. Second, in some cases I shall be literally unable to express the thoughts whose expression I wish to report. If, for instance, she was in a position to think about objects in ways which I now, not in the presence of those objects, can't think about them, I cannot say the contents of her utterances. Still, if I am trying to tell you what was said (in the ordinary sense), these constraints and limitations don't present insuperable problems: we have already remarked that someone can fairly and truly be said to have said that *p*, even though no utterance of hers had the content that *p* (according to the Fregean notion). Someone attempting to give a quite general theoretically motivated account of potential utterances of, say, 'He is hot', is, like me in the situation just envisaged, constrained by the need to be intelligible to whoever might learn from her account, and is limited by the unavailability to her of thoughts that others may have had in other times and places. Although the limitations are now in an obvious way more severe, they are of the same, not persistently problematic kind. The greater severity arises from the fact that 'having the content that ———' is, as we have seen, a stricter notion than 'says that ———'. And it arises also from the theoretically enforced need to generalize, to speak in abstraction about countless potential particular utterances. Obviously, no one can know (say) whom 'he' as demonstrative pronoun would be used as referring to on all occasions. Forced to generalize, and wishing to say something intelligible in the abstract, the theorist says that utterances of (say) 'He was tired' would be used as saying, if anything, that some contextually demonstrated person was tired, noting that such utterances would have a certain sort of content, and elaborating perhaps on this 'certain sort'.

(Of course many indexicals present questions of their own; and there is much to be said under this head, and about modes of thought which can be discriminated more finely than any linguistic devices. But there is no reason to think that these questions would need to be ignored by someone who conceives of psychology in the way suggested here. And they have not been ignored; see, e.g., Evans, 1982.)

2.5 Truth

In focusing here on the use to which an interpretational truth-theory can be put, we may seem to have lost sight of the notion of truth. We should enquire now what role this notion plays—especially in view of my suggestion (§1.1) that philosophers should avoid a position in which it requires some special accounting that *truth* and *reference* have ready application in connexion with psychological understanding.

In the literature one finds two sorts of answers to the question how *truth* fits in with *interpretation* when interpretational truth-theories are at issue. According to the first answer, advocates of interpretational truth-theories are claiming that truth is a concept to which *meaning* can be reduced, or in terms of which it can be analyzed. According to the second, it is the purest accident that a theory of truth might do what a theory of linguistic meaning or a theory of content has to do. These answers are evidently at opposite extremes: the first sees the advocate of interpretational truth-theories as forging the closest of conceptual connexions between *truth* and *content;* the second sees the advocate as having no use at all for *truth per se.* Neither answer seems correct.

The first answer is obviously incorrect. It is presumably given by those who suppose that any account of content must be a philosophical analysis, so that if truth features in the account, content must be being analyzed in terms of truth. And it is small wonder that those who hold the view that the project which introduces interpretational truth-theories is an attempt at analyzing 'content' or 'meaning' take the project to be misguided. They can be disabused of their view only if it is shown (something I have attempted to show) how and where truth enters into the project.

The second answer does not rest on any such evident misconception. I think that it is fuelled by the perfectly correct thought that what is relied on in interpretational theories for particular languages is the disquotational character of '*** is true iff ———'. Now truth is a normative notion. So if (like Soames, 1984) one distinguishes truth's disquotationality from its normativity, and tries to separate them, it looks as though only part of truth's character (and a relatively uninteresting part, it may be thought) does any work in truth-theories. It would indeed be an accident that truth was used if any property with one of truth's features (sc. disquotationality), even a property lacking one of truth's essential features (sc. normativity), might just as well have been used instead. But does truth really lose its normal, normative role in the context of interpretational truth-theories? Is disquotationality a genuinely separate feature? Admittedly, truth's normative nature does not leap from the page if one is proving theorems inside such a theory. But that should not make one suppose that it somehow goes away. Attempts to separate disquotationality from normativity ignore the fact that it is in virtue of possessing the disquotational feature that truth is the evaluative concept that it is. Consider that instead of 'Utterance *u* is true if and only if *p*', one could always say, 'Utterance *u* is true if and only if it is indeed the case that *p*'.

What is certain is that it is only by conceiving potential utterances as *evaluable* for truth that one can have a conception of an interpretational truth-theory at all. To take a single example outside the realm of language use, it seems that to believe that *p* is (very roughly) to be disposed to act in ways that would tend to satisfy one's desires in a world in which it was true that *p*. Such evidence as one has that someone believes something, then, if got from noticing ways in which she acts, relies on one's taking a view of how the world would be if what is believed were true, and of whether the world is indeed that way. How would the world be if it were true that *p*? Well, one has already said how it would be, if one has uttered a sentence with the content that *p*. What one says in saying how the world would be if a belief were evaluable as true is what one says in specifying the content of that belief, which one does in attributing the belief.

There is another way to see that truth plays its normal normative role here. Some people hold that truth is a property only of contents (or, as they may say, propositions), and they think that it follows that we ought not to predicate truth of sentences, as Tarski did. For their benefit, it is pointed out that predication of truth to a sentence as potentially uttered on an occasion could always be viewed as predication of truth to the content that the sentence is used to express. In place of 'sentence *s* as used by *X* at *t* would be true iff ———', then, we could put 'sentence *s* as used by *X* at *t* would express a content which is true iff ———'. This way of putting it makes it clear that a theory of truth can be seen as matching contents which would be expressed by subjects with contents to be expressed by interpreters. Then we realize that coming to know an interpretational truth-theory is coming to be in a position to exploit the Principle of Semantic Innocence in psychological understanding. Exploiting that principle is a matter of relying on the fact that we may use our words having their ordinary *semantic* properties in attributing beliefs to another. Everyday psychological understanding evidently makes no reference to a theory of truth. But it shares with the theorist's a reliance on the fact that utterances and states of mind are, like the utterances that report them, *truth*-evaluable, truth-*evaluable*.[12]

3. Two-task accounts of content

3.1 "Use" theories of meaning

Accounts of intentional phenomena that conform to what at the outset I christened the 'two-task idea' have gained wide acceptance in the last few years. I have presented the unitary account of content in order that it may be seen as in competition with two-task accounts. It is not usually seen as a competitor, however. When it is introduced into discussion, wrong impressions are sometimes given of its status and pretensions. I hope to correct one such impression now, before turning to look at the genesis of the two-task idea.

Many philosophers who believe in a version of the two-task idea speak of a difference between 'truth-conditional theories of meaning' and 'use theories of meaning'.[13] They may make this contrast in order to suggest that one sort of theory is to be promoted as serving one, the other as serving the other, of their two putative tasks. But they can give the impression that an account centred on a truth-conditional theory is at most a partial one in anyone's view: they seem to rule out the possibility that truth-conditional theories should be promoted as playing a central role in an account designed to elucidate the nature of mental states quite generally—as of course they are by advocates of a unitary account.

Speaking of a difference between 'truth-conditional' and 'use' theories of meaning can be misleading in a further way. For suppose it is allowed that it is possible for a person to believe in something deserving the name of 'truth-conditions theory' but to reject the two-task idea. If truth-conditional theories and use theories are then contrasted, it looks as though such a person eschews something called a 'use theory'. But this is wrong. Certainly it is wrong if a 'use theory' is associated with the name of Wittgenstein, or if it is associated with the slogan that meaning does not transcend use.

An interpretational truth-theory plays its role in an account of *(inter alia)* the *use* of language. And there is bound to be dispute between someone who supports a unitary account and someone who espouses some version of the two-task idea about how an account of language *use* is to be given. Such a dispute is part of a broader dispute about the nature of intentionality, and is reflected in a disagreement as to what the *use* of language should be thought to encompass. According to the conception already employed here, *use* includes all the countlessly many things that people are heard as doing when a fellow speaker, or a theorist supplied with a theory of content and force, comes to understand them. This is a broad conception. According to another conception of *use*, which is invoked by two-task theorists from whose standpoint 'use' and 'truth-conditions' are in opposition, use includes only such facts about what people do with language as can be stated without yet allowing that speakers relate themselves to the world. This is a narrow conception. The two very different conceptions have presumably grown up in response to different theoretical demands.

What first made use conceptions of meaning attractive was the naturalistic idea that linguistic phenomena are, as it were, in the open: an account of a language must allow (for example) that everything needed in its acquisition is accessible to those who in fact acquire it. This idea surely gives rise in the first instance to the broad conception of use: whatever might be counted as observable linguistic behaviour is a part of use. The narrow conception of use comes to be invoked (I think) when the focus is the individual language user, and her *dispositions* to linguistic behaviour are introduced. If dispositions themselves are thought of as states of individuals whose nature and correct individuation are independent of any conditions that obtain outside the individual, then the verbal behaviour towards which people can be thought of as disposed is inevitably restricted. I suggest that it is a particular individualistic conception of individuals' *dispositions* (characterized sometimes as their tacit knowledge) rather than anything in the idea of *use*, or of verbal behaviour itself, which has given rise to the newer and much narrower conception of *use*.[14]

If this is right, then it is at very best tendentious to suggest that a unitary account of content eschews a 'use' theory. On the one hand, a statement of the original, epistemological motivation for speaking of 'use' appears to require the broad conception which is employed in the unitary account. On the other hand, it may be doubted whether the narrow conception of use corresponds to anything that anyone would ordinarily recognize as 'use': there is much one can say about language use, we ordinarily think, but it is hard to say anything about it if we are banned from using modes of speech report in which we make mention of objects beyond the language user. (For example, when I tell you that someone said that Quine wrote *Word and Object*, I seem to have told you something wholly about one of her uses of language; but this is not so according to the narrow conception.)

We should not allow a terminological manoeuvre to take us from the evident fact that accounts of intentional phenomena should be directed towards *(inter alia)* language use into automatic acceptance of the idea of a disposition which can be characterized both individualistically and as something which is recognizably a disposition to use language.[15] The advocate of a unitary account of content holds that a truth-conditional theory plays a crucial role within an account of the use of any language; and she denies that there is any workable conception of language use according to which an account of use could be separated from an account of the genuinely semantical aspects of a language.

Of course, though, it is not mere terminological manoeuvering which has been thought to recommend the two-task idea. The terminology may encourage us to forget that there was ever any other idea; but it has gained its hold because of arguments that are thought to demonstrate that semantical properties are a separable aspect of explanatory mental states. I turn now to look at some such arguments— to discuss the work of three authors selected to show something of how the two-task idea has gained ground in the last decade or so.

3.2 Putnam

Putnam's paper 'The Meaning of "Meaning"' (1975) is seminal in the history of the two-task idea. Putnam there did not engage himself in the kind of rivalry that I am now trying to establish: when he criticized what he called Davidsonian semantics, he meant by 'Davidsonian semantics' a theory of meaning simply, and not the broader account (of §2 here) which makes mention of such theories.

The difficulty that Putnam professed to find with Davidsonian semantics was that 'for many words, an extensionally correct truth-definition can be given which is in no sense a theory of the meaning of the word' (1975, p. 259). Putnam's point was that either of the sentences '"Water" refers to water' and '"Water" refers to H_2O' might be used in a truth definition; we cannot distinguish between them in point of extensional correctness. But of course a theory of meaning ought not to be indifferent to which of these sentences it made use of. Putnam's point can be put another way: two truth-theories can be equally good extensionally speaking, but not interpretationally speaking. But when we put the point in this way, we shall think of Putnam only as having recorded that a truth-theory needs to be constructed so as to be sensitive to all the psychological facts if it is to capture *meaning*. Of course this is how truth-theories have been envisaged here.

Putnam introduced Davidsonian semantics into a discussion of some natural assumptions about *meaning*. Above all, he wanted to draw attention to a difficulty he saw about combining two assumptions: (i) knowing the meaning of a term is a matter of being in a certain psychological state; (ii) the meaning of a term determines its extension. In the context of this discussion, we can think of Putnam's criticism of Davidson as suggesting that Davidson paid attention to assumption (ii) at the expense of failing to acknowledge assumption (i): Davidson's account, according to Putnam, got the extension of terms right, but did so without caring about what is known by speakers of a language (speakers who, for instance, might have no concept of H_2O, yet have a concept of water). In that case, we can see that the construal of Putnam's claim about extensional correctness, just given on behalf of Davidson, puts us in a position to meet Putnam's main point. For the requirement on a theory of psychological sensitivity, which we have seen comes down to the requirement that the theory be sensitive to Fregean sense, ensures that assumption (i) is met. Since the account incorporates that sensitivity in its mode of stating precisely the *extensions* of terms, assumption (ii) is also met.

The difficulty for Davidson that Putnam thought he saw was illustrated by way of his famous Twin Earth thought experiments. An ordinary, scientifically unsophisticated speaker of English knows what is meant by 'water'—a certain stuff, in fact H_2O. We are to imagine that Twin Earth is in nearly every way just like this earth, and that the Twin Earth counterpart of our English speaker inhabits an environment which contains a liquid which on the basis of the sort of observa-tions that ordinary speakers ordinarily make cannot be distinguished from water; but the liquid on Twin Earth has a quite different chemical composition from water—it is XYZ. What would be meant by 'water' by the Twin Earth counterpart, then, will be something different from what we on Earth mean by 'water'. But, as Putnam says, what is in the head of our English speaker and what is in the head of his Twin Earth counterpart need not be relevantly different. So whatever state of a speaker constitutes knowledge of the meaning of a word, if it does indeed determine what is meant by the word, is not in the head. Many have thought that a case has now been made for splitting knowledge of meaning and other psychological states into two parts—each part corresponding to one of Putnam's two assumptions, and each part imposing its own theoretical task. But the reply on Davidson's behalf has shown already that Putnam's (i) and (ii) can be combined. What the thought experiment suggests is that a problem would arise if one combined (ii) with the further assumption that psychological states are in the head (in whatever sense it is of 'in the head' that makes it seem evident that indeed there need be no relevant differences in the heads of the Earth speaker and the Twin Earth speaker). By themselves, Twin Earth thought experiments lend no support to the two-task idea.

Notice that, given the Principle of Semantic Innocence, Putnam's argument would affect psychological states generally, and not just states of knowing meanings: the state which I on Earth attribute by saying, 'He believes that the lake fills with water each February' is, like the state which I attribute by saying, 'He knows that "water" means water', a state of the Earth speaker, but not of the Twin Earth speaker with his indistinguishable head. And of course those who have taken some version of the two-task idea to be forced on us by Twin Earth examples have wished their idea to cover psychological states generally.

3.3 Fodor

Putnam gave the name 'methodological solipsism' to the doctrine that mental states are literally in the head. And this was a doctrine that Fodor defended in his paper 'Methodological Solipsism Considered as a Research Strategy in Psychology' (in Fodor, 1980, at p. 312). The methodologically solipsist sort of psychology that Fodor hoped to promote he called Rational Psychology. The sort of psychology which is used in psychological understanding, in which reference is made to things in the world beyond the subject when mental states are imputed Fodor called Naturalistic Psychology. And he said about Naturalistic Psychology, 'It isn't a practical possibility and isn't likely to become one (1980, p. 234).

Now we know that what Fodor said about Naturalistic Psychology cannot be literally true, because Naturalistic Psychology is what we all actually use all the time. It seems that Fodor cannot really have been interested in everyday psychological understanding, and that he must only have meant that *if* we want psychology to meet certain standards—such as treating mental states as in the head—then Naturalistic Psychology must be deemed 'not a practical possibility and not likely to become one'. And yet it would be wrong to think that the Rational Psychology which Fodor favours for its practicability abjures psychological understanding. For the case Fodor makes for Rational Psychology relies on the principles that govern psychological understanding. It seems that Fodor thought, on the one hand, that the subject of the mind as we know it outside of laboratories isn't practicable, but, on the other hand, that any practicable psychology would have to embody the principles that we work with in interpreting one another as possessors of minds.

Fodor's combination of hostility and friendliness towards Naturalistic Psychology can be explained. He thought that only one aspect of Naturalistic Psychology stood in the way of its being practically possible, and that that aspect could be peeled off, as it were, retaining everything that matters to psychological explanations as we know them. After the peeling off, there would be no obstacle to psychological explanation of the ordinary sort but conforming to his desired standards. For Fodor thought that only on one construal of psychological explanations are there problems of practicability, and on their problematic construal the explanations contain something extra, not really needed for explanatory purposes. As he put it: 'It's typically an opaque construal [of a propositional attitude context] that does the explanatory work' (p. 234).[16]

Fodor's idea can be made clearer with one of his own examples. Suppose that some action of John's is explained by saying this:

John believes that Cicero was a Roman orator.

Then there is an opaque construal of the sentence on which it would be invalid to substitute 'Tully' for Cicero, and a transparent construal on which the substitution would be valid. According to Fodor, one makes reference to Cicero himself, and thus to things in the world beyond John's head, only when one intends the transparent construal to be put on one's words. And the aspect of Naturalistic Psychology to be peeled off is what is supposed to be distinctive of transparent construals—sc., roughly, reference.

Fodor's point about the connexion between opacity and explanatoriness has been registered here in the point that intersubstitutions of referring terms in the sentence which gives the content of a propositional attitude must for explanatory purposes show sensitivity to the *senses* of the words there. It is Fodor's other idea that must be questioned. This is the idea that *only* non-opaque construals make trouble for psychology—that it is only when we switch to a construal in which 'Cicero' can be replaced by 'Tully' that we have reference to Cicero, and thus in Fodor's view a threat to practicable psychology.

This other idea is in contravention of the Principle of Semantic Innocence. For according to Fodor's understanding of opacity, 'Cicero' is referred to in 'John believes of Cicero that he was a Roman orator' but not in 'John believes that Cicero was a Roman orator'. We must ask ourselves whether Fodor could really have had a reason to think that I refer to objects when I speak about them but not when I tell you what others think about them. Is it really that I refer to Cicero when I state that he was a Roman orator, but not when I state that John thinks that Cicero was a Roman orator?[17] If the answer is *No*, then it is wrong to suppose that when there is sensitivity to the sense of a term, it is not the role of that term to refer.

With the Principle of Semantic Innocence in place, the features of Naturalistic Psychology which made Fodor find it a practical impossibility cannot be made to disappear. And we have been given no reason to think that there could be such a subject as Fodor's Rational Psychology, which is supposed to embody sensitivity to sense but to make no references.[18]

3.4 McGinn

Unlike Fodor and others who adopt some version of the two-task idea, McGinn engages in the sort of rivalry that I have tried to set up here. That is to say, McGinn does not ignore the unitary account of content; in 'The Structure of Content' (1982a) he criticizes it. His criticisms take over at the point where Putnam's left off (§3.2).

McGinn acknowledges the main point of §3.2—that not any old truth theory, but only an interpretational one, is said by Davidson to serve as a theory of meaning. And McGinn is no opponent of the idea that truth-theories have a part to play in an account of meaning. But his view is that a theory of truth is 'constitutionally partial': the constraints on a theory of truth which ensure that it is interpretational are 'too strong if they are constraints on a definition of *truth*' (p. 239). McGinn means to suggest that insofar as a theory of content might be psychologically sensitive, that has nothing to do with its invocation of *truth*.

This suggestion was cast in doubt when it was argued that it is not an accident that *truth* plays the role it does in interpretational theories (§2.5). Certainly it must be conceded that, as McGinn says, there could be a definition of truth that was in some sense correct but that was not 'strongly constrained'. It would be possible, for instance, to construct a theory whose canonical theorems were true and on the pattern of '*s* is true iff *p*', which was insensitive to differences of sense; and we might see fit to call such a theory 'a theory of truth-conditions'.[19] But it would be wrong to think that the constraints imposed on a theory of truth in §2.1 that are meant to ensure its interpretationality are *extra* constraints, additional to those imposed on some other imagined theory ('of truth-conditions'). For it is not as if, in the course of making sense of people, one could become confident that one had a theory for their language which was extensionally correct, but have as yet no inkling of the senses of their terms. As we saw in §2, the idea of someone who supports the unitary account of content is that *truth* is the very notion that will furnish the theorist with materials to exploit the Principle of Semantic Innocence.

The question 'Why truth?' is thus easily answered in the context of the unitary account (cp. §1.1). To see exactly why that question is troublesome for McGinn will be to appreciate now the particular character of his own account. According to it, a theory of mind and meaning not only has a part which specifies the truth-conditions (in McGinn's sense) of utterances and states of mind, but also contains another part which is needed to explicate the explanatory role of such things—a theory of their intra-individual properties, said to specify their cognitive role. 'We view beliefs as relations to propositions that can be assigned referential truth-conditions' and, as a separate matter, 'we view beliefs as causally explanatory states of the head whose semantic properties are, from that point of view, as may be' (p. 216). The bearing of *truth*-evaluability on beliefs cannot then be accounted for in terms of their explanatory properties. In fact, McGinn's own answer to the question 'Why truth?' is that truth and reference may be located 'in the point of communication—in the intention with which assertions (and other kinds of speech acts) are made. A hearer understands a speech act as an assertion only if he interprets it as performed with a certain point or intention—viz. to convey information about the world' (p. 226).

But there seems to be a problem about invoking specifically this principle about *linguistic* understanding in explicating truth's salience in our thinking about mind and meaning. The problem is that there are principles which have an apparently similar status but which govern interpretation more generally. Where McGinn wants to say that *a* is taken to have asserted something only if she is taken to purport to put forward something true, one could equally well say that *a*'s wants are satisfied only when their contents come to be true, or *a* succeeds in doing what she tries to to the extent that the beliefs which explain her trying to do that are true.[20] But if we can recognize a place for truth when we consider non-linguistic action and think about its explanation and its point, then it seems wrong to relegate truth to a place in which it works in the minds only of those engaged in communication, and to deny that the principles which embody people's rational explicability could contain essential mention of relations between the contents of beliefs and the things in the world that the contents concern.

It is when one appreciates the Principle of Semantic Innocence at work in the area of giving psychological explanations that one seems bound to recognize the truth-evaluability of contents as indispensable from that area. Suppose I assert that Jane drove to Bedford, and then explain the action that I have asserted there was by saying that Jane believed that there was a zoo in Bedford. (It is common knowledge, let us suppose, that Jane might be hoping to visit a zoo.) Given that that which, in a simple assertion, is put forward as true is exactly that which, in an explanation of action, is put forward as a (true or false) content believed by the person whose action is to be explained (cp. §1.2), it is hard to maintain a difference of attitude towards the relevance of truth-evaluability to my presentation of the content that Jane drove to Bedford and my presentation of the content that there was a zoo in Bedford. McGinn wants to sever our understanding of how utterances can transmit knowledge about the world (as they typically do in assertions) from our understanding of how utterances can feature in explanations of people's interactions with the world (as they often do when it is said what someone thinks). But if the semantical properties of beliefs were really irrelevant to the explanatory status of beliefs, then it would seem that, in finding Jane intelligible, it would not be relevant that Bedford be seen as somewhere she drove to and somewhere she thought there was a zoo. This does seem relevant.

McGinn's premiss, which leads to the disconnexion of the semantical from the explanatory, is that 'beliefs play a role in the agent's psychology just in virtue of intrinsic properties of the implicated internal representations'. The premiss (as McGinn allows, p. 208) amounts to the methodological solipsism which Putnam seemed to recommend and which Fodor attempted to find a painless way to endorse. The issue between those who give a unitary account and the two-task theorists then comes down to an issue about whether, as the two-task theorist maintains, it is not beliefs as we know them, having truth-evaluable contents, but only some part of beliefs, or (in McGinn's version) beliefs only under some partial aspect, that we rely on in psychological understanding.

There is of course a deeper motive than any we have seen for methodological solipsism and for the two-task theorists' claims about beliefs as they figure in explanations. (If there were no such deeper motive, the two-task idea would surely not be as prevalent as it is, nor its varieties as various.) The two-task theorists share a general view about the character of any respectable causal explanation, and this is a character lacked by psychological explanations as we know them. We have then to choose between holding that psychological explanations are in good order even though they lack this character and holding that we must revise our thinking about psychological explanatory states. The two-task theorists' revision would enable us to see them as participating in the character of explanations whose features they apparently lack.[21]

Nothing said in this essay could force a choice. But we do well to remember that the view that psychological explanation is special and *sui generis* was held by some philosophers long before the two-task idea was invented. And I hope here to have made it clear that we are not lost for an account of content if we do take psychological explanation to be relevantly special. Philosophical understanding of psychological understanding, as well as psychological understanding itself, can be governed by the Principle of Semantic Innocence.[22]

Postscript: Externalism

The idea from Putnam (1975) which started the two-task idea has given rise to an enormous amount of discussion under the head of 'externalism'. To update this essay in response to all of this discussion would involve me in a range of questions with which this collection has not been concerned. Rather than attempt that task, I ask the reader to think of the two-task accounts and their various successors as examples of productions on the philosophical stage set as it was when the essay was written and as it still often is. I suggest that the stage is set very differently if the ontological conclusions of Part I here, and the conclusions about psychological explanation of Parts II and III, are accepted.

A state may be called 'externalist' if x's being in the state presupposes the existence of things which are no part of x but which exist in x's environment. Putnam's Twin Earth examples (introduced at §3.2) reveal that some states of mind are externalist in this sense. In the context of argument taking off from Putnam's particular thought experiments, 'environment' means *physical* environment. But Burge (1979) demonstrated for a person's *social* context what Putnam (1975) demonstrated for the physical environment—the determination of the psychological from outside the individual subject. And discussions of externalism have been directed towards what Burge, as well as Putnam, demonstrated.

When 'externalism' is understood simply by reference to the cases introduced by Putnam and Burge, it may be thought of as saying something negative: it summarizes what is established when the cases are treated as counterexamples to a thesis which has been called individualism.[23] Individualism would tell us that the properties a subject shares with all her 'molecule for molecule replicas' determine her intentional states. And the cases reveal that there could be a pair of psychological subjects, X and Y, who differed in respect of their intentional states of mind, although the only difference between their situations was an environmental one (X and Y themselves being 'molecule for molecule replicas').

Now the essay's unitary account of content incorporates a view about the vision required for psychological understanding—a vision which embraces more than any circumscribed psychological subject. This is surely an externalist view. But its externalism does not consist merely in its compatibility with anti-individualism as demonstrated by way of the thought experiments. The unitary account accommodates the externalist character of the propositional attitude states through its simple failure to suggest that an individual's being in such a state *should* be independent of matters external to the individual: it accommodates it effortlessly, as it were.

Externalism is often treated as something the philosopher has to make efforts to allow for. In much contemporary philosophy of mind, when externalism is discussed, the project is to render the truth of some anti-individualist thesis compatible with one or another claim in metaphysics or in epistemology which is supposed to be independently recommended.[24] Two-task accounts of content are still proposed; and many other ideas have been introduced about how features of a scientific psychology might be reconciled with the evidently externalist character of intentional states. The unitary account of content in the essay obviously plays a different role from any of these ideas: it was not offered in a spirit of reconciliation, being an account which is itself externalist (in the rough and ready sense explained). The defensibility of the unitary account of content shows, then, that there can be an intelligible externalism which has no need to engage itself specifically with such problems as may be taken to come to the surface when some particular anti-individualist thesis is formulated—when Twin Earth is postulated, for instance. Such externalism is a part of naive naturalism.

When Twin Earth examples are constructed, an assumption is put in place: two people, X and Y, are not distinguishable at the level at which subpersonal accounts of them are given. With this assumption in place, we have to imagine that the discrepancies between X's and Y's situations are not reflected in any differences between X and Y as they are described in subpersonal terms. Consideration of Twin Earth cases, then, can make it look as though any aspect of a person's being in a mental state which is not recorded in a subpersonal description is something that could be factored out as a separable contribution to a person's being as she is. And they can make it look as though the truths about X's and Y's physical environments or their social contexts (which we are to think of as having left no distinctive mark on any of X's and Y's subpersonal parts) were irrelevant causally to what X or Y might say or do. In consequence, we are encouraged to take a view of X's and Y's ordinary personal psychological states which actually would be the view appropriate for someone whose interest is in subpersonal psychology. Meanwhile, it seems quite mysterious how environment or social context could have any bearing on what a person says and does.

With Twin Earth on the scene, it is easy to underestimate the challenge the externalist character of mental states poses to a range of traditional ways of thinking about 'the place of the mind in nature'. It was Putnam (in 1975) who introduced the Twin Earth examples. But Putnam's own *Representation and Reality* (1988) may be read as showing that thinking in the style which Twin Earth assumptions encourages does not contribute to the understanding of content as it features in commonsense psychology. For Putnam argued there that a correct appreciation of the interpretive interests brought to bear in human understanding will show that there cannot be a 'naturalized' theory of commonsense psychology (such as scientific psychology purports to be). The lesson surely is that, to the extent to which the naturalizing tendency makes anti-individualism seem problematic, we must avoid the tendency. The naturalizing tendency of which I spoke at the start (in the Introduction) supplies the 'deep motive' for two-task accounts of content of which I spoke in the essay (in its penultimate paragraph). My hope is that the unitary account of content may be seen as support for *naïve* naturalism: it offers a positive account—for anyone who resists the tendency of sophisticated 'naturalizers' but still wants an account—of some of the irreducible subject matter of commonsense psychology.[25]

Notes
References
Index

Notes

Introduction

1. For an instructive (and deliberate) failure to turn up any generalizations, see Schiffer, 1987, ch. 2, §4. See also Child, 1994, on the uncodifiability of rationality, pp. 78–93.

2. This is perhaps the *locus classicus* for a view that Paul Churchland and Patricia Churchland have done much to promote. They would not themselves characterize their view as I do, as nihilistic: the Churchlands are optimistic that our present view of ourselves will be replaced by something. What sort of something that is, one can't say, however, because if they were right there would be no such thing as a view, and there would be no things remotely like ourselves. Nor can optimism really be their attitude: one can only coherently hope for what one can conceive.

I distinguish between vanishing eliminativism and banishing eliminativism in Essay 2. The eliminativists of the 1960s and 1970s were mainly the vanishers of this terminology, so that they believed that the mental could be abandoned without loss, and did not think of themselves as nihilists. But if abandoning the mental has the radical consequences I outline (which it is nowadays usually acknowledged to have), then the vanishers' attitude appears unsustainable.

3. Loar is more explicit than many functionalists are that functionalism places trust in science. When it comes to functionalism, the threat which is usually recognized is the threat of epiphenomenalism; see §5 below for my explanation why this is as hard to live with as eliminativism is.

See Fodor, 1985, for another functionalist view, and for a detailed survey of the various positions I lump together here as potentially threatening to commonsense psychology. See the beginning of Essay 10 for an explanation why I do not see fit to go into the details of the various positions. Essay 9 shows how a certain conception of subpersonal psychology can be opposed both to eliminativism and to functionalism (lumped together for present purposes).

4. Quine, 1960, pp. 219–221. When Quine speaks of the 'intentional idiom', that may suggest merely a way of talking about certain states of mind.

In fact, though, if the idiom could be faulted, then so too could all the thoughts that people have about one another as thinkers and agents, even if these thoughts are for the most part not expressed in the intentional idiom. (For the most part, they are not *expressed* at all.)

5. There is more on Dennett, including an account of the 'instrumentalist' label, in Essay 10.

6. I bring Marx in because I want to distance myself from the idea that (as I have been told) it is a sign of postmodernism to wish to get past the going versions of naturalism.

7. John McDowell (1994) contrasts what he calls bald naturalism with a naturalism whose conception of nature is premodern. His contrast, I think, subsumes the one which I make between what the 'naturalizers' of the going naturalism believe in, and naive naturalism. But they are *modern* writers, albeit outside the British Empiricist tradition, who have endeared me to the premodern conception of nature: see n. 6 above, and n. 1 to postscript to Essay 2.

8. Cp. Baker, 1987—a book which I regret I did not come across until this work was complete.

9. The continuity is shown, for example, in Papineau, 1993. In that book, naturalism is 'the view that human beings are normal parts of the natural world described by science', and naturalism is defended as a consequence of 'certain physical truisms'. The principal 'truism' is the completeness of physics, which Papineau makes the foundation of various theses of supervenience.

Supervenience theses are typically so formulated that they presuppose the ontological claims I deny: their proponents take the supervenience base to be 'physical properties', but 'physical' is understood in such a sense that mental things are not in that sense physical (not in my view). On supervenience, see further Essay 7, §6. And for an account of how supervenience theses might fare when physics is not privileged, see Morris, 1992, pp. 174ff.

1. Persons and Their States, and Events

1. This is an example where the true holism of the mental (the interdependencies there are between states of different kinds) is ignored. Often the propositional attitude states are treated separately from others (see Introduction §2). The present point is that even the understanding of propositional attitude states is restricted.

2. Crane and Mellor's thesis is that there is no defensible definition of 'physicalism' such that physicalism could deprive commonsense psychology of the ontological status of the non-mental sciences. These authors' own certainty that commonsense psychology has the relevant ontological status relies

upon their claim that nothing can rule out commonsense psychological laws (1990, pp. 200–201). This claim is surely not trivial. (Like others (Davidson, 1970, and his followers), I reject it.)

The non-triviality of physicalism itself (however misguidedly so-called) is seen when philosophers derive it from this non-trivial claim. Not that there is any necessary link between physicalism and the claim. Crane and Mellor may well be right to think that no properly ontological thesis can be got from the claim. And physicalism can be otherwise got: Davidson himself does not get it from the claim, which contradicts his thesis of anomalism as he meant it. Nevertheless, the claim has seemed to recommend 'physicalism'. (One can see that the ontological doctrine commonly known as physicalism might be arrived at either by way of Davidson's premises or by using something like the claim in Crane and Mellor, by comparing the two arguments stated sketchily at the end of §4 of Essay 8 below—Davidson's argument and a 'quicker' one. Employing a term from that essay, I could say that even if physicalism is not at issue between Crane and Mellor and me, impersonalism may be.)

3. See Steward, 1997, esp. chaps. 4 and 8. Steward's discussions of causation in part 2 of that book, as well as of ontology in part 1, often provide actual arguments against claims which I have been content to reject on the basis of their lacking any support. Steward and I are agreed about the mistaken assumptions in ontology and mistaken pictures of causality's operation upon which much current philosophy of mind rests.

4. A philosopher who refuses to treat consciousness as a residual problem, and whose 'biological naturalism' might seem to be in keeping with my own naive naturalism, is John Searle (see his 1992 book). But I cannot agree with Searle that the mysteriousness surrounding consciousness derives from our ignorance of how 'the system of neurophysiology/consciousness' works, because (as I have explained) I do not think we should ever 'find it obvious that if *the brain* was in a certain state, *it* had to be conscious' (1992, p. 102, my italics).

In the light of the following essays in Part I, it may be apparent that an attitude like Searle's to ontological reductionism (e.g., at 1992, p. 113) will strike me as blasé. For more on biologism in connexion with Searle, see Essay 10 n. 9.

2. Descartes, Rorty and the Mind-Body Fiction

1. I confine attention here to the first two chapters. If my view of Rorty's thought as presented here has been influenced by other of Rorty's writings, then (except at the postscript) these are his earlier writings in the philosophy of mind.

2. Descartes, *Sixth Set of Replies*, at p. 251, in vol. 2 of 1967.

3. Descartes, *Meditation II*, at p. 151, in vol. 2 of 1967.

4. Descartes, *Meditation VI*, at p. 196, in vol. 2 of 1967.

5. See the beginning of Williams, 1970. The distinction is useful when discussing writings about so-called Cartesian Dualism. But the distinction is arguably quite foreign to the thought of Descartes himself.

6. Descartes, *Passions of the Soul*, Article XI, at p. 336, in vol. 1 of 1967.

7. For example, Descartes, in *Reply to the Sixth Set of Objections*, at p. 253, in vol. 1 of 1967.

8. See Wilson, 1978, pp. 183–184. I try in what follows to push forward in one respect her view that much of what now goes by the name 'Cartesian Dualism' is not attributable to Descartes: I suggest that some of what deserves to go by that name is attributable to modern materialists.

9. Descartes, *Discourse on the Method*, at pp. 116–117, in vol. 1 of 1967.

10. Descartes, *Reply to the Sixth Set of Objections*, at pp. 253–254, in vol. 1 of 1967.

11. Descartes, *The Principles of Philosophy*, Part IV, Principle CXCVIII, at p. 296, in vol. 1 of 1967.

12. Descartes, Letter to Regius, December 1641, at p. 122, in 1970.

13. Nagel, 1986, pp. 32–33.

14. I am deliberately not much more explicit than Rorty is about the tenets of neo-dualism: the aim is only to make room for a position which is (1) coherent, (2) consistent with Rorty's few positive characterizations of it, and (3) plausibly actually held by some present-day philosophers. I assume that Thomas Nagel and Donald Davidson (for rather different reasons) would both count as having seen virtues in epistemic neo-dualism; and it would be hard to define the position with greater explicitness or in greater detail without losing one of them. As may be clear, I should also like neo-dualism to be true—if infelicitously named.

15. This is not to suggest that we can have a clear idea of what counts as a 'purely epistemic' thesis in this area. (Is Davidson's thesis that there are no psychophysical laws epistemic, for instance?)

16. The affinity between Descartes and the modern materialists at this point is highlighted when Descartes responds to the objection that the soul is not the sort of thing to influence matter: he says, 'If "corporeal" is taken to mean anything that can in any way affect a body, then mind too must be called corporeal in this sense' (Descartes, Letter to Hyperaspites, August 1641, at p. 112, in 1970). And the hylomorphism of Descartes (well brought out by Hoffman, 1986) may not interfere with this point of resemblance to the materialists: it can be the soul *as motive power* that plays for Descartes the role that the central nervous system plays for the materialists.

17. For the idea that nature is something strictly external to perceivers, see, e.g., Descartes, *Principles*, Part IV, CXCIX, at p. 296, in 1967.

18. 'Banishing' eliminative materialism is the position called eliminativism in my Introduction. I take 'vanishing' eliminative materialism to be a view less recently propounded; and I agree with Rorty (1979, pp. 117–119) that it is not a more plausible version of reductive materialism, but rather, as it were, another way of putting certain reductive materialist beliefs.

19. Definitely *not* all physicists' explanations, in Rorty's view: this is to allow for what in the next sentence I call the pluralism in Rorty's conception of the Physical.

20. Rorty, 1979, p. 27.

21. Rorty, then, like me, is after a position which is both naturalistic and anti-scientistic. To some, this will seem to be a hopeless objective: Putnam tells us that he meant by 'naturalistic' what McDowell means by 'scientistic' (Putnam, 1992, p. 360). But Putnam's usage may be a symptom of the extent to which the naturalizers have had a monopoly on the term 'natural'. 'Scientistic', at any rate, is a safer term for what one intends to denigrate.

Of course a position worthy of the name of naturalism is not secured simply by labelling something 'naturalism'. I have suggested here that it is harder than Rorty thinks it is to avoid the kind of naturalism which is caught up with the scientism that Rorty takes to be a legacy of the Enlightenment.

3. Physicalism, Events and Part-Whole Relations

1. For an explicit defense, see Fodor, 1973.

2. This statement is given by McDowell, 1978.

3. Davidson, 1970.

4. 'Fusion', as it is used here and throughout, can be defined in terms of 'part' (z is the fusion of x and y, if and only if x and y are parts of z, and anything which is a part of z is a part either of x or of y or of something all of whose parts are parts of either x or y). Nothing, then, turns on the choice of the word 'fusion' except what follows from our ordinary understanding of 'part' applied to particulars. ('Sum' or 'aggregate' might have been used instead of 'fusion'.)

In any sophisticated treatment, 'fusion' will be a multigrade relation, and not the simple two-place one used in (A) (at the start of §3 below). For a useful discussion, see Eberle, 1970, esp. ch. 2.

5. See (a) Hellman and Thompson, 1975 and 1971, (b) McGinn, 1980, and (c) Peacocke, 1979, p. 44. In (a) and (b), there is an assumption that the notion of parthood can do some work in arriving at physicalism; see n. 14 on

(a), and n. 20 on (b). (C) makes no such assumption, and merely introduces 'parthood' into a statement of physicalism.

6. As it stands, (A) is suited, in the presence of claims about what there basically is, to say what else there is. For many mereologists, the basic individuals will be point-sized occupants of space-time (or, ultimately, for the reductionist mereologist, the items will be space-time points). Some mereologists believe (with Quine) that an ontology whose members are identified with the contents of spatiotemporal regions (or, ultimately, with spatiotemporal regions) incorporates continuants and events alike; other mereologists (such as David Lewis, for whom point-sized occupants of space-time are point-sized bits of *matter*) take such an ontology to incorporate continuants, but hold some different theory of events. By considering (A) separately for the cases of continuants and of events, I mean to cover both of these doctrines, and also a doctrine in which, for the continuant case, the basic individuals are chemical atoms or their constituents.

7. See Goodman, 1951, p. 51.

8. For connexions between the notion of a continuant and a principle of individuation (which gives *inter alia* intelligible persistence conditions), made via the notion of a sortal concept, see Wiggins, 1980. My argument here takes such connexions for granted, and questions whether a mereologist can admit them.

9. By 'material thing' one may or may not intend what Quine intends by 'physical object' (in, e.g., Quine, 1981). Those who think that the 'contents of portions of space-time' are *material* contents will use a notion of material thing which differs from Quine's notion of physical objects in excluding events; cp. n. 6.

10. See, e.g., David Wiggins's discussion of Locke in his 1968 essay. And for a discussion of the counterexamples to (U), and arguments that they are genuine, see Doepke, 1982.

11. Some of the difficulties about regarding continuants as things with temporal parts are brought out by Geach, 1979, pp. 70–71. See also Mellor, 1981, esp. ch. 8.

12. At this point, essentialist considerations may be brought against the mereological conception (see, e.g., Wiggins, 1980, pp. 136ff.). Such considerations are used for the case of events in Boyd, 1980.

Quine, who regards continuants (his 'bodies') as a special kind of physical object (cp. n. 9), relies on reinterpreting (say) 'ring' as 'place-time of a ring'. The question I would put to Quine is: How can people's understanding of (say) 'ring', and their abilities to make references to rings, be accounted for in the terms that the reinterpretation uses?

13. A more radical suggestion might be made at this point: that we simply

eliminate continuants from our discourse. For arguments against that suggestion, see Doepke, 1982. Doepke also provides more detailed arguments supporting the conclusions of the preceding paragraphs of the text.

14. (C) is a simplified and slightly modified version of something proposed by Jarvis Thomson, 1977. The complicated antecedent is required because a proponent of (A) will wish to place some restrictions on the possibility of the inheritance by fusions of the causal properties of their parts. One can imagine all sorts of variants on (C), and (A)'s proponent might well suggest something more highly qualified. The arguments that follow do not exploit any of the deficiencies of (C) that have resulted from aiming at something relatively simple.

Hellman and Thompson, 1971 and 1975, are committed to something like (C) if they agree that events are such as to stand in causal relations. If their characterization of distinctively physicalist doctrines in those papers were correct, then even the physicalist who confined herself to the ontological doctrine of §1 would commit herself to a mereological conception of events.

15. This is only a gesture towards an argument. My remarks about causal explanation in §5 below are suggestive of further problems about combining counterfactual accounts of causation with a mereological conception of events.

16. I am thinking specifically of the account of causation in Davidson, 1967a. (This is discussed further in §7 below, in the next essay, in the postscript to Part I and in Essay 8.)

17. Of course, it may be a vague (or even unanswerable) question which microphysical events occur in the spatiotemporal region in which some given economic event occurs. In assuming that the relevant microphysical events could be specified, we make a concession to the physicalist. (For arguments designed to show that there really is vagueness of this kind in the case of some mental events, and that the vagueness creates a problem for the physicalist, see Essay 4.)

18. Cp. Fodor, 1973, who says that 'interesting generalizations . . . can often be made about events whose physical descriptions have nothing in common'. Fodor himself, in making the point, presupposed that all events have physical descriptions, which is to beg the question at issue here.

19. Compare here Putnam, 1979. In that review, Putnam considered anomalous monism, and introduced comparisons between continuants and events so far as their physical status was concerned. But I think that Putnam distracted our attention from the relevant comparisons in two ways. First, he failed to distinguish between claims about identity and claims about composition: he simply took for granted the mereological conception of continuants discussed in §§2 and 3 above, and found physicalism about continuants quite

unproblematic in consequence. Second, Putnam used the phrase 'a particular event E' to denote a (certain) repeatable thing, so that what he calls events are not always the particulars that are at issue here. I agree with Putnam on the point that physicalism about continuants is less controversial than physicalism about events (mental events, say). The rest of the present section is meant to provide an explanation of this point.

20. The argument of McGinn, 1980, may gain its plausibility from a failure to appreciate the disanalogy. McGinn defends physicalism by way of the principle that every particular is of some natural kind. Taking artifacts to provide counterexamples to this principle literally construed, he modifies it—adding to it a disjunction with the effect that the principle only requires *parts* of particulars to be of natural kinds. It is a question why we should find the modified principle compelling for the case of events; and another question whether we should be satisfied with the physicalism that could be derived from it in the case of events.

21. A comparison of events with continuants has been crucial to my argument insofar as it can be used to support the idea that it is no more plausible that a purely spatiotemporal ideology defines events than that such an ideology defines continuants. One might mention counterexamples to (U) (see §3) in the case of events in a more direct argument for the conclusion about events; for example, the simultaneous rotating and heating of a metal ball, suggested by Davidson, 1969. Such examples help to make it plain that identity questions are not to be settled by reference to purely spatiotemporal facts.

If someone accepts this point in the continuant case, it seems it ought to be easy to persuade him that continuants do not have temporal parts. But for the purpose of my argument, it may be unnecessary to persuade him of that. *Pro tanto* we do not require any exact analogue in the event case of the claim that continuants lack temporal parts; though counterexamples to (U) can still be relevant both where continuants are concerned and where events are concerned. A full discussion of event-parts and of comparisons between event-parts and continuant-parts would take one well beyond the considerations used here.

22. Boyd, 1980, cites considerations similar to those of §3 here as a ground for suspicion of Davidson's event identity claims. But Boyd's argument assumes the existence of composition relations between, for example, neural events and mental events; and I do not think we have to concede so much to the physicalist in raising the question that both Boyd and I would wish to raise. (Boyd's eventual conclusion is that 'token events . . . seem less stereotypical "individuals", and more like type events, more like "universals"'. The conclusion seems to me to be rested on a conflation of the *composition* and *re-*

alization relations. If the conclusion were correct, it might undermine the relevance of the comparisons between continuants and events.)

23. See further Essay 4.

4. Which Physical Events Are Mental Events?

1. For such argument, see, e.g., Davidson, 1970, Fodor, 1976, Wiggins, 1976 and McGinn, 1977. For the contrast between stronger and weaker physicalisms, see further Dennett, 1979, pp. xiv–xvii, and McDowell, 1978.

2. I offer further argument for the account of action outlined in this section in the first three chapters of Hornsby, 1980. There is more on *action* in Part II here.

3. I derive these conditions from recent work on the subject: see, e.g., Davis, 1979, pp. 18–22. If my statement appears very different from Davis's, then that is (a) because I avoid the locution "doing an A", which imports the false idea of particular actions as the things we do (§2.1), and (b) because I think that actions, even if they are events of trying (§2.2), are not volitions.

4. See, e.g., Peacocke, 1979, pp. 134ff., which rests upon such an assumption about uniqueness of denotation.

5. Benacerraf, 1965. In one important respect, the arithmetical case differs from the present case: it is indeterminate which sets particular numbers are because there is no unique best reduction of number theory to set theory; in the case of mental events, the indeterminacies are not owed to rival reduction and crop up one by one. This means that the analogue of certain reactions to the arithmetical case need not be considered. But in both cases the same question arises what to say about the particulars, numbers or events.

6. This argument is in Evans, 1978. Evans concludes that there cannot be vague objects. But see the next paragraph for a conception of a vague object which isn't vulnerable to his argument (albeit a conception which, I argue, cannot be sustained for the objects at issue here).

7. Kripke (1971) also was concerned to make out that his argument showed more than what I am here imagining an opponent saying is all that my argument shows. 'Mere non-identity . . . may be a weak conclusion . . . The Cartesian modal argument, however, surely can be deployed to maintain relevant stronger conclusions as well.' What I deny is that non-identity is a weak conclusion—if a weak conclusion is one that does little damage to what people believe. I should want to claim also that, having recognized that the conclusion Kripke calls weak is presupposed to most physicalists' claims (see below §5), we should be in a position to use that conclusion to explain the intuitions that serve Kripke's Cartesian modal argument; and that then there

may be no relevant stronger conclusions which the Cartesian argument could be deployed to maintain.

8. Quine, 1977, p. 190, Hellman and Thompson, 1975.

9. Peacocke, 1979, emphasizes the difficulty when he shows that neither supervenience nor determination à la Hellman and Thompson catches the notion that a physicalist wants: see n. 4, pp. 120–122. Ideas about everything's dependence on the physical are customarily given in those of supervenience. See Introduction, n. 8.

5. Action and the Mental-Physical Divide

1. In 1980 I said that 'actions are inside the body', mistakenly supposing that this gave a vivid summary statement of my view that actions are described in terms of their effects so long as they are described as actions. No doubt my summary statement abetted the idea that I think actions are 'mental'. I like to suppose that it can be retracted while leaving almost everything else intact.

2. There was an example from Putnam in n. 19 of Essay 3, see p. 229.

6. Bodily Movements, Actions and Epistemology

1. The use of 'physical' at the beginning of this sentence (and in the first paragraph of §2) is a stipulative one, which might be provisionally defined by this sentence itself.

2. My statement relies upon a distinction between things that are done (which are not particulars: I can do the same thing as you) and actions (which are particulars: your doing something cannot be the same as my doing that thing). I avoid the 'intentional under some description' terminology of Davidson, 1971a, but the criterion of actionhood I intend is his.

Some of those who engage in the controversy I am introducing believe that we should recognize some 'subintentional' items as actions, thereby recognizing more actions than Davidson's criterion defines; but they need not deny what is assumed here, that at least the items Davidson calls actions are actions.

3. The argument for this was given by Grice in his 1967 William James lectures, and by Armstrong, 1973. O'Shaughnessy, 1974, used the argument, and I attempted to state a more general version (1980, pp. 33ff.). O'Shaughnessy has since argued for a more general thesis still: he identifies actions with attempts even where the class of actions includes the subintentional (cp. n. 2); see O'Shaughnessy, 1980, vol. 2, ch. 11.

4. Notice that 'and intentionally moves her body' is doing some actual work in this sentence. For one can accept that someone's action is her intentionally doing something that she does by moving her body without affirming

that she intentionally moves her body. I am inclined to doubt that *move the body* is something that we intentionally do whenever we try to do something that requires a bodily movement. Because the claim about *trying* above is confined to what we intentionally do ('we try to do what we intentionally do'), I am not committed to thinking that whenever there is a ("physical") action, there is an event of trying to move the body—even if I confine myself to cases in which that is so.

5. The quotation is from McGinn, 1982b, p. 90. McGinn there perspicuously sets out four different views.

6. For instance, O'Shaughnessy, 1980, who accepts identities between actions and attempts, argues for them only by way of arguing against alternatives. Jackson (1982) dissents from the identity thesis without contemplating arguments other than the negative ones that O'Shaughnessy uses.

7. The generality of the schema may be doubted. (We say such things as 'I'll arrive at the station on time by telephoning for a taxi', but we don't want to identify my arriving at the station with my telephoning.) But it need not be doubted that, whatever argument can be given for the account of action individuation, it will, with some regularity, yield statements of identity between actions and events describable as someone's trying to ———.

8. This is by no means a novel thesis. Ryle must have accepted it (see 1949, ch. 5, §4).

It may be objected that we need to distinguish between attempts to move the body and attempts to bring about things beyond the body. That which is here called the attempt is someone's trying to wiggle her finger; and (it will be said) this can be distinct from her action, even if her action is to be identified with, say, her trying to get someone's attention. I think that there are difficulties about treating *trying to move the body* as a special case. But one's view of this matter is likely to depend upon whether one thinks that any moving of the body that is an action is an intentional moving of the body (cp. n. 4 above), and upon whether one accepts that we can have a uniform account of *trying to* of the kind suggested below (penultimate paragraph of §2).

9. This is evidently McGinn's motive when he writes, 'The composite conception of action . . . seems to meet our desideratum of displaying actions as inherently psychophysical more successfully than [three other conceptions]' (1982b, p. 90).

Notice that someone might think that there was a point in insisting that persons are inherently psychophysical but be dissatisfied with a conception of a person (actually Descartes's) as composed out of something mental and something physical. It must then be possible to give serious content to a claim that something is psychophysical without introducing any notion such as composition to say how the psychological and the physical exist together.

10. Arguments are offered for an account of individuation of actions that regards as parts of actions things that on the present account are the consequences of actions. But these are not arguments for the specific claim that *movements* are parts of actions.

O'Shaughnessy accepts the claim of identity of the action with the attempt and takes the movement to be part of the action; but he happily concedes that there is no straightforward specification of the action-minus-movement. This he calls a non-autonomous part, and he is not affected by the argument of the present paragraph. O'Shaughnessy's own argument for this view relies on the rejection of alternatives.

11. Another possible reason may be given which bypasses any questions about the status of the attempt. Here I mean the consideration stated by McGinn when he says that a theory that identifies actions with movements 'fails to register the essential activity of actions' (1982b, p. 88). It may be that this consideration gains some of its force from the idea that movements are "mere" movements—an idea that I challenge in §5 and in the postscript below. Still, there does seem to be something right in the suggestion that there are certain predications that we can make of actions, but not of movements. For the kinds of predication that might be mentioned here, see O'Shaughnessy, 1980, vol. 2, p. 128. (It is true that O'Shaughnessy sets out these features in the course of preparing to argue for the conclusion that actions are *not* distinct from movements. But, given O'Shaughnessy's views, the non-distinctness in question cannot be identity; cf. n. 10.)

12. One may have a view of "deviant chains" that would lead one to qualify this.

13. This imports the idea that it is possible for someone to try to move her body and fail to do so. More controversial than that is the thesis that if someone succeeds in moving her body, then the very event that occurred and that was her trying to move her body could still have occurred even if she had not succeeded. (See Smith, 1983.)

14. Acceptance of the thesis called more controversial in n. 13 may lead to a cleaner argument than that presented here against the idea that the action is both the attempt and the movement. It may also affect our view of the idea considered in the previous paragraph that the movement is a part of the action; and here it will make a difference whether one is with O'Shaughnessy in accepting the action/attempt identities, or with McGinn in denying them.

McGinn, 1982b, p. 89, argues as follows against the identity of action with attempt: 'The trying could occur without the movement; but in those circumstances the action would not have occurred. In short, tryings are contingently successful, but actions are necessarily successful'. Now the claim in the last four words is not 'Necessarily there is nothing to which "action" applies unless there is a movement'; if this were the claim, it would be compatible with the idea that the trying/action might occur without the movement. The claim must be: 'Any event that is an action could not have failed to be an action'; in this case, the claim itself may be disputed, and the argument now also requires the thesis about trying that I have called 'more controversial' (at n. 13).

15. In the first two chapters of my 1980 book I offered considerations different from any used or alluded to here in favour of the view that actions cause movements.

16. See, e.g., O'Shaughnessy, 1980, vol. 2, pp. 130ff; and McGinn (1982b), who writes: 'We can see someone's actions when we see him move his body; but on [this] theory [which identifies actions with attempts] all you see are the consequences of the agent's actions, never the actions themselves, since the tryings with which actions are identified are purely inner events invisible to the naked eye' (pp. 88–89). In chap. 7 of *Actions*, I responded to the objection that my view had the absurd consequence that actions are invisible. But there I made the claim that 'actions occur inside the body,' misguidedly supposing that this was a vivid summary statement of my view. With that claim to one side, the defense against the objection can be conducted rather better: see Essay 5.

17. Philosophers single out the word 'action' to stand for events in a certain class (see the beginning of §1 above). The word does not play that role in every use, and one does not preserve the sense of sentences if one switches between the philosopher's carefully delimited use and other uses; see Essay 5, §3. Here I think we have a case in point: I suggest that when we say that actions are visible, finding that obviously correct, we do not use 'action' in the delimited way. (This is not to say that it is false in any sense that actions are visible.)

18. I take it that 'x saw a moving his finger' is to be assimilated to 'x saw a move his finger' (from which it differs in aspect), and not to 'x saw a's moving of his finger': in this last construction, but only here, the whole of what follows 'saw' is a noun phrase in extensional position. I take it also that 'x saw a ϕ', unlike 'x saw that a ϕ-d', requires sight by x of a for its truth.

19. It seems as if McGinn thinks that the overtness of movements guarantees the overtness of attempts-plus-movements. For he thinks that attempts are hidden (see the quotation in n. 16 above), but that attempts-plus-movements, which in his own view are actions, are visible. McGinn might use the principle that if a thing is visible it has a visible part. But this principle, though it may be correct for material objects, seems to have less to recommend it for events. (Suppose someone was worried that he could not see actions because he thought that they went on inside us. It is not obvious that he would be reassured if he was then told that only parts of them go on inside

us—especially if he were told that the psychological part of an action is always on the inside.)

Similarly, O'Shaughnessy thinks that to allow that actions 'encompass' movements is to ensure that actions are visible (1980, vol. 2, p. 132). (Though he does not identify actions with attempts-plus-movements—cf. n. 10.)

20. 'At best directly' is deliberately vague. The epistemological outlook that I describe here is associated with many different views about how we have knowledge of others and how much of it we have. (One's view of how much is not determined by the outlook because it depends on how seriously one is able to take the predicament that the outlook creates, and on how one conceives knowledge of one's mind, etc.)

21. See, e.g., Taylor, 1964, ch. 3, n. 1, pp. 55–56.

22. Until it is decided whether actions are distinct from bodily movements, it remains an open question whether a distinction between actions and movements is in fact (as I believe) a distinction between items within the realm of events.

An ambiguity in 'move' (see Essay 5, §3) can be acknowledged even by those who deny the distinctness of actions and movements, and who thus deny that the ambiguity corresponds to any distinction between items within the realm of events. This shows that we may have to detect two possible sources of ambiguity in 'behaviour', even if we deny that one of them proves to correspond to the distinction 'within the realm of events' just mentioned in the text.

23. Similarly, one has made no advance in exposing the traitor if one knows only that one has seen the traitor. This point derives from the extensionality of the '*x* sees *a*' construction (cp. n. 18). (If our interest were in epistemology at its most general—do we see things in an external material world?—then we should have to concern ourselves with questions framed using the extensional construction. I assume that someone who raises questions about the visibility of actions doesn't [*pro hac vice*] have an interest in epistemology at its most general.)

24. This doesn't yet contradict someone who holds that there is, for any bodily movement, a colourless characterization of it. But see postscript to this essay. Here I confine myself to arguing against those who think that we *must* start with colourless characterizations of movements if we distinguish these from actions.

25. See Cook, 1969, and McDowell, 1982. See also Long, 1964.

26. Other arguments are given against the thesis (see, e.g., O'Shaughnessy, 1980, vol. 2, ch. 11). I should hope to use a consideration of the kind in §3 above in reply (see n. 17).

27. I say *some* people. It is possible that someone should think that the ar-

gument of §3 is inconclusive but not want to frame his response to that argument in the terms of the objector who speaks at the start of §4.

28. For a full discussion, and for arguments for its compatibility with causal accounts of perception, see Child, 1994, pp. 143–153.

29. This reason is at work in Moore, 1993, who seeks a 'reductive' thesis about actions: the phrase 'ordinary physical world' is taken from him (p. 83). But a neutral conception of bodily movements is not the property of reductionists alone: see below. I respond to Moore's reductionism in Hornsby, 1994.

30. A full discussion of the two disjunctive conceptions would need to speak to phenomenology. In the case of perception, it is the *anti*-disjunctivist who places great weight on the fact that perceptions and hallucinations do not seem any different to the subject. When it comes to action, it may be that the *disjunctivist* will argue from phenomenology: bodily movements are special among effects of action in being objects of proprioception. There is much more to be said here.

31. See McDowell, 1988 and 1994, for the epistemology that disjunctive accounts make available.

32. 'Facts about their occurrence', because we have to see people *in action* for their states of mind to be disclosed to us. Really there is no need to place any emphasis on bodily movements to give a satisfactory account of common-sense psychological knowledge of others. Bodily movements are only actually prominent in accounts which a disjunctive conception of them enables one to oppose.

7. Physicalist Thinking and Conceptions of Behaviour

1. I have changed the order of Kim's sentences. For a similar argument, given in the course of a defense of functionalism, see Loar, 1981, p. 88.

2. It may be said that this counterexample is importantly different from the examples that were Kim's concern, because in the counterexample it is only in the presence of the explanans that we come to be able to separate necessary conditions for the obtaining of the explanandum. But this feature may also be present in psychological cases. We can know that someone turned on the burner (and know what psychological explanation there is of that) without knowing what sort of bodily movement on her part resulted in the burner's being on.

3. Where Lewis uses 'state' I use 'type of state' because I make no assumption that functionalists are committed to any type identities of Lewis's sort.

4. 'Bodily movements' is used by Loar and others; 'motor responses' by Lewis in 1972.

5. There is little here that is uncontroversial. (See Essay 6.) What I assume now is that we can distinguish the denotation of descriptions such as '*a*'s raising her arm', which are actions, from the denotation of such descriptions as '*a*'s arm's rising', which are not actions.

6. Loar uses a technical, theoretical psychological notion of *willing*, whereas my exposition uses *trying*. Loar's view of theoretical psychology is discussed in §5. For arguments (in effect) that 'try' has many of the properties needed for the two-stage account of action production, see chaps. 3 and 4 of my 1980 book.

7. Loar's argument for narrowing down psychological explanation (see n. 1) introduces *basic actions*, which Loar calls 'primary explananda'. He says that non-basic things are explained by 'independent facts', that is, facts that are not themselves psychologically explained. The question for Loar is quite parallel to that for Kim: is the reason offered for extricating independent facts from non-basic things not also a reason for extricating non-psychological facts even from basic things?

There are two points about Loar's terminology: (a) I have spoken of *basic things (done)*, rather than *basic actions*, because actions themselves, assuming these are particulars, do not stand to one another in relations of relative basicness (see Hornsby, 1981); (b) it may be that Loar himself does not distinguish actions from bodies' movements, as my exposition of functionalism has suggested that functionalists do.

I state the second stage of a functionalist's account of output as I do because I think that (on occasion) an agent's ϕ-ing is the same as her trying to ϕ and not the same as a movement of the ϕ-type. Still, the consequent of the conditional might read '*a* ϕs'—only then the conditional cannot be supposed to take one from cause to effect (unless one denies that, on occasion, events of trying simply are actions). At any rate, the argument addressed to Kim and Loar requires only that some condition relating to the agent's body's functioning, as well as some condition relating to the agent's mind, is necessary for the occurrence of an action. To accept this much, no stand need be taken on the controversies alluded to in n. 5 or on the details of a correct formulation of the two-stage account of action production.

8. See my account of what I there called *teleologically* basic descriptions of actions in chap. 6 of my 1980 book. And notice that I make no assumption to the effect that all beliefs are linguistically expressible by their possessors.

If bodily movement descriptions of actions are not basic, then there will be some *non-bodily* basic descriptions for functionalists to use in describing outputs. But if the functionalist does use output O-terms which touch on regions beyond the agent's body, then (a) it will become more implausible that his 'simple ability' conditions are 'purely psychological', and (b) this will do nothing to supply the richness that functionalists seem to want to find in their notion of behaviour (see below).

9. I am relying here on such claims as are made for examples by Strawson and Warnock in Pears, ed., 1963: our system of classifying actions is grounded in quite different interests from any system of bodily movement classification. I do not conclude, as they did, that actions are not bodily movements; but I do take their claim to show the irreducibility of movements-classified-by-someone-interested-in-action to movements-classified-by-the-scientists-interested-in-movements-*per-se*.

10. It may be pointed out that complexity could be derived from complexity in descriptions of *inputs*. (Functionalists insist that stimulus terms as well as behavioural ones are needed to characterize the mental ones: this is a respect in which functionalists are thought to differ from behaviourists which I have not singled out for attention.) But I think that there are things to be said about *perception* which lead in the same direction as the things I have said about *action* and which should show that the functionalist cannot make anything of this point. And the argument I actually give is meant to rely on the fact that my opponents themselves believe that more detail is needed in *output* specifications than (so I say) they are entitled to.

11. This explains the technicalities in Loar's account (see n. 6). Loar's suggestion is that if a theory well confirmed by experiments in theoretical psychology and neurophysiology were true of a person, and certain of the functional states of the theory satisfied the full complement of the constraints imposed by common sense as necessary conditions of having beliefs and desires, then it would be correct to count those functional states as beliefs and desires.

12. The 'certain' beliefs are (intuitively, and leaving out modifications that would be required to accommodate fortuitously false beliefs) those whose truth is required for the agent's trying to ϕ to result in the agent's ϕ-ing.

It is easy to miss the point about the ramification of worldly conditions if one thinks about explanation as we know it and forgets about the predictive aspirations of functionalists' output generalizations. When we know the explanation of an agent's doing something, we are in a position to specify a small number of beliefs which enter the explanation of her doing that, and only some of these are beliefs whose truth values bear on whether she has actually done the thing. But this is not the position of someone who hopes for a general, predictive theory of what agents do. Consider a functionalist who hoped to derive actual mental-physical identities for the case of a particular person at a particular time. He might start with a list of types of state which were instantiated in the person at that time. For any type of state on that list, he will say (counterfactually) that its instance would interact thus and so *if*. . . .

Thus *possible* events of trying must be seen (at *t*) as such as to be produced in a person (at a time later than *t*) by way of beliefs that the person may lack (at *t*).

Some people seem to forget that a functionalist's psychological theory must make mention of all the types of mental state there are. I have put the matter as I have here because it may help to remind one of this. It shows, I think, that someone who responded to the argument of Essay 4 by suggesting that a more broadly based functionalism is needed to discover identities of actions with neural events would need to invoke 'type-type psychophysical correlations'.

13. I say that there is no warrant for the detail. But I should acknowledge that I have an argument only insofar as I am in a position to ask (rhetorically), 'What reason could there be for supposing that the detail is warranted?' ('What reason could there be for supposing that theoretical psychology can dictate to common sense?') Of course the committed proponent of scientific materialism thinks that there are reasons where I see none: he supposes that metaphysical principles provide the warrant. I try to engage with his position in §§8 and 9.

14. McDowell also argues that if expositions such as Loar's seem to undermine Davidson's claims about the mental's anomalousness, then that could only be an illusion. He focuses attention on 'internal constraints', whereas I have focused on 'output generalizations'. See McDowell, 1985.

15. The argument is in McGinn, 1982b, p. 29, though McGinn himself would not endorse the argument just as it stands (see n. 17).

16. Of course anyone can, if he wants, put commonsense descriptions of behaviour together with scientific descriptions of behaviour and call what he arrives at descriptions of behaviour. What cannot be guaranteed, however, is that, having assembled a notion of behaviour by reference to two explanatory schemes, one has then accorded some stable sense to 'explanation of behaviour' or 'behavioural disposition'. (I have not said that no one is entitled to the functionalists' conception of behaviour; I have only questioned whether one is entitled to suppose that it can be put to the use to which functionalists put it.)

17. See, for example, McGinn, 1982a. McGinn himself argues that the notion of *content* is decomposable into explanatory and truth-conditional aspects. The explanatory states he envisages do not have semantic content by virtue of their explanatory role, and the arguments below apply to his position inasmuch as this is so. See further Essay 12.

18. The story that mental terms were actually introduced as theoretical terms is called a myth by Lewis. In support of the idea that it is a good myth (sc. that our terms for mental states mean just what they would if the myth were true), Lewis says that if it were a good myth it would explain the appeal of Rylean behaviourism. But the appeal of Rylean behaviourism cannot be

separated from its use of a broad and everyday notion of behaviour; and this is a notion which ought not to be available to one who tells the mythical story.

19. That this is a point about psychological explanation, rather than about 'head-world correlations', will be apparent only if one takes a relaxed view of psychological explanation; see §2.

20. Lewis is sensible to the fact that intentional notions must be precluded from accounts of behaviour if they are to be put to a theoretical use. He wrote: "There is an ambiguity in the term 'behaviour'. . . . I am using it to refer to raw behaviour—body movements and the like . . .; not to behaviour specified partly in terms of the agent's intentions. . . . That Karl's fingers move on certain trajectories and exert certain forces is what I call 'behaviour'; that he signs a cheque is not" (1974, at p. 114 in 1983). What Lewis seems to want to rule out from 'raw' behavioural descriptions are only instances of 'φ' such that any event of someone's φ-ing is an event of her intentionally φ-ing. There is no need to deny that this ruling can give us a notion of behaviour. What I do deny is that such a ruling provides us with a notion that might have been used by someone ignorant of all commonsense psychological truths. I deny, then, that Lewis has found a notion fit for his 'good myth'. (Of course there *is* a notion of behaviour [or anyway of *output*] that we can imagine applied in utter independence of any interest in persons; but with this [very raw] notion, we return to one on which we get no real purchase when we state commonsense psychological accounts.)

21. What Descartes's commentators are typically most anxious to remind us of is that Descartes should not have held both that mind and body are substances whose essences are distinct, and that mind and body causally interact. Williams is an exception: he describes a difficulty which is independent of Descartes's treating the mind as soul-like, and which depends only upon Descartes's thinking that all the transactions between the mental and the physical happen, as it were, at an interface. See the discussion of *terminal* interactionism (as Williams says we might call it) in Williams, 1978, pp. 288–292.

8. Agency and Causal Explanation

1. Or again, free agency, if not agency itself, may be thought to be subverted: it is said that the impersonal point of view, insofar as it treats actions as happenings, and treats any happening as inevitable of occurrence, exposes freedom as an illusion.

My immediate concern is with the problem that Nagel discusses under the head of Autonomy (Nagel, 1986, ch. 7, §2, to which page references are given below). I agree with Nagel that 'the essential source of the problem is a view of persons and their actions as part of the order of nature, *causally determined or not*' (p. 110, my italics); but I leave it open whether there might be a separate threat to freedom such as would be suggested by the first sentence of this note. (In Nagel's own terms, the problem I discuss here is one about freedom: he distinguishes a question about agency, which he puts aside, from two problems about freedom, of which autonomy is the first.)

2. The doubt I am thinking of here is what leads to eliminative materialism. But any philosopher who begins with the assumption that psychological explanation requires vindication through connexion with physical science aims at such subsumption; if some such philosophers are not eliminativists it is because they do not doubt that the requirement can be met. See §7 below.

3. I assume the criterion of actionhood in Davidson, 1971a: I take 'There is some description under which the event is intentional' to be equivalent to 'There is something the agent intentionally does'.

4. McGinn, 1979, p. 26, distinguished four different theses about the explanatoriness/causal status of rational explanations. He and many others have subsequently put to work the particular (putative) distinction I am concerned with here; see below.

5. The argument is in Davidson, 1963, p. 9. Not that 'because' is everywhere a causal notion. Where action explanation is concerned, there may be more to say to ensure that causation has been at work when the explanatory claim can be made. But this is supported when it is seen (a) that the 'because' goes alongside other, recognizably causal idioms (His belief *led* him to . . .'; 'Her desire *moved* her to . . .'; 'Her reason was *operative*'); (b) that the explanations rely on a network of empirical interdependencies, recorded in counterfactuals ('If she had not wanted ———, but had still believed that ———, then . . .').

6. These are the writers to whom Davidson was responding in his 1963 article, and whom he cited there, p. 3, n. 1. And of course their view is still held by some today (e.g., Stoutland, 1976).

7. This was the thesis guaranteeing the availability of 'purely causal' statements that Davidson arrived at in his 1963 article. I discuss some details of Davidson's own position in the appendix to this essay.

8. For serious, valiant, exhaustive, but eventually abortive attempts to make sense of the idea of causal interaction between states of persons, see W. S. Robinson, 1990. My brief remarks here can only gesture towards the problems that Robinson uncovers. See also Steward, 1997. (Occurrences of 'state' in this essay are of two sorts: (i) those that come into descriptions of views opposed to my own, and (ii) those that rely on our ordinary conception of a mental state—something a person can be in, so that a state is not a particular.)

9. It is a good question why people should think that recognizing the dependences we do is not enough to ensure that we have a case of the operation of causality. Hume taught that the conception we have of necessity, as a putative ingredient of our idea of causality, is a figment, since, he said, there is no impression to which our conception corresponds. Many philosophers are happy to reply to Hume that insofar as we take necessity to be inextricable from causality, we do not take it to be an isolable, perceptible ingredient of causal transactions: searching for necessity among impressions is not the way to uncover our understanding of causation. But even when this reply has been given, the idea that our understanding of causality resides in the putative objects wherein an impression of necessity was supposed by Hume to be sought is not renounced.

10. Many have alleged the commitment in one or another version. Smith, 1984, is responsible for the particular formulation of the claim quoted above, at the end of §3. Some write as if Davidson had deliberately and explicitly committed himself to it (e.g., Lennon, 1990); others as if it required argument to demonstrate his commitment (e.g., Honderich, 1982). Some, like Smith, think that the alleged commitment does no damage; but most hold it against Davidson, and say that it shows that in his view the mental is epiphenomenal (e.g., H. Robinson, 1982). But whatever the status or consequence of his commitment is supposed to be, an enormous volume of writing suggests that Davidson must in consistency allow that reason explanation is not causal explanation.

11. It is often assumed that whereas the states and events that precede actions must be treated by an argument for monism, actions themselves can be left out. But I think that it is only a prejudice about the nature of mind that leads to the idea that *being in mental states* is problematic whereas *doing things intentionally* is not.

12. See, e.g., Davidson, 1970, p. 219, where he speaks of generalizations which support explanations, but which are heteronomic, that is, not stated in a form and vocabulary that points to a finished law. For more on this, see the appendix below.

13. Consider Lepore and Loewer's 1987 attempted reconciliation of (a) mental items' subsumability under laws, and (b) mental properties' being both anomalous and causally efficacious. For these authors, the causal relevance of mental states consists in the truth of counterfactuals each to the effect of an item's being such that if it had lacked some property, then some event would have lacked some property. We find, then, that the claims that serve to underpin rational explanations make no essential mention of a person.

Thinking of the objective of propositional attitude explanation as I suggest, we must take it for granted that content is both explanatory and externally fixed (where content is that which is specified when it is said what people think or want or hope or . . .). I gesture here towards the idea that my remarks have wider application: that they embody externalism, see postscript to Essay 12.

14. I attempted to show that the reductionist would have trouble making a plausible case anyway in Essay 4.

15. Where we talk, for example, about 'human action' (general, no plural), this is another use again from the two I have separated. (Presumably we find this general use in 'action explanation'. So where something is an instance of action explanation, it is actually wrong to think of it as an explanation of an action in either of the two senses of 'an action' that I have distinguished.)

Dretske, 1988, holds that actions are not events, but complex causal processes. His argument is that a bit of behaviour is a complex process, and he assumes that philosophers had always meant a bit of behaviour by 'action'. Dretske is relying on the assumption I am questioning: the assumption that the things we naturally say can readily be expressed as claims about actions.

16. Presumably, though, it would be allowed that it takes some argument, or at least explication, to get someone to agree that bodily movements are effects of actions—as both Lewis and I think.

17. I have extracted the words 'causal explanation' at the ellipsis. Nagel assumes that one who admits that action explanation is not of the 'objective' kind denies that it is causal. The assumption is not compulsory.

18. Nagel appreciates this: 'The sense of an internal explanation persists—an explanation insulated from the external view which is complete in itself and renders illegitimate all further requests for explanation of my action as an event in the world' (1986, p. 117). But instead of taking this to show the irrelevance of the external perspective, he takes it to be another sign of the conflict.

Nagel entertains the idea that someone who insists that the external perspective be brought to bear in the domain of reasons may be using a very limited conception of what an explanation is (1986, p. 117). But he says that anyone who considers herself entitled to a broader conception is under an obligation to show why the language of belief and desire doesn't introduce 'descriptions [merely] of how it seemed to the agent'. I suspect that Nagel thinks this obligation arises because he takes the internal view to be ultimately a first-personal one. See §7, and the end of Essay 10.

19. For ways to make these ideas precise, see Moore, 1987. The target at the end of Moore's paper is the 'absolute conception' of reality. Belief that such a conception ought to be attainable is surely one source of the view that actions are impersonally apparent; compare McDowell, 1985, p. 395. But as-

pirations more limited than aspirations to this putative conception are all that are required to generate the pressure I am trying to counteract, or so, at least, my argument assumes.

20. There is evidence that some universalizing assumption may serve for Davidson to ground his nomological principle in the ease with which he moves from 'nomological' to 'physical': compare Johnston, 1985, p. 411.

21. For the relation between the conclusion here and (a) present-day versions of physicalism, and (b) Descartes's dualism, see Essays 4 and 2 respectively.

22. See Clark, 1989, for the idea that cognitive psychology may proceed without any of the standard assumptions about connexions between folk psychology and brain science.

9. Personal and Subpersonal Levels

1. In his 1994 book, Campbell connects reductionist views of the self with exclusion of the kind of understanding that is brought to bear when a person is seen, say, to have arrived at a conclusion. The depersonalization which I am here accusing opponents of is encountered also in the various theories of personal identity against which Campbell ably argues (1994, ch. 5, esp. 5.3).

2. Where it is thought that neuroscientific subpersonal Psychology must tell the same truths as commonsense psychology, we find eliminativism. Where it is thought that functionalist subpersonal Psychology tells the same truths as commonsense psychology, we find functionalism. But whereas eliminativism is arrived at via a metaphysical doctrine about where the truth must really reside (combined with recognition that commonsense psychology has no place there), functionalism is usually rested in a doctrine about the nature of commonsense psychology itself. If someone's metaphysics assured her that commonsense psychology *had* to be susceptible to functionalist treatment, then, by acknowledging the possibility that it could not be so treated, she would allow for the threat of eliminativism. This explains why eliminativism and functionalism could be lumped together in my Introduction, see n. 4 there. But see also Baker, 1987, for a different way to distinguish eliminativism from functionalism.

3. I say 'laboratory Psychologists' meaning to exclude experiments the interpretation of whose results uses commonsense psychological concepts (e.g., in Social Psychology).

4. One aim of Peacocke, 1992, is to bring together philosophical and empirical psychological concerns by treating people's possession of concepts in such a way that its 'subpersonal, computational basis' can be enquired after. Peacocke says (in a note at p. 240) that he uses subpersonal in the part-whole

way that Dennett defined in 1978, p. 153 (see Essay 10). But I find it impossible to read all of Peacocke's uses of 'subpersonal' in line with that definition. How should one understand, for instance, the idea at pp. 57–58 that a person subpersonally possesses information? (When I have spoken here of the distinction that Dennett intended, I have meant Dennett 1969; see further Essay 10.)

10. Dennett's Naturalism

1. For the position Dennett reaches when he sides with Dawkins, see Dennett, 1987a, and Hornsby, 1992. Someone who settles for the modest degree of biologism advocated here should feel no inclination to say that human beings are '*merely* biological beings'. We should not say that unless we thought that the understanding of persons used only biological or sociobiological explanations. Darwin's theory can show that a correct account of human beings must introduce nothing supernatural, without making us think that any correct account of human beings is itself shot through with Darwinian explanations. (Some people not only think that, but, paradoxically enough, use it to ground their beliefs about how human beings ought to live.)

2. These were questions about 'what the attitudes *are*'. When Dennett characterized the subpersonal in his 1981 article, he distinguished between intentional system theory and subpersonal cognitive psychology. In subpersonal intentional system theory, the intentional stance is taken, but towards subsystems: see the quotation in the text. Subpersonal cognitive psychology, by contrast, is 'a concrete, microtheoretical science of the actual realization of those intentional systems' (1981, p. 57). Dennett's belief in such a science (having the title 'cognitive'), in combination with his view that intentional systems are to be found at personal and subpersonal levels alike, is what makes me think that he broaches the questions that Fodor calls hard. Strictly, though, to make allowance for Dennett's instrumentalism, one must think of these now not as questions about what the attitudes *are*, but as questions about what the attitudes seem to be, or what it is as if they were.

3. This is an attempt at an untendentious statement of Dennett's irrealism. Dennett's own version is in the next sentence's quotation (got from a place where Dennett is trying to make light of his Instrumentalism). Dennett's evolutionary views (glossed over at the end of §1.1 as irrelevant to what he shares with the naive naturalist) are actually crucial to the kind of Instrumentalism he advances. For criticism of his argument from evolution, see Hornsby, 1992.

4. 'Particular beliefs or desires' means particular fillings for '——' in '*a* believes that ——', so that there are not any particulars ('items') here. A

state of *believing that p* is attributed when the belief that *p* is attributed; but the state in question (being a species of property) is categorically different from a state of the sort that most orthodox naturalists speak as if a belief were.

5. I say 'somehow' because we now have the idea that I earlier said was 'fairly incredible'. If the psychophysical character of concepts used from the intentional stance is granted (see Essay 4), then it should be evident that in fact nothing could be in a position to see meaningful behaviour in advance of being in a position to attribute beliefs and desires to persons. But we must assume that a stance-taker has somehow acquired the concepts.

6. The adoption of a design stance in biology is not always to be treated as adoption of an *intentional* stance, however: see Hornsby, 1992. So even where it is only as if an animal believed something, the animal can genuinely possess other animal properties.

7. Actually, it does not remove *all* of Dennett's putative grounds: see n. 3 above. Here I have dealt rather swiftly with Dennett's irrealism. For more discussion of interpretationism, see Child, 1992, ch. 1. (Child reads Dennett as a non-constitutive interpretationist, whereas I have read him as, in Child's sense, a constitutive one.)

8. In connecting consciousness with P-predicates in Strawson's sense, I am thinking of a property of self-conscious beings. There must then be more to be said about non-human animals. If, with me, you think that the first-person introducing considerations of 3.1 have no application to non-human animals, then you will take them to be excluded from those considerations, as thermostats are; but you will not then assimilate animals to thermostats—see n. 6.

Those who think that non-human animals are persons (in a sense of 'person' associated with Strawson's P-predicates) would draw the line between genuine and 'as if' intentionality in a different place from me. Different arguments from any in the foreground here—such as those that Davidson has given, connecting satisfaction of intentional P-predicates with the use of language—would be needed against them.

Sometimes communication between non-human animals has been treated by thinking of the animals *as if* they took the intentional stance. If the considerations of 3.1 are to work as I mean them to, then it has to be excluded that such a treatment is being offered when those considerations are advanced. The necessary exclusion is made when the considerations are seen to rely upon the intentional stance's *genuinely* being taken. (This is different from relying upon the genuineness of the possession of intentional properties by those towards which the stance is taken: a distinction between genuine and 'as if' possession of intentional properties can be introduced by the considerations, and need not be prior to them.) In my own view, a double 'as if' is at work when it is supposed that a non-human animal *takes* the intentional stance.

9. 'Sort of' because I do not know how we are supposed to think of the word demons and content demons who 'wring sentences from us' in Dennett's 1991 account. My description of Dennett as 'striving to locate consciousness at the inside' obviously does not tell the whole story. If I am right that Dennett should allow his naturalism to remain naive, then there could be no need for a project with exactly the ambitions that Dennett's may be taken to have. In his account of selves in ch. 13 (1991), the consequences of Dennett's kind of reductionism are written large at the personal level, and it becomes clear that much is lost from naive naturalism by Dennett's reconstructions. But I can be in sympathy with some such project.

Searle is another philosopher who locates consciousness at the level of people's materialistic innards; but, unlike others in this category, he wants a biological view of human beings to prevail (1992). It is not Searle's biological view, however, which informs his approach to consciousness, but rather his idea of a 'causally emergent feature system' (pp. 112–113). I would dispute not only Searle's approach but also his belief in the pervasiveness of explanations of macro-phenomena in terms of micro-phenomena (see Essay 11, §3).

10. Nagel was the philosopher Dennett singled out as introducing mysteries where he found none.

11. Causation in Intuitive Physics and in Commonsense Psychology

1. 'Theory of mind' is the going terminology in developmental psychology. See, e.g., Whiten, 1991. By 'intuitive physics' here I mean a subject matter which stands to the physical as 'theory of mind' (or commonsense psychology) may be thought to stand to the mental: I do not mean only the *generalizations* about the physical world that physics proper may contest. ('Folk physics' would not be inappropriate here, then: see Introduction, on 'folk psychology'.)

2. The thesis of externalism (see postscript to Essay 12) may be supposed to demonstrate the special need to extract purely causal statements in the psychological case. The thought is that only the 'intrinsic' properties of something could determine its causal powers (see Introduction, §4). It seems to me that the thought relies upon failing to consider rational explanation in its ordinary setting.

3. See Strawson, 1985. My attempts to discredit the Nomological Character of Causality in Part I, and 'universalizing' assumptions about causation in Essay 8, are relevant here.

12. Semantic Innocence and Psychological Understanding

1. Block, 1986; Field, 1977; Fodor, 1980; Harman, 1982; Loar, 1981, 1982; McGinn, 1982; Putnam, 1975; Schiffer, 1980.

I have not tried to keep track of all the variants. And I have not taken account of changes of views of these authors over the years.

2. It can be hard to disentangle terminological from genuine differences among those who hold the idea. The word 'content' is used differently by different two-task theorists: v.i., n. 6.

3. There is a discussion of answers to this question, and an answer of his own, in §3 of McGinn, 1982a. I discuss McGinn's own answer in §3.4 below.

4. See, for what may be the first use of this notion, Field, 1977.

5. The claim that truth-theories can do duty as theories of meaning pervades Davidson's essays collected together in Davidson, 1984. My debt to these writings will be evident.

6. I assume, then, (i) that a state's having the content it does is what enables it to play the explanatory role that it does, and (ii) that a state's content is what is specified in a 'that' clause when it is ascribed. Two-task theorists are prevented by their philosophical position from holding that (i) and (ii) are both true. And sometimes 'content' is used so that (i) is preserved, sometimes so that (ii) is.

7. Davidson spoke of our 'pre-Fregean semantic innocence'; and Barwise and Perry, 1983, who are responsible for naming the Principle, take their anti-Fregean stance to be all of a piece with their endorsement of the principle. It may then be questioned whether I have any right to help myself to a *Fregean* notion of content (below).

Well, Davidson's point was that Frege's view that words in 'that' clauses refer to their sense should not be allowed to supplant our naive view that they refer there to what they ordinarily refer to. But once the Fregean notion of content is in place, the effect of Davidson's paratactic analysis is to ensure that matches as to content are what determine intersubstitutions in 'that' clauses. This of course is exactly the result achieved by Frege by having words there refer to their senses. (For a demonstration of how much in harmony Frege and Davidson may be, see McDowell, 1980. And I should myself question whether Barwise and Perry have respected the Principle at the end of the day, although I cannot enter into this here.)

8. This would require qualification in a more precise account. There can be determinants of what is done with words which are not determinants of content but which are more or less accidentally language specific. (E.g., it might be that a particular tone of voice conventionally signalling that a question was to be taken as a polite request was used by all and only the speakers of some language.)

9. The notion of 'strict and literal saying' is sometimes introduced to escape the falsehood. But it is not the case that 'say' has any strict and literal sense of its own to be called on; so 'strict and literal saying', if invoked, requires stipulations such as I have introduced for 'content'.

10. I think that the fact that there is so much more which determines what is said than which determines what content an utterance has is part of what has led to the anarchism that one finds in (for instance) Baker and Hacker, 1984. It is as if the vast discrepancy between what an account of the content of utterances yields (on the one hand) and what is required in an account of speech acts (on the other) leads these authors to think that there is nothing stable about our language stock which we rely on in being understood.

11. Thus we need not think, what Wettstein claims (1986, p. 205), that 'our practices of substituting one name for another are not nearly as restrictive . . . as Fregeans would lead us to believe'. Fregeans may distinguish between the restrictions imposed in one's accounts of natural language semantics and psychological understanding and the relaxations permitted by our practices.

12. I make no attempt here to accommodate utterances of non-indicative sentences or those propositional attitude states whose objects are not straightforwardly truth-evaluable. For some useful considerations about how the analogue of content for utterances in the imperative mood relates to the analogue of content for desires and intentions (considerations thus pertaining to the unification of semantics and psychology), see Hamblin, 1987.

13. See some of the work in the 1982 issue of the *Notre Dame Journal of Philosophical Logic* (in which Loar, 1982, is found).

14. For an example of this use of 'use', and attributions of it to others, see McGinn, 1982a, pp. 240–242.

15. In Essay 7 I drew attention to equivocations on 'behaviour'. If use is linguistic behaviour, so that use is what linguistic behavioural dispositions give rise to, then the two notions of use are parallel to the two conceptions of 'behaviour' that I distinguished there in criticizing modern physicalisms. (I tried there to put pressure on the two-task theorists' view of explanation which is discussed at the end of §3.4.)

Notice that talk of dispositions itself *need* not have altered anything: *of course* speakers of a common language are all *disposed* in some same ways by virtue of sharing a language.

16. Fodor's talk of opaque vs. transparent construals indicates that he thought that there is an ambiguity in, for example, 'John believes that Cicero was a Roman orator,' according as intersubstitution of 'Tully' for 'Cicero' is not or is permitted. (Disambiguation can then be achieved with 'John believes of Cicero that he was a Roman orator', in which intersubstitution is permit-

ted.) But this is questionable. The appearance that there is a transparent reading may be fostered by the laxity in ordinary reports (see §1.4 above)—an inevitable and more considerable laxity when reporter and reported are differently situated (see §1.6 above). It may then be that there are not two readings of sentences like 'John believes that Cicero . . .', but variations in how licit it is to proceed as if one had the transparent style of report.

17. It might be held that this puts the point in a question-begging way: of course 'he' refers here, because that is the only way back-reference could be secured. But the onus is put on those who deny the Principle of Semantic Innocence: they owe us an account of how 'he' *could* secure such back-reference.

Fodor (1980) comes close to acknowledging the Principle when he says that 'the intuitive opaque taxonomy is actually what you might call "semi-transparent"' (p. 238). But what is at issue at present is whether an "entirely functional taxonomy" of the propositional attitude states is the same as any "pretheoretic" one.

18. Fodor has come to give a different account of these matters. I criticize his earlier one because I find that the phenomenon of opacity still leads people to suppose that reference can be pulled apart from sense. (I should want to bring the Principle of Semantic Innocence to bear in a discussion of Fodor's 1987 account.)

19. If we did use the term 'truth-conditions' in this way, we should *eo ipso* be committed to McGinn's claim that 'it is no defect in a statement of truth-conditions that the expressions used differ merely in cognitive role (sense) from the expressions mentioned' (p. 239).

20. These are rough and readily stated principles, stated so as to connect with the thought that a belief that *p* disposes one to act in ways that will satisfy one's desires if it is true that *p* (cp. §2.5). See Essay 7, p. 122.

21. For more on this choice, see the editorial introduction to Pettit and McDowell, 1986.

22. For more on the costs of the two-task idea, see McDowell, 1986, §§6–8.

23. My terminology ignores the many distinctions that have been made between different species of externalism and different versions of anti-individualism. In other contexts, these distinctions are important (although they do not seem to be marked by any uniform terminology in the literature).

Some glosses on externalism incorporate philosophical opinions not contained in any recognizably anti-individualist thesis. Consider, for example, Fodor, fourteen years on from the paper discussed in the essay: 'It is . . . the heart of externalism that *semantics isn't part of psychology*' (1994, p. 38).

24. A thesis in epistemology which is supposed to need reconciling with externalism is 'self-knowledge'. The philosophers' project in this case is to

render a person's usually authoritative knowledge about the contents of her own thought compatible with externalism. The supposed difficulty about doing this cannot be blamed directly on a false view about the scope of what is 'naturalizable', so that there is more to be said under this head: I think that the idea of Semantic Innocence used in the essay will again be crucial.

25. If one deems a subject matter irreducible, one obviously shies away from giving an ambitious account of the subject matter. The unitary account of content's title to be at least 'an account' depends upon its showing how utterances conceived of as describable in non-contentful ways (in quotation marks, as it were) have a place in people's contentful interactions. It is important, though, not to overestimate its ambitions: there is a danger of supposing that in introducing utterances conceived in non-contentful ways, the account might itself be located in 'the objective, materialistic, third-person world of the physical sciences'—to use Dennett's phrase. But Essay 10 gives an argument against the idea that understanding people could be a matter of taking a certain stance towards what is impersonally present. (Despite its lack of ambitions, the unitary account's title to be an account ensures that it is not part of "minimalism" about truth or meaning. But that is another story: see Hornsby, 1996.)

References

Akins, Kathleen. 1993. 'What Is It Like to Be Boring and Myopic?'. In Bo Dahlbom, ed., *Dennett and His Critics: Demystifying the Mind*. Oxford: Blackwell, pp. 124–160.

Armstrong, D. M. 1968. *A Materialist Theory of the Mind*. London: Routledge and Kegan Paul.

———— 1973. 'Acting and Trying'. In his *Philosophical Papers*, vol. 2. Cambridge, England: Cambridge University Press, pp. 68–88.

Baker, G. P., and P. M. S. Hacker. 1984. *Language, Sense and Nonsense*. Oxford: Blackwell.

Baker, Lynne Rudder. 1987. *Saving Belief: A Critique of Physicalism*. Princeton: Princeton University Press.

Barwise, John, and John Perry. 1983. *Situations and Attitudes*. Cambridge, Mass.: M.I.T. Press.

Benacerraf, Paul. 1965. 'What Numbers Could Not Be'. *Philosophical Review*, 74, pp. 47–73.

Block, Ned. 1986. 'Advertisement for a Semantics for Psychology'. *Midwest Studies in Philosophy*. Minneapolis: University of Minnesota Press, pp. 615–678.

Boyd, Richard. 1980. 'Materialism without Reductionism: What Physicalism Does Not Entail'. In Ned Block, ed., *Readings in Philosophy of Psychology*, vol. 1. London: Methuen, pp. 67–106.

Brand, Myles. 1984. *Intending and Acting*. Cambridge, Mass.: M.I.T. Press.

Brewer, Bill. 1993. 'The Integration of Social Wisdom and Action'. In Naomi Eilan, Rosaleen McCarthy and Bill Brewer, eds., *Spatial Representation*. Oxford and Cambridge, Mass.: Blackwell, pp. 294–316.

Burge, Tyler. 1979. 'Individualism and the Mental'. In P. French, T. Melhing and H. Wettstein, eds., *Midwest Studies in Philosophy, IV: Studies in Metaphysics*. Minneapolis: University of Minnesota Press.

Campbell, John. 1988. 'Is Sense Transparent?'. *The Proceedings of the Aristotelian Society*, 88, pp. 273–292.

———— 1994. *Past, Space, and Self*. Cambridge, Mass., and London: M.I.T. Press.

Child, William. 1994. *Causality, Interpretation and the Mind.* Oxford: Clarendon Press.

Churchland, P. M. 1981. 'Eliminative Materialism and the Propositional Attitudes'. *Journal of Philosophy*, 78, pp. 67–90.

Churchland, P. S. 1986. *Neurophilosophy.* Cambridge, Mass.: M.I.T. Press.

Clark, Andy. 1989. *Microcognition.* Cambridge, Mass.: M.I.T. Press.

Cook, John W. 1969. 'Human Beings'. In Peter Winch, ed., *Studies in the Philosophy of Wittgenstein.* London: Routledge and Kegan Paul.

Cottingham, John. 1986. *Descartes.* Oxford: Blackwell.

Crane, Tim and Hugh Mellor. 1990. 'There Is No Question of Physicalism'. *Mind*, 99, pp. 185–206.

Davidson, Donald. 1963. 'Actions, Reasons and Causes'. *Journal of Philosophy*, 60, pp. 685–700. Reprinted in Davidson (1980), pp. 3–19, to which page references in the text and notes refer.

——— 1967a. 'Causal Relations'. *Journal of Philosophy*, 64, pp. 691–703. Reprinted in Davidson (1980), pp. 149–162, to which page references in the text and notes refer.

——— 1967b. 'Truth and Meaning'. *Synthese*, 17, pp. 304–323. Reprinted in Davidson (1984), pp. 17–36, to which page references in the text and notes refer.

——— 1968. 'On Saying That'. *Synthese*, 19, pp. 130–146. Reprinted in Davidson (1984), pp. 93–108, to which page references in the text and notes refer.

——— 1969. 'The Individuation of Events'. In N. Rescher, ed., *Essays in Honour of Hempel.* Dordrecht: Reidel, pp. 216–234. Reprinted in Davidson (1980), pp. 163–180, to which page references in the text and notes refer.

——— 1970. 'Mental Events'. In L. Foster and J. W. Swanson, eds., *Experience and Theory.* Amherst: University of Massachusetts Press, pp. 79–101. Reprinted in Davidson (1980), pp. 207–228, to which page references in the text and notes refer.

——— 1971a. 'Agency'. In R. Binkley, R. Bronaugh and A. Marras, eds., *Agent, Action and Reason.* Toronto: University of Toronto Press. Reprinted in Davidson (1980), pp. 43–61, to which page references in the text and notes refer.

——— 1971b. 'Psychology as Philosophy'. In C. S. Brown, ed., *Philosophy of Psychology.* London and Basingstoke: Macmillan Press. Reprinted in Davidson (1980), pp. 229–244, to which page references in the text and notes refer.

——— 1973a. 'The Material Mind'. In P. Suppes et al., eds., *Logic, Methodology and the Philosophy of Science*, vol. 4. Amsterdam: North Holland Publishing Company. Reprinted in Davidson (1980), pp. 245–259, to which page references in the text and notes refer.

—— 1973b. 'Freedom to Act'. In T. Honderich, ed., *Essays on Freedom of Action*. London: Routledge and Kegan Paul, pp. 139–156. Reprinted in Davidson (1980), pp. 63–81, to which page references in the text and notes refer.

—— 1974. 'On the Very Idea of a Conceptual Scheme'. In *Proceedings and Addresses of the American Philosophical Association*, 47. Reprinted in Davidson (1984), pp. 183–198, to which page references in the text and notes refer.

—— 1980. *Essays on Actions and Events*. Oxford: Clarendon Press.

—— 1984. *Inquiries into Truth and Interpretation*. Oxford: Clarendon Press.

—— 1985. 'Reply to J. J. C. Smart'. In B. Vermazen and M. B. Hintikka, eds., *Essays on Davidson: Actions and Events*. Oxford: Oxford University Press.

Davis, L. H. 1979. *Action Theory*. Englewood Cliffs, N.J.: Prentice Hall.

Dennett, Daniel. 1969. *Content and Consciousness*. London, Boston and Henley: Routledge and Kegan Paul (2nd ed., 1986).

—— 1978a. 'Artificial Intelligence as Philosophy and as Psychology'. In Martin Kingle, ed., *Philosophical Perspectives on Artificial Intelligence*. New York: Humanities Press and Harvester Press. Reprinted in Dennett (1979), pp. 109–126.

—— 1978b. 'Towards a Cognitive Theory of Consciousness'. In C. Wade Savage, ed., *Perception and Cognition: Issues in the Foundations of Psychology*. Minneapolis: University of Minnesota Press. Reprinted in Dennett (1979), to which page references in the text and notes refer.

—— 1979. *Brainstorms*. Hassocks: Harvester Press.

—— 1981. 'Three Kinds of Intentional Psychology'. In R. Healey, ed., *Reduction, Time and Reality*. Cambridge, England: Cambridge University Press. Reprinted in Dennett (1987c), pp. 43–68, to which page references in the text and notes refer.

—— 1987a. 'Evolution, Error and Intentionality'. In Y. Wilks and D. Partridge, eds., *Source Book on the Foundations of Artificial Intelligence*. Cambridge, England: Cambridge University Press. Reprinted in Dennett (1987c), pp. 287–321, to which page references in the text and notes refer.

—— 1987b. 'Setting Off on the Right Foot'. Introduction to Dennett (1987c), pp. 1–11.

—— 1987c. *The Intentional Stance*. Cambridge, Mass.: M.I.T. Press.

—— 1991a. *Consciousness Explained*. Boston, Toronto and London: Little, Brown and Company.

—— 1991b. 'Real Patterns'. *Journal of Philosophy*, 88, pp. 27–51.

Descartes, Rene. 1967. *The Philosophical Works of Descartes,* trans. Elisabeth Haldane and G. R. T. Ross. Cambridge, England: Cambridge University Press.

—— 1970. *Descartes' Philosophical Letters,* trans. and ed. Anthony Kenny. Oxford: Clarendon Press.

Doepke, F. C. 1982. 'Spatially Coinciding Objects'. *Ratio,* 24, pp. 45–60.

Dretske, Fred. 1988. *Explaining Behavior: Reasons in a World of Causes.* Cambridge, Mass.: M.I.T. Press.

Duff, R. A. 1990. *Intention, Agency and Criminal Liability: Philosophy of Action and the Criminal Law.* Oxford: Blackwell.

Eberle, Rolf. 1970. *Nominalistic Systems.* Dordrecht: Reidel.

Evans, Gareth. 1978. 'Can There Be Vague Objects?'. *Analysis,* 38, p. 208.

—— 1982. *The Varieties of Reference.* Oxford: Oxford University Press.

Field, Henry. 1977. 'Logic, Meaning and Conceptual Role'. *Journal of Philosophy,* 74, pp. 379–409.

Flanagan, Owen. 1992. *Consciousness Reconsidered.* Cambridge, Mass.: M.I.T. Press.

Fodor, Jerry. 1973. 'Special Sciences, or the Disunity of Science as a Working Hypothesis'. *Synthese,* 28, pp. 97–115. Reprinted in Fodor (1981), pp. 127–145, to which page references in the text and notes refer.

—— 1976. *The Language of Thought.* Hassocks: Harvester Press.

—— 1980. 'Methodological Solipsism Considered as a Research Strategy in Cognitive Psychology'. *The Behavioral and Brain Sciences,* 3. Reprinted in Fodor (1981), pp. 225–253, to which page references in the text and notes refer.

—— 1981. *Representations.* Brighton: Harvester Press.

—— 1985. 'Fodor's Guide to Mental Representation'. *Mind,* 94, pp. 57–97. Reprinted in Fodor (1990), pp. 3–29, to which page references in the text and notes refer.

—— 1987. *Psychosemantics: The Problem of Meaning in the Philosophy of Mind.* Cambridge, Mass.: M.I.T. Press.

—— 1990. *A Theory of Content and Other Essays.* Cambridge, Mass.: M.I.T. Press.

—— 1994. *The Elm and the Expert: Mentalese and Its Semantics.* Cambridge, Mass.: M.I.T. Press.

Geach, P. T. 1979. *Truth, Love and Immortality.* London: Hutchinson.

Goodman, Nelson. 1951. *The Structure of Appearance.* Cambridge, Mass.: Harvard University Press.

Grice, H. P. 1967. The William James Lectures, published as *Studies in the Ways of Words.* Cambridge, Mass.: Harvard University Press (1989).

Hamblin, C. L. 1987. *Imperatives.* Oxford: Blackwell.

Harman, Gilbert. 1974. 'Meaning and Semantics'. In M. Munitz and P. Unger, eds., *Semantics and Philosophy*. New York: New York University Press.

—— 1982. 'Conceptual Role Semantics'. *Notre Dame Journal of Formal Logic*, XXIII, pp. 242–256.

Hellman, G., and F. W. Thompson. 1971. 'Physicalist Materialism'. *Nous*, 11, pp. 309–345.

—— 1975. 'Physicalism: Ontology, Determination and Reduction'. *Journal of Philosophy*, 72, pp. 551–564.

Hoffman, Paul. 1986. 'The Unity of Descartes' Man'. *Philosophical Review*, 95, pp. 339–371.

Honderich, Ted. 1982. 'The Argument for Anomalous Monism'. *Analysis*, 42, pp. 59–64.

Hornsby, Jennifer. 1980. *Actions*. London: Routledge and Kegan Paul.

—— 1981. 'Action and Ability'. In R. Haller, ed., *Language, Logic and Philosophy*. Dordrecht: Reidel, pp. 387–398.

—— 1992. 'Physics, Biology, and Common-Sense Psychology'. In David Charles and Kathleen Lennon, eds., *Reduction, Explanation, and Realism*. Oxford: Clarendon Press.

—— 1993. 'On What's Intentionally Done'. In Stephen Shute, John Gardner and Jeremy Horder, eds., *Action and Value in Criminal Law*. Oxford: Clarendon Press, pp. 57–74.

—— 1994. 'Action and Aberration'. *University of Pennsylvania Law Review*, 142, pp. 1719–1747.

—— 1996. 'Truth: The Identity Theory'. *Proceedings of the Aristotelian Society*, 97, pp. 1–24.

Jackson, Frank. 1982. 'Acting, Trying and Essentialism'. *Inquiry*, 25, pp. 255–270.

Jarvis Thomson, Judith. 1977. *Acts and Other Events*. Cornell: Cornell University Press.

Johnston, Mark. 1985. 'Why Having a Mind Matters'. In E. Lepore and B. McLaughlin, eds., *Actions and Events: Perspectives on the Philosophy of Donald Davidson*. Oxford: Blackwell, pp. 408–426.

Kim, Jaegwon. 1982. 'Psychophysical Supervenience'. *Philosophical Studies*, 41, pp. 51–70.

Kripke, Saul. 1971. 'Identity and Necessity'. In Milton K. Munitz, ed., *Identity and Individuation*. New York: New York University Press.

Lennon, Kathleen. 1990. *Explaining Human Action*. London: Duckworth.

Lepore, E., and B. Loewer. 1987. 'Mind Matters'. *Journal of Philosophy*, 84, pp. 630–642.

Lewis, David. 1972. 'Psychophysical and Theoretical Identifications'. *Australasian Journal of Philosophy*, 1, pp. 249–258.

—— 1974. 'Radical Interpretation'. *Synthese*, 23, pp. 331–344. Reprinted in Lewis, 1983, pp. 108–118.

—— 1983. *Philosophical Papers*, vol. 1. Oxford: Clarendon Press.

—— 1986. *Philosophical Papers*, vol. 2. Oxford: Clarendon Press.

Loar, Brian. 1981. *Mind and Meaning*. Cambridge, England: Cambridge University Press.

—— 1982. 'Conceptual Role and Truth Conditions'. *Notre Dame Journal of Formal Logic*, XXIII, pp. 272–283.

Long, Douglas C. 1964. 'The Philosophical Concept of the Human Body'. *Philosophical Review*, 73, pp. 321–337.

McCulloch, Gregory. 1990. 'Dennett's Little Grains of Salt'. *Philosophical Quarterly*, 40, pp. 1–12.

McDowell, John. 1978. 'Physicalism and Primitive Denotation: Field on Tarski'. *Erkenntnis*, 13, pp. 131–152.

—— 1980. 'Quotation and Saying That'. In Mark Platts, ed., *Reference, Truth and Reality*. London: Routledge and Kegan Paul, pp. 206–237.

—— 1982. 'Criteria, Defeasibility and Knowledge'. *Proceedings of the British Academy*, 68, pp. 455–479. Reprinted with revisions and additions in Jonathan Dancy, ed., *Perceptual Content*. Oxford: Oxford University Press (1988), pp. 209–219, to which page references in the text and notes refer.

—— 1985. 'Functionalism and Anomalous Monism'. In E. Lepore and B. McLaughlin, eds., *Actions and Events: Perspectives on the Philosophy of Donald Davidson*. Oxford: Blackwell, pp. 387–398.

—— 1986. 'Singular Thought and the Extent of Inner Space'. In Philip Pettit and John McDowell, eds., *Subject, Thought and Context*. Oxford: Oxford University Press, pp. 137–168.

—— 1994. *Mind and World*. Cambridge, Mass.: Harvard University Press.

McGinn, Colin. 1977. 'Mental States, Natural Kinds and Psychophysical Laws'. *Proceedings of the Aristotelian Society*, supp. vol. LII.

—— 1979. 'Action and Its Explanation'. In N. Bolton, ed., *Philosophical Problems in Psychology*. London: Methuen, pp. 20–42.

—— 1980. 'Philosophical Materialism'. *Synthese*, 44, pp. 173–206.

—— 1982a. 'The Structure of Content'. In Andrew Woodfield, ed., *Thought and Object*. Oxford: Oxford University Press.

—— 1982b. *The Character of Mind*. Oxford: Oxford University Press.

Marx, Karl. 1971. *Early Texts*, trans. and ed. D. McLellan. Oxford: Blackwell.

Mellor, D. H. 1981. *Real Time*. Cambridge, England: Cambridge University Press.

Moore, Adrian. 1987. 'Points of View'. *Philosophical Quarterly*, 37, pp. 1–20.

Moore, Michael. 1993. *Act and Crime: The Philosophy of Action and Its Implications for Criminal Law*. Oxford: Clarendon Press.

Morris, Michael. 1992. *The Good and the True*. Oxford: Clarendon Press.

Nagel, Thomas. 1986. *The View from Nowhere*. Cambridge, England: Cambridge University Press.

O'Shaughnessy, Brian. 1974. 'Trying (as the Mental "Pineal Gland")'. *Journal of Philosophy*, 71, pp. 365–386.

—— 1980. *The Will*. Cambridge, England: Cambridge University Press, 2 vols.

Papineau, David. 1993. *Philosophical Naturalism*. Oxford: Blackwell.

Peacocke, Christopher. 1979. *Holistic Explanation: Action, Space, Interpretation*. Oxford: Oxford University Press.

—— 1992. *A Study of Concepts*. Cambridge, Mass.: M.I.T. Press.

Pears, D. F., ed. 1963. *Freedom of the Will*. London: Macmillan.

Putnam, Hilary. 1975. 'The Meaning of "Meaning"'. In Keith Gunderson, ed., *Language, Mind and Knowledge: Minnesota Studies in the Philosophy of Science*, vol. VII. Minneapolis: University of Minnesota Press. Reprinted in his *Philosophical Papers, Vol. II: Mind, Language and Reality*. Cambridge, England: Cambridge University Press, pp. 215–271, to which page references in the text and notes refer.

—— 1979. 'Reflections on Goodman's "Ways of Worldmaking"'. *Journal of Philosophy*, 76, pp. 603–618.

—— 1982. 'Computational Psychology and Interpretation Theory'. In his *Philosophical Papers, Vol. III: Realism and Reason*. Cambridge, England: Cambridge University Press.

—— 1988. *Representation and Reality*. Cambridge, Mass.: M.I.T. Press.

—— 1992. Reply to John McDowell. *Philosophical Topics*, 20, pp. 358–361.

Quine, W. V. O. 1960. *Word and Object*. Cambridge, Mass.: M.I.T. Press.

—— 1977. 'Facts of the Matter'. In R. W. Shahan and K. R. Merrill, eds., *Philosophy in America from Edwards to Quine*. Oklahoma: Oklahoma University Press.

—— 1981. 'Things and Their Place in Theories'. In his *Theories and Things*. Cambridge, Mass.: Harvard University Press, pp. 1–23.

Robinson, Howard. 1982. *Matter and Sense*. Cambridge, England: Cambridge University Press.

Robinson, W. S. 1990. 'States and Beliefs'. *Mind*, 99, pp. 33–51.

Rorty, Richard. 1979. *Philosophy and the Mirror of Nature*. Princeton: Princeton University Press.

—— 1987. 'Non-Reductive Physicalism'. In *Theorie der Subjectivitat: A Festschrift for Dieter Henrich*. Konrad Cramer et al., eds., Frankfurt: Suhrkamp, pp. 278–296. Reprinted in his (1991) *Objectivity, Relativism and Truth: Philosophical Papers, vol. I*. Cambridge, England: Cambridge University Press, pp. 113–125, to which page references in the text and notes refer.

Ryle, Gilbert. 1949. *The Concept of Mind*. London: Hutchinson.

Schiffer, Stephen. 1980. 'Truth and the Theory of Content'. In H. Parret and J. Bouverese, eds., *Meaning and Understanding*. Berlin and New York: Walter de Gruyter, pp. 204–222.

———— 1987. *Remnants of Meaning*. Cambridge, Mass.: M.I.T. Press.

Searle, J. R. 1992. *The Rediscovery of the Mind*. Cambridge, Mass.: M.I.T. Press.

Smith, Michael. 1983. 'Actions, Attempts and Internal Events'. *Analysis*, 43, pp. 142–146.

Smith, Peter. 1984. 'Anomalous Monism and Epiphenomenalism: A Reply to Honderich'. *Analysis*, 44, pp. 83–86.

Soames, Scott. 1984. 'What Is a Theory of Truth?'. *Journal of Philosophy*, 81, pp. 411–429.

Steward, Helen. 1997. *The Ontology of Mind: Events, States, and Processes*. Oxford: Clarendon Press.

Stoutland, F. 1976. 'The Causation of Behaviour'. In *Essays on Wittgenstein in the Honor of G. H. Von Wright (Acta Philosophica Fennica,* 28), pp. 286–325.

Strawson, P. F. 1959. *Individuals*. London: Methuen.

———— 1985. 'Causation and Explanation'. In B. Vermazen and M. Hintikka, eds., *Essays on Davidson: Actions and Events*. Oxford: Oxford University Press, pp. 115–135.

Taylor, Charles. 1964. *The Explanation of Behaviour*. London: Routledge and Kegan Paul.

Wettstein, Howard. 1986. 'Has Semantics Rested on a Mistake?'. *Journal of Philosophy*, 81, pp. 185–209.

Whiten, A., ed. 1991. 'Natural Theories of Mind: Evolution, Development and Simulation of Everyday Mind Reading'. Oxford: Blackwell.

Wiggins, David. 1968. 'On Being at the Same Place at the Same Time'. *Philosophical Review*, 77, pp. 90–95.

———— 1976. 'Identity, Necessity and Physicalism'. In S. Korner, ed., *Philosophy of Logic*. Oxford: Blackwell, pp. 96–132.

———— 1980. *Sameness and Substance*. Oxford: Blackwell.

Williams, Bernard. 1970. 'Are Persons Bodies?'. In S. Spicker, ed., *The Philosophy of the Body*. Chicago: Quadrant Books. Reprinted in his (1973) *Problems of the Self*. Cambridge, England: Cambridge University Press, pp. 64–81, to which page references in the text and notes refer.

———— 1978. *Descartes: The Project of Pure Enquiry*. Harmondsworth: Penguin.

Wilson, Margaret. 1978. *Descartes*. London: Routledge and Kegan Paul.

Wittgenstein, Ludwig. 1953. *Philosophical Investigations*. Oxford: Oxford University Press.

Subject Index

Name Index